MORE MAP ON INSIDE BACK COVER

HARLOW IN HOLLYWOOD

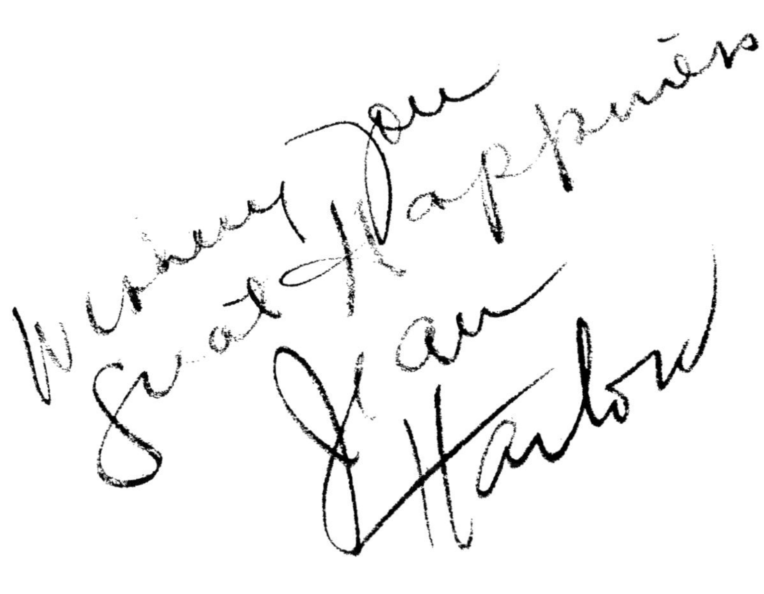
Wishing you great Happiness
Jean Harlow

Jean Harlow wakes up to stardom in *Bombshell,* the 1933 film based on her improbable lifestyle.

HARLOW IN HOLLYWOOD

The Blonde Bombshell in the Glamour Capital
1928–1937

Darrell Rooney · Mark A. Vieira

ACP
ANGEL CITY PRESS

This 1934 Russell Ball photograph shows Harlow posing in her living room with a photo of her ubiquitous mother, Jean Bello.

To my family,
and to Sharon, Mallory, and Briony Barnes,
descendants of the Kansas Carpenter family.

— Darrell Rooney

To my mother,
who explained Jean Harlow's "quizzical" eyebrows,
and to my father,
who explained "classic."

— Mark A. Vieira

Photographer James Doolittle made this color portrait of Jean Harlow in the spring of 1937 for a cover of *Screen Play Magazine*, but ultimately a different pose was used.

COVER IMAGE
Jean Harlow poses in Bullocks Wilshire for George Hurrell. This 1935 photograph captures the quintessential Hollywood star, store, and photographer.

ENDPAPERS FRONT AND BACK
This reworking of the 1937 Starland Map shows the numerous places touched by the presence of the legendary Jean Harlow.

Contents

Preface

Jean Harlow. The name resonates. Blonde Bombshell. Platinum Blonde. The labels applied by press agents during Harlow's seven-year career carry a charge seventy years later. An actress who died in 1937 still has currency in American culture. Her films make new fans, whether seen in revival theaters, on cable television, or on DVD. Chat rooms debate her attributes. Her photographs sell at all levels of the collecting world—vintage prints for as much as fourteen thousand dollars, and camera negatives for as much as fifty thousand. The first blonde sex symbol has transcended history and become a legend. A dozen books have been written about Harlow, some fallacious, others sincere. The definitive biography is David Stenn's 1993 *Bombshell: The Life and Death of Jean Harlow*, a painstakingly researched work that dispels the lies that tarnished the legend. But no book has addressed the aspect of Harlow that made her a star: her image. No book has shown the environment that created this symbol. Numerous books have dwelt on the milieus of Monroe and Madonna, but none has looked at the star who created the mold. *Harlow in Hollywood* is the first book devoted to both the Harlow image and the city that spawned it.

The person behind the image was Harlean Carpenter. She was born in 1911, the daughter of a Kansas City dentist and a socialite who wanted to be a movie actress. Harlean first came to Los Angeles at age ten, when her parents divorced. In 1927, her mother, the first Jean Harlow, became Mrs. Marino Bello in Chicago. Harlean dropped out of school, eloped with a rich boy, and returned to Los Angeles. In behavior that would become a pattern, Harlean left her husband for the dubious shelter of her mother and stepfather's home. When Harlean's tow-headed beauty began to attract attention, Jean Bello imposed her ambitions on her daughter. Harlean Carpenter became the second Jean Harlow, a movie extra at Hal Roach Studios and Paramount, and then at Metropolitan Studios, where Howard Hughes discovered her and cast her in his aviation epic, *Hell's Angels* (1930). Even though the teenager's hair was still ash-blonde, a publicist coined the phrase "Platinum Blonde." *Hell's Angels* was a huge hit, and, because she projected an unlikely combination of sensuality and innocence, nineteen-year-old Jean Harlow became a sensation.

Harlow should have been groomed as a major star, but Hughes had no investment in that process. This was the specialty of Metro-Goldwyn-Mayer, where an erudite producer named Paul Bern assigned her to drama coaches and crafted films to showcase her. In the process of refining her image, the forty-two-year-old Bern fell in love with her. Two months after marrying her, Bern committed suicide. In another of the strange turns that marked Harlow's career, she did not fall from grace. She survived the scandal. Energized by this publicity, M-G-M elevated her to the level her mother had envisioned. Harlow became a star of the first rank, publicized and imitated. In the worst year of the Great Depression, women found the money to go platinum.

Harlow's screen performances soon caught up to the potency of her image, thanks to innate talent and resourceful filmmakers. Harlow's next husband came from the film industry, even though previous romances had included gangland figures, writers, and prizefighters. Her marriage to cinematographer Harold Rosson lasted eight months. Neither he nor the studio could overcome Harlow's mother, a relentless manipulator who had the temerity to force a salary strike. After Harlow reached an accord with M-G-M, her career continued to soar. She was earning three thousand dollars a week, her films averaging profits of half a million. She was honored with three thousand fan letters a week and a sexy *Time* Magazine cover. To her friends, Harlow was a cheerful, unpretentious girl, an avid reader who liked to wisecrack and party. Her private challenge was balancing dreams of domesticity with the demands of a mother who spent her salary before it was paid.

When a grassroots movement mandated less sexy movies, Harlow modified her image. The Platinum Blonde became the Brownette, playing a series of dramatic roles. While making these films, she fell in love with actor William Powell, who was forty-four. In 1936, Harlow developed health problems. By

Looking as if she has found a new home, Harlow strolls the Metro-Goldwyn-Mayer studio lot in April 1932.

1937, her stressful life had worsened them. Her stepfather had bankrupted her. Powell was unwilling to marry her. She was working nonstop and drinking heavily. Another series of illnesses pushed her system to the breaking point. In May 1937, while filming *Saratoga* with frequent costar Clark Gable, she fell ill—but forced herself to work. When she collapsed on the set, she was misdiagnosed. By the time the true cause of her illness was discovered, her condition was untreatable. She died at the tragically premature age of twenty-six.

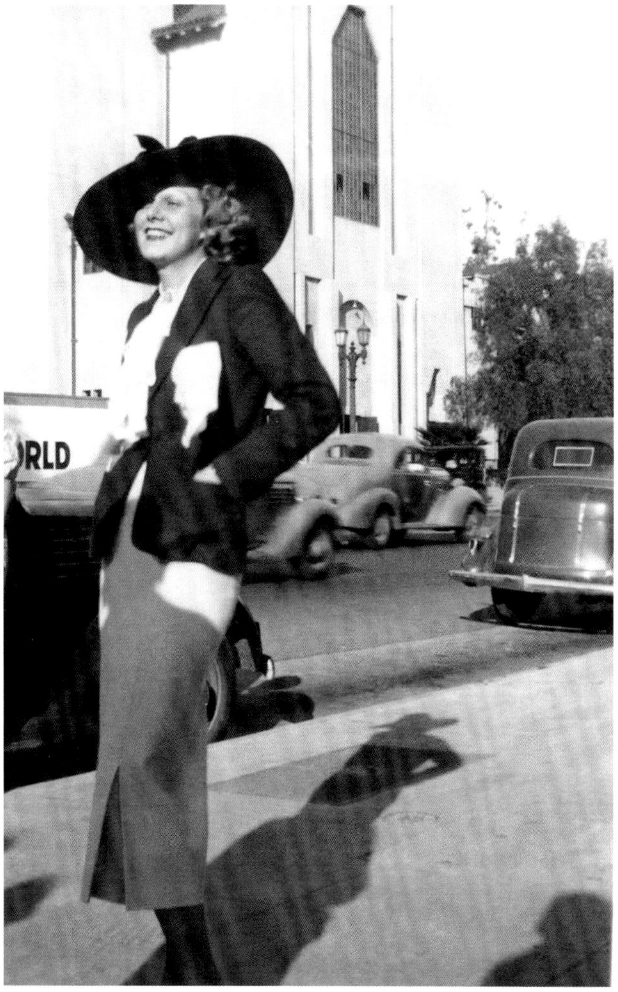

Harlow leaves Jim's Beauty Salon on Sunset Boulevard (across the street from Blessed Sacrament Church) on a Sunday afternoon in 1935.

This is the story of Jean Harlow the person. But what of Los Angeles, the city that made her famous? A look at the best of her photographs reveals a young woman being defined by—and defining—an equally young city. Just as she retained a childlike openness, Los Angeles remained a brash daughter of expansion and promotion, giving birth to a district that exists as much in the mind as on a map. This is also the story of a twentieth-century icon told in terms of the city that forged that icon. Using previously unpublished letters and documents—many in Harlow's own words—the text of *Harlow in Hollywood* tells a new version of her life story. An array of heretofore-unseen photographs shows how her destiny became intertwined with the film industry and its urban culture. Hollywood was—and is—a unique environment. Had Harlow become a Broadway star, she would have been a different entity. Her magic arc was uniquely Hollywood. Here, then, is the story of that arc, from the date palms of Gramercy Place to the topiaries of Beverly Hills, from the white-on-white Art Deco sets of *Dinner at Eight* to the Georgian façade of "the Whitest House in Hollywood," from the trompe l'oeil walls of the Café Trocadero to the sprayed stucco walls of George Hurrell's studio…all the unique, colorful settings that comprise the life of *Harlow in Hollywood*.

Harlow rode a horse in Arizona for this scene in *Bombshell*,
but most of her brief life was spent in the glare of Hollywood spotlights.

Introduction

The story of Jean Harlow in Hollywood begins in Kansas City, Kansas, with her mother, who was also named Jean Harlow. The first Jean Harlow was born in 1889 to Samuel "Skip" Harlow and his wife, the former Ella Williams. Skip, an affluent real estate developer, was strong willed, almost autocratic. Ella dabbled in painting and music, taking care never to oppose him. He kept her in check with harsh words and an occasional slap in the face. He watched his daughter Jean, too. When he saw her becoming a beauty, he began to groom her for marriage.

The first Jean's assets were impressive: looks, breeding, and money. Suitors began lining up, but the buxom brunette had other ideas. She knew she affected people. Kansas City friends were mesmerized by her beauty. Strangers stared at her and followed her. She learned to manipulate and control, becoming a skilled actress, affecting compliance while plotting escape. She became involved with a railroad conductor, a symbol of travel and freedom. Before she could flee Kansas City, she was found out by the one person she could not control: her father. Skip Harlow broke up the affair and ordered his recalcitrant child to marry someone respectable. On October 1, 1908, the first Jean Harlow became the wife of Mont Clair Carpenter, an Iowa-born dentist with a practice in Kansas City, Missouri. The Presbyterian wedding service was conducted in the Harlow home at 930 Orville Avenue in Kansas City, Kansas. The newlyweds lived almost two years in her parents' second home at 3344 Olive Street in Kansas City, Missouri, before buying their first home, which was nearby, at 4409 Gillham Road.

Even as a married woman, the first Jean could not escape her father's influence. He wanted a grandson. The newlyweds complied, planning for a boy who would be named Harlow Carpenter. On March 3, 1911, at 7:40 P.M., a child was born—a girl. When Skip objected to the idea of a second Jean, the infant was named Harlean. The war of wills had begun.

Despite this, Harlean was blessed with the proverbial sunny disposition. She was soon known as "the Baby." Not until she entered school did she realize that her name was not Baby but Harlean. Skip was also devoted to the Baby. "My grandfather was my absolute slave," Harlean recalled later. "He came home from his real estate brokerage once, and sometimes twice a day, to see how his 'Baby' was getting along." His many gifts to Harlean included an ermine bedspread; his attention to the child was restrained compared to her mother's. Jean Carpenter was obsessive. "The Baby was complete consummation to me and for me," she said later. "She was the perfection I had wanted and so beautifully got. She alone was enough."

In truth, Jean Carpenter was bitterly frustrated. She had not wanted to marry Mont. Now she was stuck in a loveless marriage—yet still subject to her father's tyranny. She focused on Harlean, treating her as a friend and confidante. To outsiders,

This photograph of the Carpenter family was made in Kansas City, Missouri, in 1912. One-year-old Harlean Carpenter is flanked by her mother, Jean Harlow Carpenter, and her father, Mont Clair Carpenter.

the attachment had a feverish, almost morbid quality. Mother and daughter were absorbed in each other, almost to the exclusion of everyone else. When Jean threw a birthday party for Harlean, Jean fussed over Harlean and ignored her little friends; they went home to their mothers and said they never wanted to go back. "We were always together, the Baby and I," said Jean years later. "All of our waking hours. I crept into bed with her and stayed with her until she fell asleep. Then I would steal away quietly, fearful that I might disturb her." In 1917, Jean enrolled Harlean in Miss Barstow's School for Girls, but the child found it difficult to make friends. Her parents did not socialize, and other children's parents were unwilling to visit the Carpenters, even though they lived in an eighteen-room home at 1312 East 79th Street. As a result, little Harlean made friends of domestics and pets. For the rest of her life, she would be more at ease with working-class people and animals than she would with her peers.

Most of her isolation was due to her mother. "Harlean's father was a highly respected man in Kansas City," said Harlean's schoolmate Dorothy P. Smith. "His wife was not." Another schoolmate, Nancy Jane Hargis, remembered Jean Carpenter as "common, sort of a floozy." Another friend, Mary Scott, recalled rumors that Jean had "lots of, shall we say, 'beaus'." Jean was able to parlay her beauty into adventures, but not into freedom. "She couldn't wait to leave Kansas City," said Smith. Yet none of her romances offered a way out. Frustrated, Jean made her daughter into a tiny version of herself. "Harlean was always overdressed," recalled classmate Agnes Low. "She always had fancy clothes. The rest of us wore plain, homemade clothes." The child sensed her mother's frustration. "Mother and I became more than mother and daughter," Harlean said. "We grew to be real friends. Perhaps it was because I was rather mature for my age and Mother knew that I understood the unhappiness she was feeling." In the end, nothing could assuage Jean Carpenter's discontent. In 1922, she filed for divorce, winning sole custody of Harlean and alimony of two hundred dollars a month. It meant little to her that Harlean longed for her father. Jean would not allow Harlean to see him. When Jean found photos with Mont in them, she ripped off his head. Less than a year later, Mother put Baby on a train and headed for Los Angeles.

The newly liberated Jean Carpenter chose the West Coast instead of Chicago or New York because she hoped to become a film actress. Even though she had never appeared in so much as a school play, years of compliments had convinced her that she was beautiful enough for the movies. Now she was traveling to Hollywood without even a letter of introduction, believing her magnetism would draw opportunity.

The sidelong glance that would become a Jean Harlow hallmark was already visible in 1914, when Harlean Carpenter posed for this winsome portrait.

She was just one of many hopefuls. In 1923 women from all over America were going to Hollywood. To the arriving Midwesterner, this unincorporated district of Los Angeles looked like a sprawling orange grove, but it was already an industrial center. Box-office receipts that year totaled $336 million. The film industry was America's sixth largest. Though there were more than fifty studios, they offered little hope of work to the thousands of women who came to Hollywood. Casting directors turned them away at the studio gates, leaving them to eke out their livings as waitresses, dance hall hostesses, or prostitutes. Still they kept coming. The 1920s had already seen women win the right to vote, and, increasingly, the right to work alongside men. They were also winning the right to smoke, to drink, and to raise hemlines.

Jean availed herself of these new freedoms. She was divorced and traveling cross-country to make her own way. She thought herself a modern woman but expressed interest in neither voting nor working. Acting in films was only a means to an end. Hollywood was full of rich men. She was going to find one.

Jean Carpenter took Harlean to the Empire Studio at 427 South Main Street in Los Angeles for this portrait of a determined mother and daughter.

After arriving in Los Angeles, Jean moved herself and Harlean into a rooming house at 1015 South Gramercy Place, a respectable middle-class home at the southwest corner of Olympic Boulevard. Jean then enrolled her child in the progressive Hollywood School for Girls at 1749 North La Brea Avenue, a block north of Hollywood Boulevard. Harlean's schoolmates included Agnes deMille, daughter of director William deMille; Katherine DeMille, adopted daughter of producer-director Cecil B. DeMille; Irene Mayer, daughter of producer Louis B. Mayer; and Evelyn Flebbe, daughter of scenarist Beulah Marie Dix. Surprisingly, the student body included two boys, Douglas Fairbanks, Jr., and Joel McCrea.

One evening, mother and daughter found themselves at the Egyptian Theatre on Hollywood Boulevard, watching stars arrive for a premiere. "When Pola Negri swept into the foyer," recalled Harlean, "my heart stopped. She was a queen. Bowing to right and left. Even throwing kisses. I was crazy to get a glimpse of this exotic woman."

While Harlean attended school, Jean made the rounds of casting offices. She began to realize that at thirty-four, she had arrived too late. The average movie recruit was in her late teens. Jean's florid beauty was better suited to the stage, but she had no training, only ambition. She had already focused attention on her child. Now she began to transfer ambition to her. Harlean was a likely prospect. Even as an adolescent, her appearance was unique and her appeal powerful.

Barbara ("Bobbe") Brown was Harlean's age and would be a family friend and employee for many years, but her first notion of Harlean was that of an infant. "My father had invited some men over," recalled Brown, "and while they were playing cards, Mrs. Carpenter stopped by and mentioned that 'the Baby' would be there soon. So I expected a tiny little baby. [Then] the doorbell rang and there was this *amazing* girl with white-blonde hair and gorgeous green eyes. The men just stared."

"Harlean was excessively blonde," wrote Evelyn Flebbe. "She had the first young white hair anyone had ever seen." Harlean's confidence and bearing were also unusual. Uniforms had been introduced to the school, but she refused to wear hers in a demure, conventional fashion "The uniform never looked on anybody the way it looked on her," wrote Flebbe. "Other girls broke the rules against pinning your middy blouse tight at the waist, but only on Harlean did this overcome the package-like effect." Flebbe's father was one of many men who noticed the precocious child. His real estate office was near the school. "After school, the girls would wander by," he said. "They all just walked. Except Harlean. She sashayed."

Jean brought Harlean back to Missouri each summer, and then returned to Los Angeles, each time moving into a cheaper apartment. Skip Harlow was less than pleased about his granddaughter's evolution. She was becoming noticeably aware of men. One of her classmates recalled that although Harlean was a good student and elected vice-president of her eight-grade class, "she was very boy-conscious." One afternoon Flebbe overheard an exchange between Harlean and her friend Marge in the study hall. "The average young millionaire of nineteen or twenty isn't going to throw himself

This snapshot of twelve-year-old Harlean was taken in front of her Gramercy Place home in 1923.

and his fortune at your feet," Marge told Harlean.

Harlean's attitude could be expected. Her mother was herself looking for a rich man, the ultimate component of her facts of life. As Harlean ripened, Jean sat her down for the latest in a series of woman-to-woman talks. "When I was a small girl she began my sex education," Harlean recalled. "I never had any distorted ideas about it. Mother told me things in a frank and open manner, gradually as I was old enough to understand. I never had any false impressions. I think all children should be educated in that way and not be permitted to get their facts of life from the gutter." Alarmed by Harlean's accelerating maturity and the nomadic existence to which Jean was subjecting her, Skip gave Jean an ultimatum: move back or be disinherited.

In 1925, mother and daughter returned to Kansas City. Harlean was enrolled in a French convent called Notre Dame de Sion. After four unpleasant months she was moved to Miss Bigelow's Private School, where she was one of six pampered students. In the summer of 1926, she was sent to Camp Cha-Ton-Ka in Michigamme on the south shore of Lake Michigan. When she paraded around the camp in a new skirt her mother had bought her in Chicago, the other girls threatened to throw her in the lake. Harlean defied them. They threw her in. The good-natured child laughed at herself and did her best to gain acceptance. It was one of the few times in her life when she escaped her mother's influence. "She tried so hard to be like the rest of us," recalled her friend Virginia Woodbridge. "She'd never been allowed to be. She wasn't permitted to have friends or be normal. She was made to be a woman before she was a teenager. She'd tell us about the men she had dates with. They were in their twenties and thirties."

When the first Jean found photos with Mont in them, she ripped off his head.

The summer hiatus was significant for a number of reasons. Harlean and one other girl contracted scarlet fever. Harlean was ill for a period of three weeks, during which her mother came and cared for her. Her recovery was slow but apparently complete. There was no thought of lingering effects or long-term damage to vital organs such as her kidneys.

Jean Carpenter was not a welcome presence in the camp. Both children and adults found her bossy and single-minded. After her mother's departure, Harlean felt sufficiently well to embark on a romance with a sixteen-year-old boy who was camping across the lake. It ended in a sexual experience, most likely her first. She was fifteen.

At summer's end, Jean Carpenter came to fetch Harlean. While changing trains in Chicago, they visited the Sherman Hotel. During dinner at its restaurant, the College Inn, Jean was approached by a swarthy forty-three-year-old man named Marino Bello. He was the brother-in-law of the manager and employed as a maitre d'hôtel but was not introducing himself on behalf of the establishment. He was attracted to Jean. A week later he was visiting her in Kansas City. Skip Harlow took one look at Bello, decided he was an unsavory character, and threatened to take custody of Harlean. He only relented when she was enrolled in Ferry Hall, a girls' finishing school in Lake Forest. For Jean it was

The Witzel Studio, a Hollywood institution itself, made this portrait of Harlean Carpenter's volleyball team at the Hollywood School for Girls. Harlean can be seen in the back row, second from left, her hand on the shoulder of Katherine ("Katie") DeMille, daughter of director Cecil B. DeMille.

a convenient distance from Highland Park, where Bello lived, albeit with his wife. Jean used visits to Harlean to cover an affair with Bello. During the same period, even though Harlean was living in a girls' dormitory, she was dating a boy named Howard Baldwin. "I've been so damned busy," she wrote him, "that I've not had one moment till now to write and try and thank you for my beautiful roses and my lovely letter. Oh Howard, my dear, these things mean so much to me, especially in the condition I've been in. Flu is devilish when you once get it." From all evidence, her interest in him was casual, the effusiveness of her letters more indicative of her mother's tutelage than of any real affection.

In December 1926, Bello's wife divorced him, citing physical cruelty. A month later, Jean Harlow Carpenter became Jean Bello. Harlean took it in stride. She was doing well in school. "I remember seeing her geometry papers," recalled Virginia L. Stuebe, "all with A's on them, beautifully done." She was liked by her classmates, even though she found most of them naïve. "She had associated with older people so much," recalled schoolmate Virginia Bosch, "that she automatically gravitated to the older and more sophisticated among us."

Inevitably, Harlean encountered a young man who had the requisite combination of looks, sophistication, and money. Charles Fremont McGrew II was the twenty-year-old heir of millionaire parents who had drowned when he was sixteen. "Chuck" was within months of claiming his inheritance when Harlean's schoolmate Jadda Leland introduced them. Harlean was as impressed by McGrew's epicene beauty as he was by her blinding blondeness. "It was love—or infatuation—at first sight," recalled Bosch. "From then on Harlean monopolized the one telephone in the dorm."

Marino Bello thought there was a wealthier prospect for Harlean, his boss's brother. Jean pushed Harlean to go on dates with him, but Harlean was in the throes of first love. On September 21, 1927, Harlean and Chuck drove around with elopement on their minds. Finally, in Waukegan, they found a justice of the peace who would perform a late-night ceremony. "Just to give you an idea of the solemnity of our wedding," said Harlean, "a radio next door to the justice's office was blaring 'The St. Louis Blues.'"

In November, Chuck turned twenty-one and received the first installment of his inheritance, the sum of two hundred thousand dollars. Harlean was achieving the fantasy her mother had nurtured. In December, though, there was a troubling episode. McGrew drank so much bootleg liquor at a Christmas party that he had to be carried to bed and could not function for two days. In January of 1928, the newlyweds boarded a ship in New York for a honeymoon cruise, sailing through the Panama Canal and ending in Los Angeles. Several days into the voyage, McGrew drank himself insensible. Harlean braved it out, making friends with newlyweds Ivor and Rosalie Roy McCray.

Harlean's second move to Los Angeles was quite different from her first. She had no need to curry favor. She may have been sixteen, but she was wealthy. On February 10, Chuck dipped into the trust fund and made a down payment of six thousand dollars on a seventeen-thousand-dollar home at 618 North Linden Drive in Beverly Hills. "We were more like two children playing at housekeeping than a settled married couple," said Harlean. "Since there was no necessity for Chuck to work, we had twenty-four hours in which to play. Our life was one continuous party." Not surprisingly, there was more insensate drunkenness. Harlean had no one to consult about McGrew's behavior. For the first time in her life, she had no maternal support. Her mother's aunt, Jetta Belle Chadsey, lived on Imperial Highway in a far-flung part of Los Angeles County. Harlean was still in touch with Bobbe Brown, but the teenager could offer no help. "Harlean was only sixteen, but she seemed years older," said Brown. "She was the mistress of a Beverly Hills mansion, with a retinue of servants, a town car, and everything, while I was still going to high school." It was only a matter of time before the inevitable happened. Harlean made a desperate call to her mother. "I'm stifling, Mommie," she cried. By April, Jean and Marino Bello were living in Beverly Hills—and living off Harlean. The Bellos' house at 300 North Maple Drive was not far from the McGrews. Jean Bello soon became a regular presence in the young couple's home.

In February, Harlean hosted a luncheon for her friends. Rosalie Roy was a guest. A child bride, like Harlean, Roy was seeking her own identity. In 1928, this meant finding a job. As Roy was leaving Harlean's party, she mentioned an appointment in Hollywood. Harlean had a new LaSalle convertible coupe, so she offered Rosalie Roy a lift. It was supposed to be a drive to another district. Instead, it was a visit to another world.

When Rosalie Roy asked for a ride in early 1928, she set a career in motion.

In the spring of 1928, Harlean Carpenter McGrew posed for this snapshot in front of 618 North Linden Drive in Beverly Hills. She had recently moved to the Spanish bungalow with her young husband Chuck.

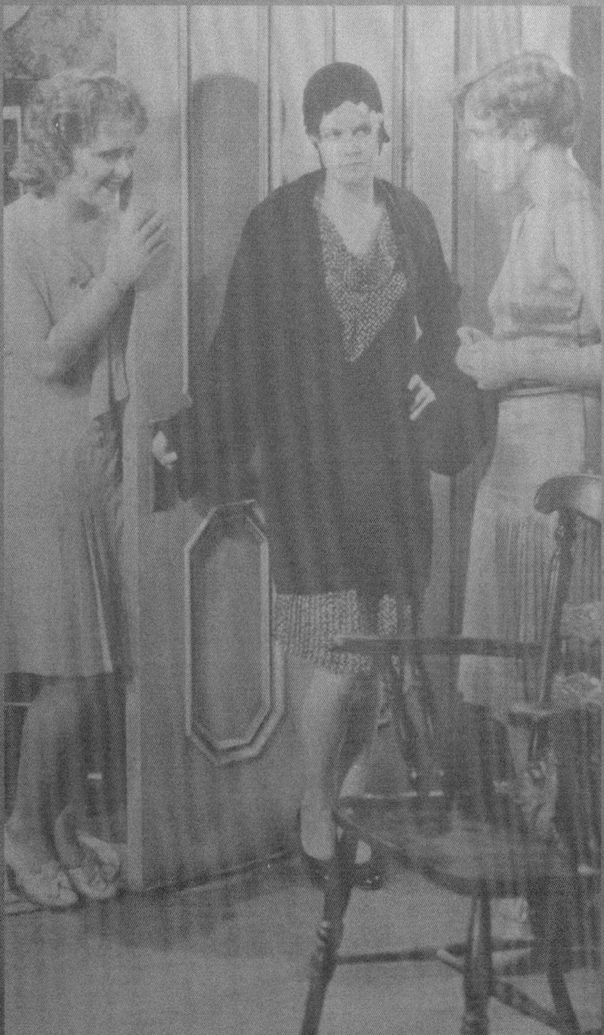

I

The Ash-blonde Starlet

- Hollywood 1928
- A Trip to Griffith Park

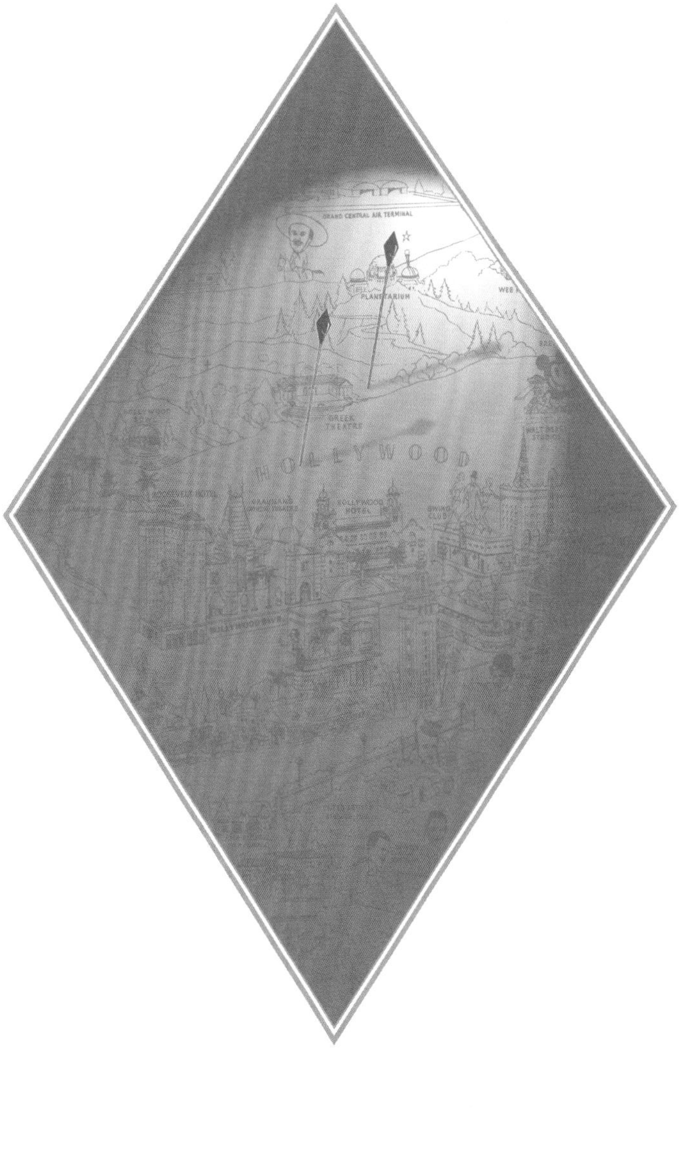

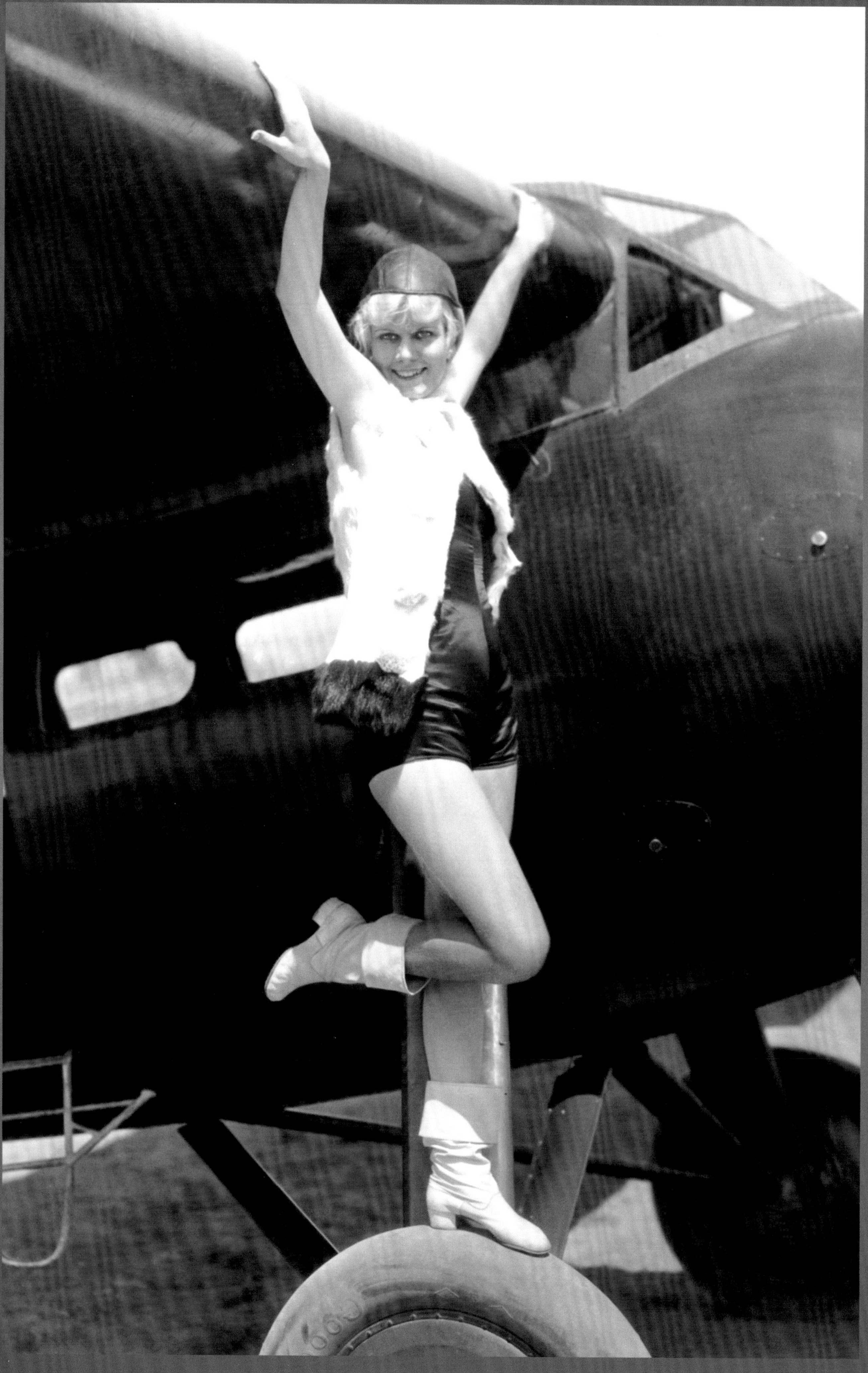

• Hollywood 1928 •

The William Fox Studios sat in arrogant splendor where Western Avenue meets Sunset Boulevard. The Fox lot was so large that it encompassed both sides of Western, dwarfing the orchards along Sunset. On the east side of Western was an assortment of exotic outdoor settings, roofless structures built to fool the eye of the camera. On the west side, behind an Italianate façade, were casting offices, writers' bungalows, and "dark" stages. The studio's most popular stars were Janet Gaynor and Charles Farrell, the team discovered and groomed by William Fox. The egotistical mogul owned a thousand movie houses, a three-hundred-acre complex in West Los Angeles, and the Movietone sound patent. This was the thriving studio where Harlean McGrew brought Rosalie Roy for an appointment.

Harlean was only one of a hundred beautiful people visiting the Fox lot that afternoon in late February 1928. Yet, as she waited for Rosalie Roy, she began to attract attention. People walking by her car stared at her. When Roy emerged from her interview, she was accompanied by two Fox executives, one of whom was a casting director named Ryan. He asked Roy to introduce him to Harlean. He was surprised that a girl with Harlean's looks was not seeking film work. After a little coaxing, Harlean accepted a letter of introduction to Dave Allen, the head of the Central Casting Bureau. The bureau was located in the Louis B. Mayer Building at Hollywood and Western, two minutes from Fox. Harlean had no interest in going there. She went home and dropped the letter in a drawer.

At a luncheon a week later, Harlean told her new friends about the letter. One of them bet $250 that she would not go to Central Casting. Piqued, Harlean went the next day. When she registered with the bureau, she was asked what name she would use. "Jean Harlow," she replied offhandedly. "A few days later," recalled Harlean, "the phone bell rang and a strange voice asked for Miss Harlow. At first, in my surprise, I said that there was no Miss Harlow in the house. Then I remembered." There was now a second Jean Harlow, the one who would become a star.

Her first work in front of a movie camera came immediately, as a dress extra in the George O'Brien film *Honor Bound.* The film was released in April 1928, and she did nothing more than stand in the background and look appealing. But she *was* appealing. *And* unique. On the set of a subsequent film, an assistant director saw her. "The most beautiful girl ever is sitting on a swing over there," he said to the director. "Walk by and take a look." Each look led to a job. Each job led to another. At first McGrew was tolerant of the attention Harlean attracted. "People used to turn around on the streets and look at her in wonderment," McGrew said later. "We were very happy—for a time." He thought her work harmless; it did not interfere with his partying.

Harlean worked as an extra throughout the summer of 1928, aided by an introduction to Joe Egli, the casting director at Paramount. He suggested she apply at Hal Roach Studios, which was located at 8822 Washington Boulevard in Culver City. It was there that Harlean played bit parts in numerous short films, among them, *Thundering Toupees* (1929) with Edgar Kennedy and *Chasing Husbands* (1928) with Charley Chase. Her salary was $12.50 a day. She registered so well on film that Roach offered her a five-year contract. She was still

[OPPOSITE] A part of a starlet's job was to be photographed in "cheesecake" poses.

underage, so, on December 26, 1928, McGrew cosigned. The contract gave him an excuse to celebrate. He drove Harlean to San Francisco and checked into the Hotel St. Francis for a New Year's binge. His drinking ignited arguments. Harlean threatened to leave him. He threw glasses and bottles at her and wrecked the hotel room.

Working at Roach's "Fun Factory," Harlean made four two-reel comedies with Roach's biggest stars, Stan Laurel and Oliver ("Babe") Hardy. She learned about comedy from them. "There was a friendliness and camaraderie about that small studio entirely different from the impersonality of the large places," recalled Harlean. "No one was too busy to help and advise. Stan and Babe realized my ignorance and did everything in their power to make me feel at home and at ease."

Harlean was less at ease in her own home. McGrew had become resentful of her work and of Jean Bello's constant presence. He gave Harlean an ultimatum. She went to Roach and requested a release from her contract. "It's breaking up my marriage," she said. "What can I do?" On March 2, 1929, the sympathetic Roach released her, perhaps aware that Jean Bello wanted Harlean out of the contract more than McGrew did. Jean Bello envisioned something more than a small comedy studio for her daughter. There were five major studios in Hollywood. She was determined to get Harlean into one.

Harlean McGrew posed with her mother Jean Bello in front of the North Linden Drive home.

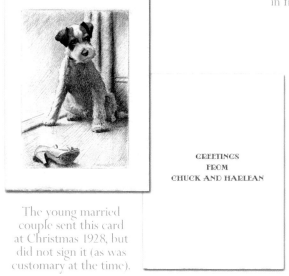

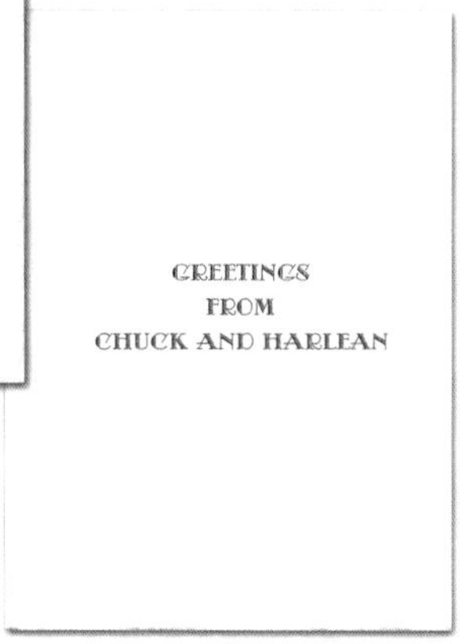
GREETINGS
FROM
CHUCK AND HARLEAN

The young married couple sent this card at Christmas 1928, but did not sign it (as was customary at the time).

Harlean literally stood out from the other extra girls in this publicity still for Hal Roach's *Chasing Husbands* (1928).

Skip Harlow went to a Kansas City theater to see his granddaughter act with Laurel and Hardy in *Double Whoopee* (1929). He was outraged when he saw Harlean dressed only in a teddy.

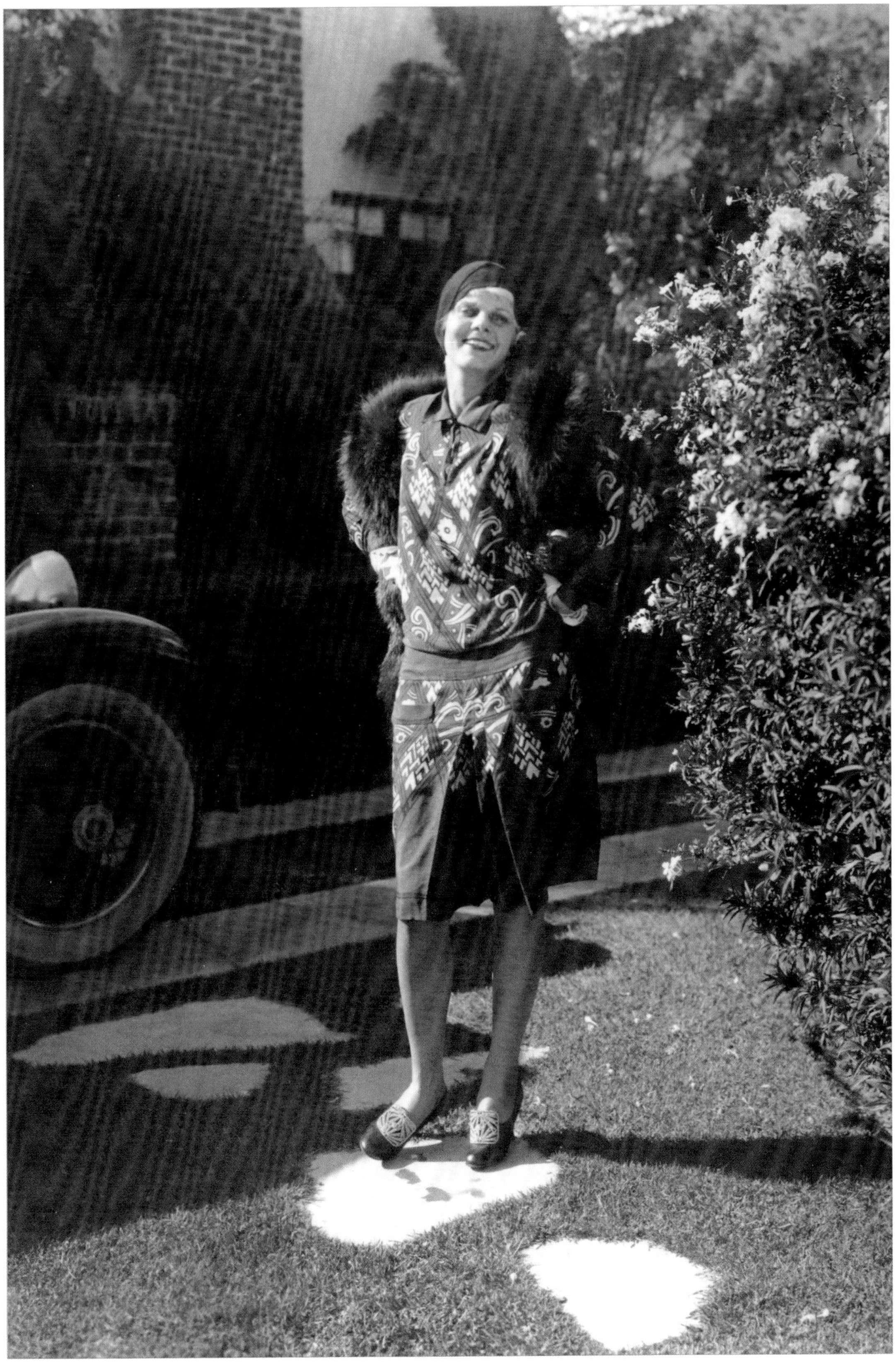

When Harlean McGrew posed in front of her North Linden Drive home in early 1929, she was a starlet with a five-year contract. It would soon be abrogated.

• A Trip to Griffith Park •

In the spring of 1929, Jean Bello pushed Harlean back into extra work at Fox, where her former classmate Evelyn Flebbe saw her one day. "This is not the glowing way to go," Flebbe said to herself. To get better work, Harlean needed photographs. Jean Bello interviewed photographers. Most were employed by the studios, but some, like Edwin Bower Hesser, were freelance artists who offered interpretations not found in studio galleries. Hesser's painterly portfolio included creamy images of Corinne Griffith, Mae Murray, and Gloria Swanson. It also included "art studies" of hungry starlets. Adela Rogers St. Johns, a popular novelist and journalist, knew Hesser's reputation. "He was a pleasant, plump little man," wrote St. Johns, "artistic to his fingertips and harmless as a kitten. But he had a passion for photographing ladies with as few clothes on as possible."

Jean Bello decided that photographs by Hesser, even seminude, would open doors for Harlean, but she would have to be of legal age before she could disrobe for an artist. Harlean turned eighteen on March 3, 1929. Over the objections of Chuck McGrew, Jean scheduled a session with Hesser. The fractious McGrew need not have worried, at least about the photographer's intentions. Hesser brought his wife to the session.

Griffith Park's craggy terrain was an ideal setting for Hesser's classically influenced images. Ten years earlier, while completing his military service, he had made a short film, *The Triumph of Venus*, depicting godly love in Greece. His still photography was shot in the same style. He accomplished it not with the imposing 8x10 view camera favored by portraitists and pictorialists, but with a small Graflex, which was easier to carry over rocky terrain. It used 4x5 film packs rather than sheet film, so there were no heavy film holders. Hesser also used the popular soft focus lens, transforming his subjects from scantily clad flappers to latter-day goddesses.

Shortly after this, Harlean became pregnant. Mother Jean saw more potential in Harlean's career than she did in motherhood. She applied pressure. Harlean caved in. An abortion was arranged. "I wanted that child that was taken from me," Harlean said later. McGrew's response to Jean Bello's manipulation was to attack Harlean. She asked for a fox fur piece to wear on screen. He yelled at her. "What do you think I'm made of? Money? To hell with you!" The arguing escalated. So did the drinking. His mother-in-law stepped in. Harlean moved out.

On June 11, Harlean and Chuck McGrew filed for a legal separation. On June 15, McGrew entered into a property settlement in which he agreed to give Harlean the house, the roadster, and $375 a month. McGrew's grandfather managed his trust fund. Harlean had just moved back into Linden Drive when the McGrew trust rejected her claim. In August, the McGrews stopped the alimony payments and McGrew left Los Angeles. Harlean had no choice but to sell the house at a loss. She moved in with the Bellos and continued to work.

Meanwhile, her own grandfather, Skip Harlow, had just seen her on the screen in Laurel and Hardy's *Double Whoopee*. He grew angry seeing her in her underwear and threatened to disinherit her. "Poor grandfather," said Harlean. "Those teddies

[opposite] In the spring of 1929, Harlean McGrew posed in the wilds of Griffith Park for pictorialist Edwin Bower Hesser. The three-thousand-acre park was built on land donated in 1896 by the eccentric Griffith J. Griffith, a Welsh immigrant who had made a fortune in mining and Los Angeles land speculation.

were too much for him." Jean Bello prevailed upon her father to visit her and Harlean so he could see that they were not living in "Good Times Land." Skip came out, saw painfully respectable Beverly Hills, and calmed down. "He didn't find it half as bad as it was painted," said Harlean.

In October 1929, Roach released a film he had shot in February, another Laurel and Hardy short called *Bacon Grabbers*. Its release had been delayed by the addition of music and sound effects, but it was significant for another reason. It was the first film in which Harlean Carpenter received screen credit as Jean Harlow.

Her first talking film had been shot at Paramount over the summer. *The Saturday Night Kid* (1929) starred Clara Bow, the Brooklyn-born "It Girl." Bow was frightened by the advent of sound and keenly aware of the competition that Harlean represented. "Who's gonna see me next ta her?" Bow asked assistant director Arthur Jacobson. Bow demanded that Harlean be taken off the picture, but relented and eventually warmed to the cheerful Harlean.

The film's male lead, James Hall, was working simultaneously on this film and on *Hell's Angels* (1930), the World War I epic being produced by Howard Hughes. Begun in 1927 as a silent film, it was in limbo because of "talkie" technology. Hughes had just decided to reshoot the principal scenes with sound. His leading lady, the Swedish-born Greta Nissen, had a heavy accent and was consequently unsuitable for the role of an English girl. Hughes needed a new actress. The call went out. Tests were shot. Ben Lyon, who was also a lead in *Hell's Angels*, made dozens of them, but none of the aspirants appealed to Hughes.

In late October of 1929, Lyon was still working on *Hell's Angels*. Hughes had rented facilities at Metropolitan, a small studio located at 1040 North Las Palmas in Hollywood. One

Harlean had just turned eighteen when she posed for Hesser, who apparently wanted to portray her as a dryad, a wood nymph.

day, during a break in shooting, Lyon was walking around the lot. He chanced to visit the sound stage where an Al Christie comedy was being made. "They were shooting a ballroom scene with about two hundred extras," recalled Lyon. "Suddenly my eyes riveted on a girl in the middle of the crowd, a blonde in a tight-fitting black satin gown. I walked over to her, and she gave me a suspicious sort of 'Keep your ground, buddy' stare as I asked her: 'How would you like to play the lead in *Hell's Angels*?'"

"What's the deal?" asked Harlean Carpenter (aka Jean Harlow).

"Tell me," said Lyon. "What time do you break for lunch?"

"12:30. Why?"

"Make it a ten-minute snack."

At 12:40 Harlean was standing in front of long, tall Howard Hughes. He stared at her without visible interest and then turned to Lyon. "Let her have a voice test," said Hughes. "You've made tests with everybody else. Make one with her. In fact, you direct it. Make it tonight."

Lyon coached Harlean during her breaks on the Christie set and arranged to make a test shot on the *Hell's Angels* set that night with the film's head cinematographer Tony Gaudio. Joseph Moncure March, who was writing the new dialogue, watched the test. "Tony yelled for lights," recalled March, "and the girl entered, framed in the doorway. She had almost albino blond hair and a puffy, somewhat sulky little face." No one on the set found Harlean impressive. "She's got the shape of a dustpan," sneered one crewmember.

A few days later, Harlean returned to the office of Caddo Productions, Hughes's company. After a few minutes, she emerged and walked over to her mother, who was waiting in her car on the Metropolitan lot. "Mommie," Harlean said in a daze. "I got the part. I got the part!"

Harlean was uninhibited and enjoyed nudity. At ease with her own body, she brought an innocent sensuality to poses that could have been merely erotic.

[OPPOSITE] While not a trained dancer, Harlean's natural grace enabled her to accomplish neoclassic attitudes.

Harlow's first speaking part was in *The Saturday Night Kid*, (1929) which starred the reigning sex symbol, Clara Bow. Also in the cast was a young stage actress named Jean Arthur.

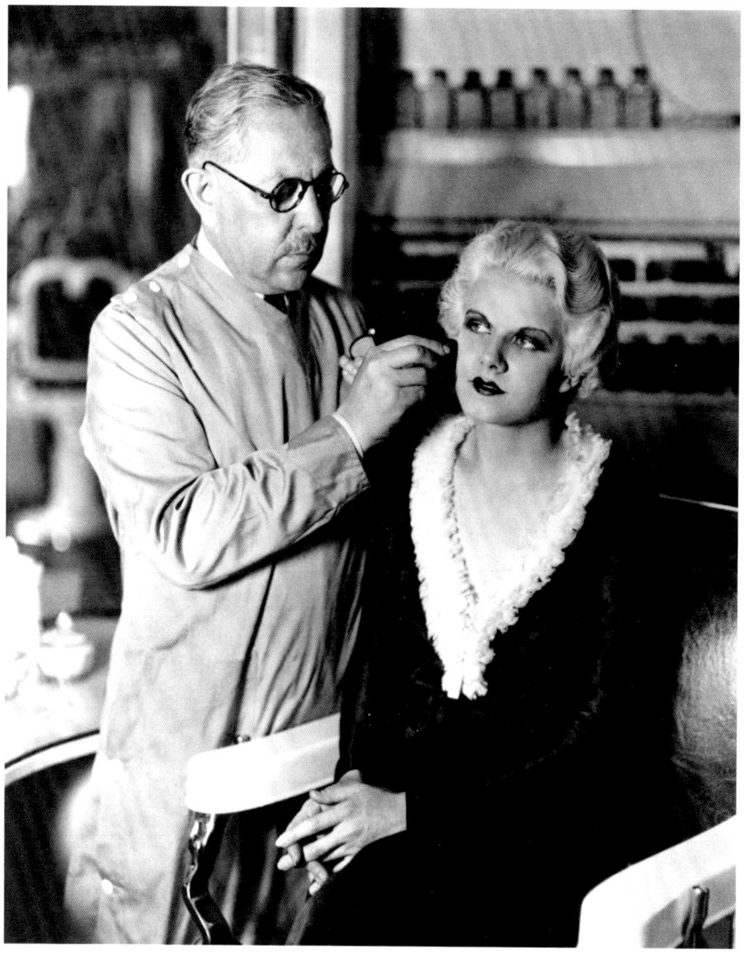

Using her mother's name, the newly christened Jean Harlow posed with Max Factor at his makeup studio, which was located at 326 South Hill Street in Los Angeles. At this time, many Hollywood institutions, even premieres, still called downtown home.

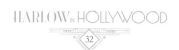

[OPPOSITE]
This Preston Duncan portrait appeared in the May 1930 issue of *Film Fun* magazine.

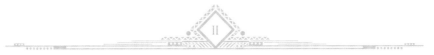

II

The Platinum Blonde

- Biplanes over Hollywood
- Yesterday's Sensation

• Biplanes over Hollywood •

In October 1929, Harlean Carpenter had been working in Hollywood for a year and a half. To the casual observer, she was several people. Her mother's "Baby." Mrs. Chuck McGrew. A bit player called Jean Harlow. On October 24, she consolidated these identities to fulfill her mother's dream. She signed a contract with the Caddo Company as "Harlean Carpenter McGrew, known professionally as Jean Harlow." This was significant. In so doing, she acknowledged that her identity would no longer be her own. "Jean Harlow" would be the creation of her mother, of a motion picture company, and of the American public. Not surprisingly, she began to sign her personal correspondence with the ambiguous "Me." Her most frequent complaint during the course of her brief life would be that people mistook Jean Harlow for her.

No one mistook Howard Hughes for anyone else. Like Chuck McGrew, he was the heir of rich parents who had died when he was a teenager. Unlike McGrew, he was a genius whose intoxication came not from alcohol but from invention, speed, and altitude. At twenty-five, Hughes was worth many millions, the only Hollywood studio head who had not worked his way up from East Coast nickelodeons. He had come from Texas to the film capital to make films with his own money and had done precisely that. He did it well, winning an Academy Award with his second, *Two Arabian Nights* (1928). Now he was engaged in an endeavor so grandiose that envious moguls were calling it "Howard's Folly."

There had been war epics, including *The Big Parade* (1925), *What Price Glory?* (1926), and *Wings* (1927). Hughes was making the epic to end them all. *Hell's Angels* would be big, bold, and brutal, an aviation saga made by an aviator. William Wellman had utilized sixty planes in *Wings*. Hughes was shooting his dogfight scenes with eighty-seven fighters, a Gotha bomber, a Zeppelin, and 137 pilots, including himself. After an on-camera crash, he spent a few days in a hospital. He would also spend $3.75 million on *Hell's Angels*. Only *Ben-Hur* (1925) had cost more, $3.9 million. But *Ben-Hur* had cost no human lives. *Hell's Angels* took the lives of three pilots and one mechanic. The resulting scenes were unprecedented in their bloody, sickening realism.

The scenes of the fliers' private lives were something else. Directing dialogue was beyond Hughes's ability. He could modify a microphone to record a Gnome Monosoupape motor, but he could not tell an actor how to read a line. He needed a dialogue director, so he hired James Whale, who had made a London hit of R.C. Sherriff's war play *Journey's End*. Himself a veteran, Whale was in Hollywood to direct the film version for Tiffany Studios. Whale became the first film director to exact a serious performance from Jean Harlow—or to try.

Harlow's accent was the first problem. Growing up on the border of Kansas and Missouri, she had acquired an unmistakably regional accent, far from the "mid-Atlantic" tones of reigning favorites such as Ruth Chatterton. Instead of pronouncing the word *corner* as "cohrnehr," she pronounced it "cwohneh." The second problem was that Whale disliked the character Harlow was playing, a sluttish rich girl he described as a pig. The third problem was Harlow's inability to act. Her only experience was

[Opposite] Jean Harlow's hair-and-makeup test for her role in the 1930 Howard Hughes production *Hell's Angels* was captured in a portrait.

as a comic foil. Her line readings were unconvincing and she knew it. Whale worked with her for a week, taking pains to disguise his contempt for the frightened girl. At one point she had to play a seduction scene. "Tell me," she pleaded. "Tell me how to do it."

"My dear girl," Whale responded, "I can tell you how to be an actress, but I cannot tell you how to be a woman."

Whale departed Caddo on November 4, leaving Harlow to coaches who were more patient but less skilled. Harlow became frustrated, trying to play a character the likes of whom she had never met. As conceived by screenwriter Joseph Moncure March, the rich girl Helen was a caricature of sexuality. Harlow may have looked flashy, but she was essentially reserved. Ben Lyon was acting these scenes with her. "She used to carry with her," he recalled, "a little satchel containing four or five books of poetry, famous prose, or some special branch of the classics that she was studying at the time." Obviously, the image of a bookworm was not going to sell a sexy epic to the public. Hughes had recently hired a publicity director named Lincoln Quarberg. After numerous false starts, Quarberg came up with the catchphrase "Platinum Blonde." Harlow didn't think much of it, but her mother urged her to cooperate by lightening her hair. Before long, Jean Bello would be bleaching her own hair.

Hughes thought enough of Harlow to shoot one of her scenes in Multicolor. The two-color process required three times as much light as black-and-white, so Klieg lights were used. Standing in front of a bank of these lights exposed Harlow to ultraviolet light and powdery dust from the burning carbon. "Each night I went home with inflamed eyes and a headache," Harlow said later. "Soon my vision began troubling

Harlow's risibly sexy scenes with Ben Lyon in *Hell's Angels* were a peculiar counterpoint to its grimly realistic war scenes.

The *Hell's Angels* advertising campaign was as didactic as it was direct. "Those two words, 'Sex Appeal,' coupled with my name in electric lights over Hollywood Boulevard, made me feel very bitter," said Harlow later.

Howard Hughes sent Harlow around the country to publicize *Hell's Angels*. She was welcomed to Seattle by its mayor, Frank Reynolds.

me. I went to see a doctor. His diagnosis was almost unbelievable. The conjunctiva, the membrane covering my eyeballs, had been burned."

Harlow should have been more irritated with Hughes. He was only paying her $150 a week, had no projects to offer, and rejected requests for her services from other studios. From the Metro-Goldwyn-Mayer studios in Culver City (M-G-M) came word that Paul Bern, right-hand man of production head Irving Thalberg, wanted to interview Harlow. When Hughes let her go to M-G-M for an interview, she didn't get the part (it was a period picture), but she realized that Bern's interest in her was different than the panting-dog attention she usually attracted. "The next evening he telephoned me," recalled Harlow. "He'd secured my number from [actress] Leatrice Joy, a mutual friend. He asked my mother for permission to take me out." Their date was unusually pleasant—and unusual—for the brand-new sex symbol. "Paul was most gentlemanly."

In early 1930, after filming had ended, Harlow spent her time off with Jean Bello. When her mother went shopping, which bored her, Harlow visited Caddo, watching post-production progress. Hughes had contracted Sid Grauman to stage the *Hell's Angels* premiere in his Chinese Theatre on Hollywood Boulevard. Grauman's publicity office was across the street, in the Hollywood Professional Building. Harlow occasionally went there to watch the veteran art director George Holl paint sexy advertising art for the theater forecourt. She was drawn to older men and to artists.

Hughes had spent too much on his epic to sell it short. He and Grauman envisioned the premiere to end all premieres, touting *Hell's Angels* as a four-million-dollar masterpiece with a cast of twenty thousand. What hyperbole could not accomplish, money could. Hughes spent seventy-five thousand dollars to take over Hollywood for a night.

On Tuesday, May 27, 1930, fifteen blocks of Hollywood Boulevard, from Vine Street to La Brea Avenue, were cordoned off and illuminated by the blinding blue-white rays of 135 sun arcs. One towering light standard was stationed every fifty feet along the boulevard. Large model airplanes hung from wires stretched across the street. Red and green searchlights aimed upward, catching a squadron of warplanes as they buzzed overhead. One monoplane drew smoke circles. Two others shot off flares and fireworks. As a crowd of fifty thousand lined the streets, police reserves tried to maintain order. When a limousine full of stars was recognized, fans screamed and pressed forward. Motorcycle cops turned on sirens and urged them back. A detachment of National Guardsmen and another of Marines moved in. The crowds stayed behind barricades. More limousines crept toward the theater, but traffic was so congested that it took them an hour to arrive. When they did, they paid eleven dollars and were escorted up a green carpet to a waiting microphone. Among the stars who spoke to a radio audience were Gloria Swanson, Charles Chaplin, Mary Pickford, Gary Cooper, Clara Bow, and Joan Crawford. After this array of glamour, Harlow's entrance was still arresting. Accompanied by Paul Bern and followed by Marino and Jean Bello, she was a high-contrast image: waves of platinum blonde hair, a mass of white orchids, a white chiffon gown, and a white velvet cape trimmed with white fox fur. She spoke clearly and calmly into the microphone, then entered the theater. No one could tell that she was terrified.

"How I got through that night I'll never know," Harlow said later. "I should have been the happiest girl alive, but like a big baby, I sat there silent and glum, like I was on my way to the dentist. I don't remember seeing the picture at all. I sat through the entire affair in a cold perspiration trying to realize that that girl on the screen was really me." Whoever she was, the girl on the screen caused as much comment as the spectacular scenes of airborne warfare, but not from the critics, who either ignored her or jeered at her. The public responded to her and began writing. Her mother had to hire family friend Bobbe Brown to help with the mail. Most of it was positive, but some of it upset her. "Because I played a hussy in *Hell's Angels*, people seem ready to accept me as such a girl in real life," she told an interviewer. "In my next picture I don't want to play such a fearfully cynical and frank part. I would like the girl to be a little sympathetic." Yet she had to admit that the role of Helen had brought her what everyone in Hollywood craves: fame.

While Harlow tried to grasp her public image, her private life unraveled. She had started divorce proceedings on November 7, 1929, charging Chuck McGrew with cruelty and intemperance. At 4:00 A.M. on June 28, 1930, he appeared at the Bellos' home, pounding on the door of the maid's room. Marino Bello let McGrew in. Harlow and Jean Bello joined them in the living room. McGrew was drunk and contentious, taunting them that he was on his way to Chicago, where they could not serve papers on him. He was too drunk to notice that while Harlow was pouring him coffee, Jean Bello was in another room dialing a telephone. Within a half hour, an attorney arrived and served papers on McGrew. He stomped out and then in a fit of rage smashed his auto into Harlow's LaSalle.

For all his misbehavior, McGrew sincerely wanted to reconcile with his wife. Jean Bello kept him at bay, seeing only an impediment to her daughter's career. McGrew went to court and charged his wife with breaking an agreement by posing for indecent photographs during their marriage. Harlow countered that Edwin Bower Hesser was an art photographer and that she had posed for him with her husband's knowledge. Meanwhile, Marino Bello discovered that his wife was planning to divorce him; she had found evidence of philandering. He chose this moment to offer as-yet-unpublished Hesser photographs to the opposing side; or at least he threatened to. In either case, he was not about to be pushed out of the family just as Harlow was becoming a cash cow. Jean Bello backed down. The court actions dragged on. Harlean and Chuck McGrew's divorce decree would finally be granted on January 30, 1931.

No harm had been done to Harlow's name or career. Hughes had kept her on the move, promoting *Hell's Angels* with a three-month tour of vaudeville theaters and movie houses. Jean Harlow in person was proving as popular as the siren on the screen. With her newfound fame, her name began appearing above Ben Lyon's and James Hall's in *Hell's Angels* advertising. Ironically, the artist who had painted the credits for the film itself misspelled her name as "Harlowe," the first and last time this would happen.

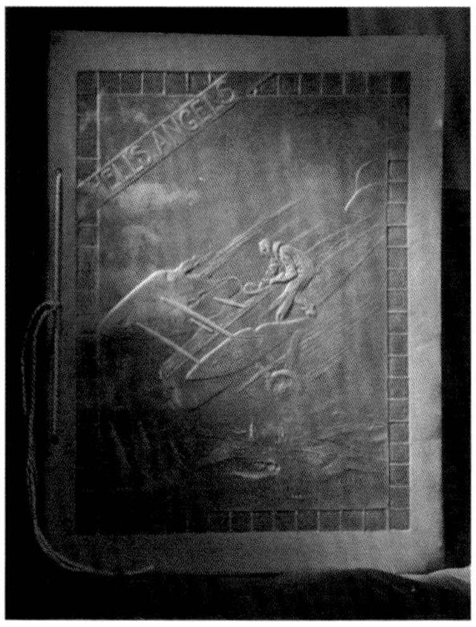

An original drawing by Clayton Knight graced the embossed leather cover of the *Hell's Angels* premiere program.

The premiere of *Hell's Angels* at Grauman's Chinese Theatre on May 27, 1930, was itself a super-production, one that remains unsurpassed for extravagance, imagination, and audacity.

On seeing Harlow arrive at the *Hell's Angels* premiere with M-G-M producer Paul Bern (visible at left), Hollywood columnist Dorothy Manners wrote: "At last the world sees Jean Harlow, whose future begins now."

• Yesterday's Sensation •

Jean Harlow expected that *Hell's Angels* would bring her bigger and better roles. With Paul Bern on her side, this looked likely. In December of 1930, Harlow went to M-G-M to play in George Hill's *The Secret Six* (1931), one of the first films to exploit the public's interest in organized crime. She would play a gangster's moll who helps a crusading reporter. Playing the reporter's sidekick was twenty-nine-year-old Clark Gable. After ten years of road companies and Broadway, he had just signed a contract with M-G-M. When he was introduced to Harlow he said, "You're not at all the kind of girl I'd imagined." Harlow was beginning to realize the effect that *Hell's Angels* was having on her career. "I feel as though I were burlesquing every siren act that has ever been done," she told an interviewer. "Producers will think of me only as this sort of person." Ralph Wheelwright, publicist on *The Secret Six*, was surprised by the difference between Harlow and her screen image. "Jean was never cheap, vulgar, or trampy," recalled Wheelwright.

Harlow was nervous working at the imposing M-G-M studios, so Gable tried to bolster her confidence. "I remember Jean would ask me at the end of a scene, 'How'm I doin'?'" said Gable. "We had to criticize each other. We were not among the chosen few who saw the daily rushes." The processed film of the day's work was usually viewed in a screening room the following afternoon, but only by the film's supervisor, director, and cameraman. "The rushes were only for important people," said Harlow. "We just did our day's work and went home." One day Wallace Beery, the film's star, snapped at Harlow over a minor mistake. "Without hesitation, she flared right back at him," recalled Gable. Like most bullies, Beery backed down when confronted. Yet Harlow was unable to confront her mother, who was pushing her harder than ever.

The Secret Six was well made and well received, but it did little to advance Harlow's career. As soon as she finished filming, Hughes shipped her off for a personal appearance at the Chicago opening of *Hell's Angels*, whereupon she was yanked back to Hollywood for retakes on *The Secret Six*. Hughes then loaned her to Universal.

Tod Browning had just finished *Dracula* (1931) when he began to direct Harlow and Lew Ayres in a boxing story called *Iron Man* (1931). He was told to hurry it along. Universal was feeling the pinch of the Great Depression. It made sense to increase the marketability of this film by decreasing the yardage of Harlow's costumes. One day, during the filming, a trade journalist was stopped at the door of the soundstage. "Miss Harlow is insufficiently clad to permit visitors on the set," he was told. She was not insufficiently clad for the cameras, however. Harlow knew the score. "Howard Hughes was loaning me out for $2500 a week," she said. "I was getting $150. But he was loaning me for cheap parts where I didn't wear any clothes." In one scene, Harlow is punched by a gangster. "It got a scream from one femme member of the audience," reported *Variety*. Other audiences reacted with "delighted applause." Even more discouraging were the reviews. *The New York Times* film critic Andre Sennwald wrote: "It is unfortunate that Jean Harlow, whose virtues as an actress are limited to her blonde beauty, has to carry a good share of this picture."

Jean Bello hired a voice coach to work with Harlow. What she really needed was a sympathetic director. After working with the distracted Browning, she was sent to Warner Bros. for a few scenes in William Wellman's gangster film *The Public Enemy* (1931). She fared worse with Wellman, who had neither the time nor the inclination to work past her newly stilted diction. "She was a little bit standoffish," recalled Joan Blondell, who soon realized that Harlow was cowed by the Broadway veterans in the cast: Blondell, James Cagney, and Edward Woods. She fought with

[Opposite] "Miss Harlow is insufficiently clad to permit visitors on the set," a publicist told a disappointed journalist outside the *Iron Man* stage.

Jean Harlow posed with Kiowa Chief Wopope at the 1931 Ramona Pageant in the Hemet-San Jacinto Valley.

these producers are sending out!"

Howard Hughes had moved the Caddo Company into the United Artists lot at Santa Monica Boulevard and Formosa Avenue. He might as well have moved to the moon. Jean Bello was furious at his lack of interest in her daughter's career. At this point, she decided to take control. She appointed her husband to be Harlow's manager and began firing off telegrams to Hughes demanding the cancellation of the contract. Hughes, of course, refused. He was making too much money loaning Harlow to other companies.

Harlow spent May and June on a personal appearance tour that passed through Chicago, New York, and Detroit. She told anyone who would listen that she wanted to "escape the blonde vampire typing which *Hell's Angels* has tagged for me." While performing at the Oriental Theatre in Chicago, she was introduced to members of the underworld by none other than Marino Bello. One mobster she met was Abner "Longy" Zwillman, the head of a gang in Newark, New Jersey. His gentlemanly demeanor belied a violent past that included the

Wellman and the Warner Bros. studio over the revealing scenes planned for her. "They'll probably never let me make another picture for them," said Harlow. "The moment I was signed, they changed the script to undress me." Her resistance was viewed as odd by her fellow actors, since she appeared to be quite unselfconscious about her body. Cagney eyed her breasts and asked her: "How do you hold those things up?" "I ice them," replied Harlow. Keeping her breasts at the correct elevation required this practice, one that Jean Bello had no qualms about performing.

For all her acting deficiencies, Harlow made the usual impression in *Public Enemy*. Critics dismissed her, and young women—the primary percentage of cinema audiences—imitated her. Her next loan-out was to the Fox Film Corporation for a trashy film called *Goldie* (1931). "The character I played was the same detestable, unsympathetic girl," said Harlow, who in the course of the film was called a tramp, beaten, and even branded. Harlow wrote a friend in Chicago: "Don't go to see *Goldie*. I won't. We hear such terrible things about it. It's no wonder the picture shows are empty. The trash

Johnny Hamp and his orchestra were headlining at the Cocoanut Grove nightclub in the Ambassador when this photo was taken of him and Harlow on the golf links.

near-fatal beating of an African-American pimp. Against the wishes of her mother, Harlow had an affair with him. Zwillman expressed his affection for the twenty-year-old actress with gifts such as a Scottish terrier and a red Cadillac roadster. When Harlow complained that she was sick of playing unsavory characters, Zwillman got in touch with Harry Cohn, the head of Columbia Pictures. An under-the-table loan of five hundred thousand dollars to Cohn sealed a deal for two pictures. Hughes got $1000 a week from Cohn, but he refused to give Harlow any more than the $250 that her 1931 contract stipulated. The difference was made up by Longy Zwillman.

Harlow's first film for Columbia was a comedy called *Gallagher*, directed by Frank Capra, the only director granted any latitude by the crude, dictatorial Cohn. Capra found Harlow aloof at first. So did cameraman Joseph Walker and the nominal stars of the film, Loretta Young and Robert Williams. Once again the insecure girl was trying to pass herself off as a sophisticate. The impression lasted all of two days. Then she warmed to her coworkers. "Jean Harlow loved to laugh,"

One of Harlow's first visits to the Agua Caliente resort in Tijuana took place on March 29, 1931. She attended the horse races with entertainer Hap O'Connor.

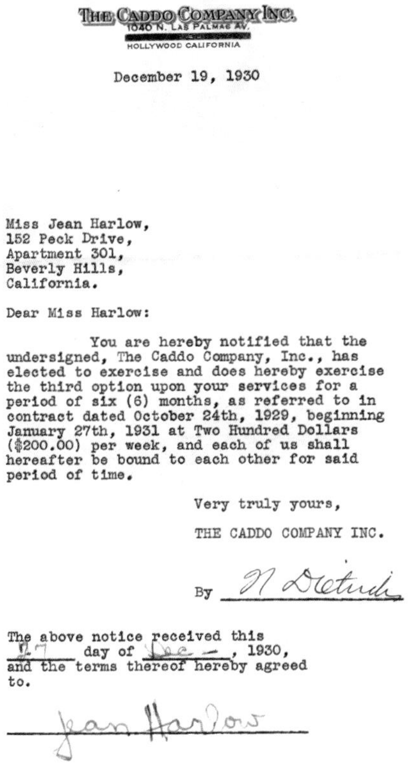

THE CADDO COMPANY INC.
1040 N. LAS PALMAS AV.
HOLLYWOOD CALIFORNIA

December 19, 1930

Miss Jean Harlow,
152 Peck Drive,
Apartment 301,
Beverly Hills,
California.

Dear Miss Harlow:

You are hereby notified that the undersigned, The Caddo Company, Inc., has elected to exercise and does hereby exercise the third option upon your services for a period of six (6) months, as referred to in contract dated October 24th, 1929, beginning January 27th, 1931 at Two Hundred Dollars ($200.00) per week, and each of us shall hereafter be bound to each other for said period of time.

Very truly yours,

THE CADDO COMPANY INC.

By N Dietrich

The above notice received this 27 day of Dec, 1930, and the terms thereof hereby agreed to.

Jean Harlow

By their 1929 contract, Howard Hughes paid Harlow $100 a week, with an increase of $50 per week every six months. By late 1931, her popularity soaring, she still earned only $250 a week—but Hughes charged other studios $1000 for her work.

remembered Capra. "She was just a child. She wanted to learn all the time. She was absolutely ignorant of stage sayings. She pronounced words very oddly, very childlike—like 'liberry' instead of library. And when her scenes were finished, she'd stick around and watch the others." Marino and Jean Bello visited the set only once. "That was enough," said Capra. "I could tell the whole story right there. She was dominated. She wanted her mother, she loved her mother, and she wanted to be near her mother. And her mother and the husband made all the deals. I felt pity for her."

Jean Harlow was becoming a commodity. Despite negative acting reviews, she was hugely popular. Platinum Blonde clubs were springing up across the country. Hughes had Lincoln Quarberg devise a publicity campaign, and, accordingly, Columbia changed the name of the film from *Gallagher* to *Platinum Blonde*. A ten thousand dollar prize was offered to any beautician who could match Harlow's unique shade of platinum. She had recently begun a ritual. Every Sunday she would go to Jim's Beauty Parlor at 6769 Sunset Boulevard. While there, her hair was bleached with an unfriendly mixture of chemicals that might include peroxide, ammonia, or Lux flakes.

Her second Columbia film was first titled *Blonde Baby*. To avoid confusion with *Platinum Blonde,* it was released as *Three Wise Girls* (1932). "I've decided I'm going to be an actress, not a professional sex vulture," said Harlow. "If I don't, I'll get a job as a clothes model." Zwillman persuaded Columbia that Harlow was worth more to them as an actress than as a model, so she got the sympathetic role in *Three Wise Girls*. "For once I'm a nice girl," she said. "A little country girl who comes to the big city, jerks sodas at a fountain, and goes back home just as sweet and pure as when she left." The two films did fairly good box office. The critics were not impressed. "Jean Harlow, as the original small town girl (looking exactly like a big city siren) fails to turn

Bern convinced Howard Hughes to loan Harlow to M-G-M for *The Secret Six*. She appeared with Johnny Mack Brown (seen here) and a newly signed stage actor named Clark Gable.

Harlow was seen at numerous 1931 events with M-G-M producer Paul Bern.

In Universal's *Iron Man* (1931), Harlow displayed none of this charm; she was cast as a boxer's scheming wife.

Universal Pictures in 1931.

Iron Man art director Charles Hall designed this set to show the affluence of the boxer played by Lew Ayres.

Harlow disliked playing a "sex vulture" in *Iron Man*, but she managed to look the part.

William Wellman went to Hollywood Boulevard to shoot this scene of Harlow, Edward Woods, and James Cagney for *The Public Enemy*.

Harlow posed with Johnny and Ruth Hamp for a Tijuana souvenir photo.

Harlow went to Fox Film to play in *Goldie* (1931) with Warren Hymer (seen here) and Spencer Tracy. "The trash these producers are sending out!" she knowingly told a friend.

Elmer Fryer shot this fashion photograph of Harlow wearing an Earl Luick gown from *The Public Enemy*. (1931)

This Ray Jones photograph shows Harlow wearing a Vera West gown.

Warner Bros. 1931.

Fox Films 1931.

On April 1, 1931, six months after completing *The Secret Six*, Harlow was brought back to M-G-M for a portrait sitting with Clarence Bull, mostly because producer Paul Bern saw potential in the actress. Harlow wore natural eyebrows designed by Fox Film, where she was working on a Spencer Tracy vehicle called *Goldie*.

Harlow's stepfather Marino Bello struck a proprietary pose in front of 1353 Club View Drive, but Harlow's film work paid the rent. The nearby club was the Los Angeles Country Club on Wilshire Boulevard.

HOUSES—
For Sale
West and Northwest —50-A

OUR MASTERPIECE
Overlooking Los Angeles
COUNTRY CLUB

MAGNIFICENT TEN-ROOM ENGLISH STONE - TRIM HOUSE. PERPETUAL VIEW OF COUNTRY CLUB, CITY, SEA AND MOUNTAINS.
No detail has been overlooked to make this the perfect home. Large rooms, finest hardwood trim, steel casement windows, full tile kitchen, 4 bedrooms, 3 beautiful baths, den, breakfast room opening to stone floor pergola, stone solarium, immense terrace overlooking the world.
The low price will surprise you. Drive out Wilshire Blvd. past L. A. Country Club. Turn left at first street, 1 block.
1353 CLUB VIEW DRIVE
OXford 1028

On November 24, 1929, the *Los Angeles Times* advertised this home on Club View Drive in Los Angeles.

Twenty-year-old Harlow posed in front of her new residence.

in an adequate performance," wrote a critic in *Film Weekly*. "She does not even begin to act."

"More than anything in the world I want to learn to act," said Harlow. "If I have any luck at all, I ought to be good for five years on the screen. And then, well, I'd like to buy a little tract of land somewhere in California and build a rambling house. But not Spanish. I'd like a couple of good saddle horses, half a dozen wire-haired dogs, and half a dozen cats."

The Columbia deal was finished. So was the dalliance with the gangster. No offers were coming in. Harlow turned to Paul Bern. The best he could offer her was the role of a circus aerialist who marries (and poisons) a midget in Tod Browning's *Freaks* (1932). Harlow was repelled by the prospect of a horror film. Bern looked around and found her the role of a mobster's sexy girlfriend in the upcoming Charles Brabin film, *The City Sentinel*. On November 5, 1931, Harlow signed with M-G-M for the one film. After a year of striving, she was back where she had started, playing a gun moll. "I was ruining my chances for any real success on the screen," she said. "I felt that the public would soon grow tired of me."

Harlow named her Great Dane Bleak because she bought him on an overcast day.

The step-down living room featured a mahogany-beamed ceiling.

Jean Bello furnished Harlow's Club View Drive home to her own taste. The screen on the right hid a bar.

Harlow posed for a "home layout" session in her bedroom.

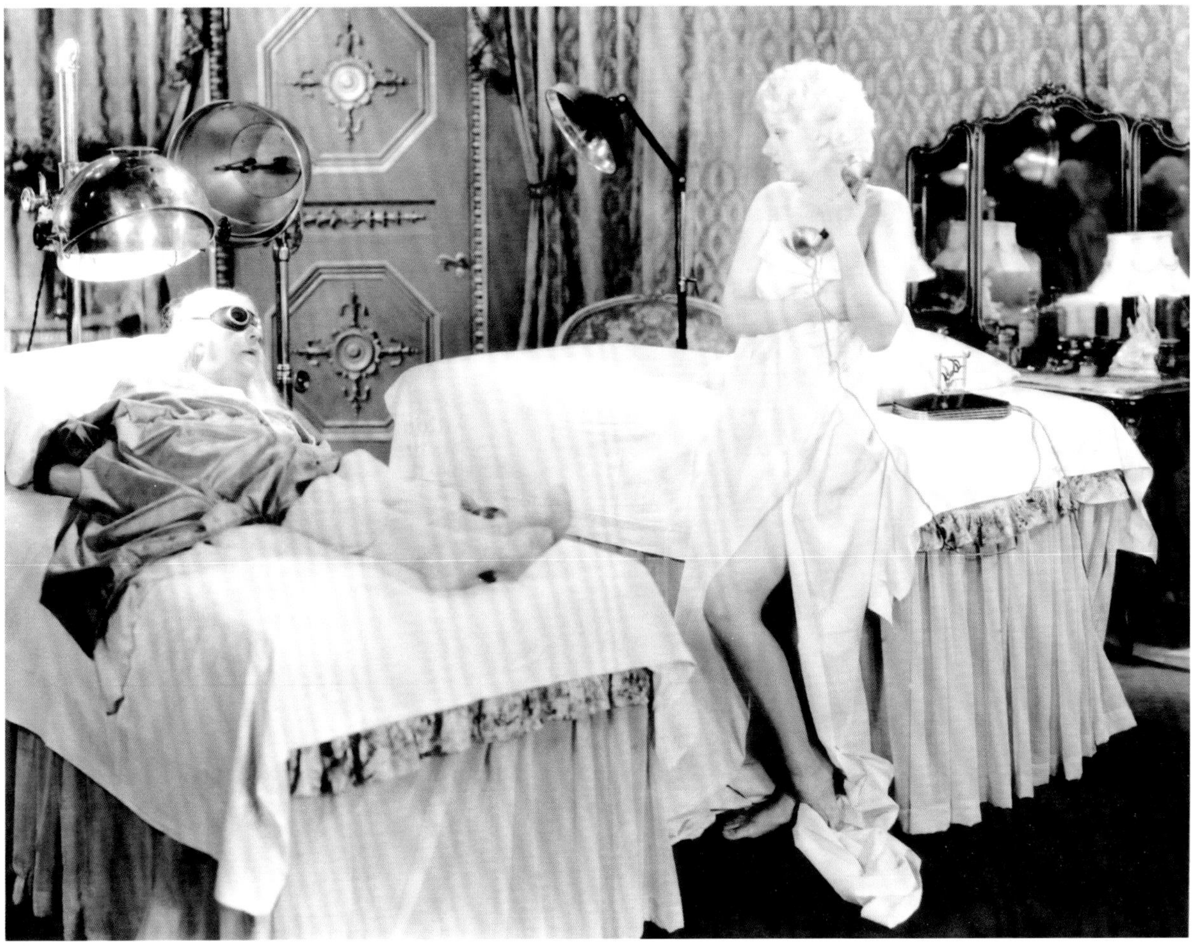

A gangster got Harlow into Columbia Pictures, where she had an opportunity to play something more than a half-dressed baby vamp. In Frank Capra's *Platinum Blonde*, she played a rich girl and Louise Closser Hale played her wacky mother.

Located at Sunset Boulevard and Gower Street, Columbia was the smallest of the so-called "Major Minor" studios.

Harlow's second Columbia film was *Three Wise Girls* (1932). She was supposed to be a "good girl," but her sexy allure was still in evidence.

[OPPOSITE] Preston Duncan made this portrait to publicize Fox Film's *Goldie*.

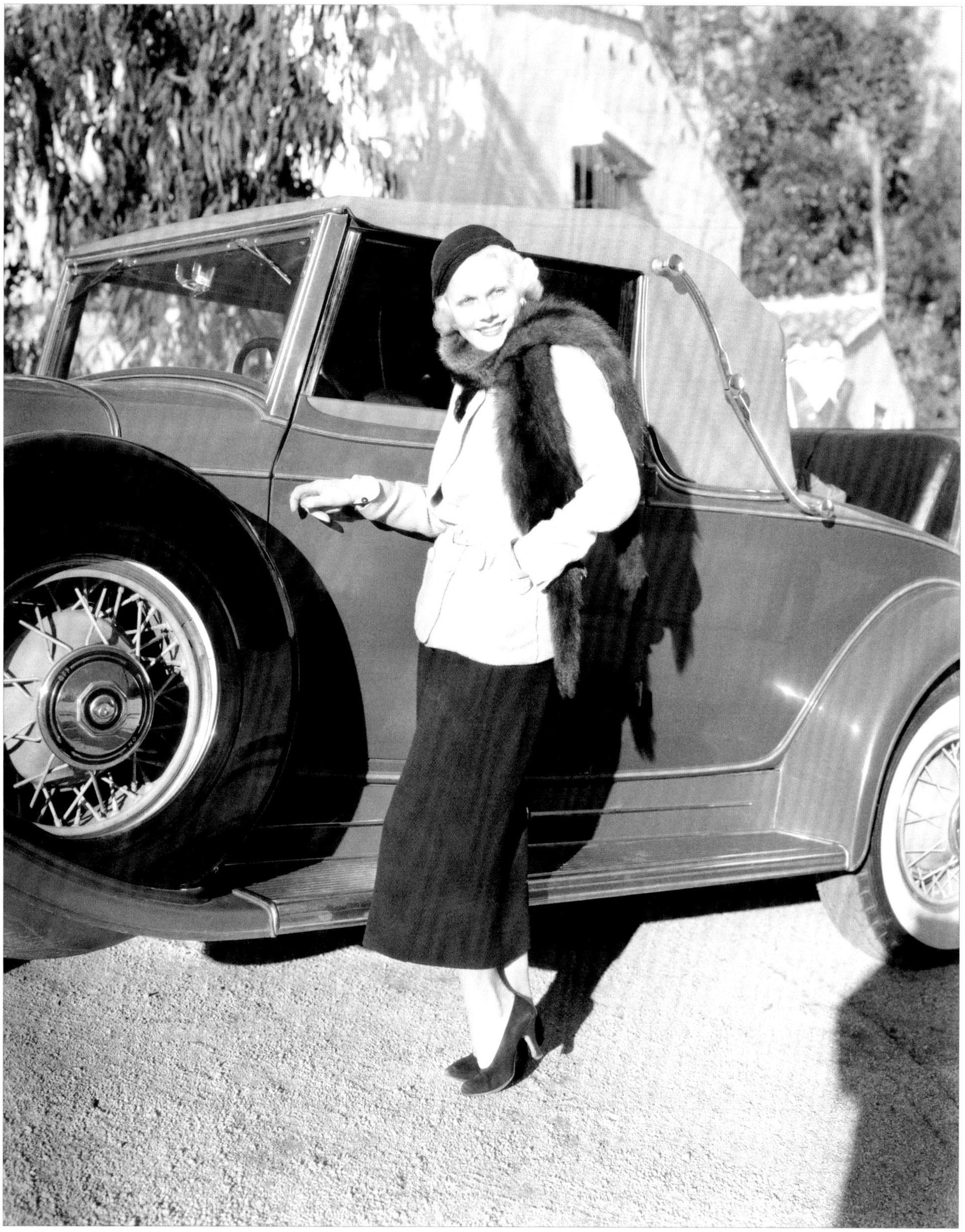

On December 3, 1931, Clarence Sinclair Bull photographed Harlow with her new Cadillac roadster.

[OPPOSITE] *Platinum Blonde* capitalized on Harlow's renowned hair color.

III

The Star

- Club View Drive to Culver City
- Tragedy on Easton Drive

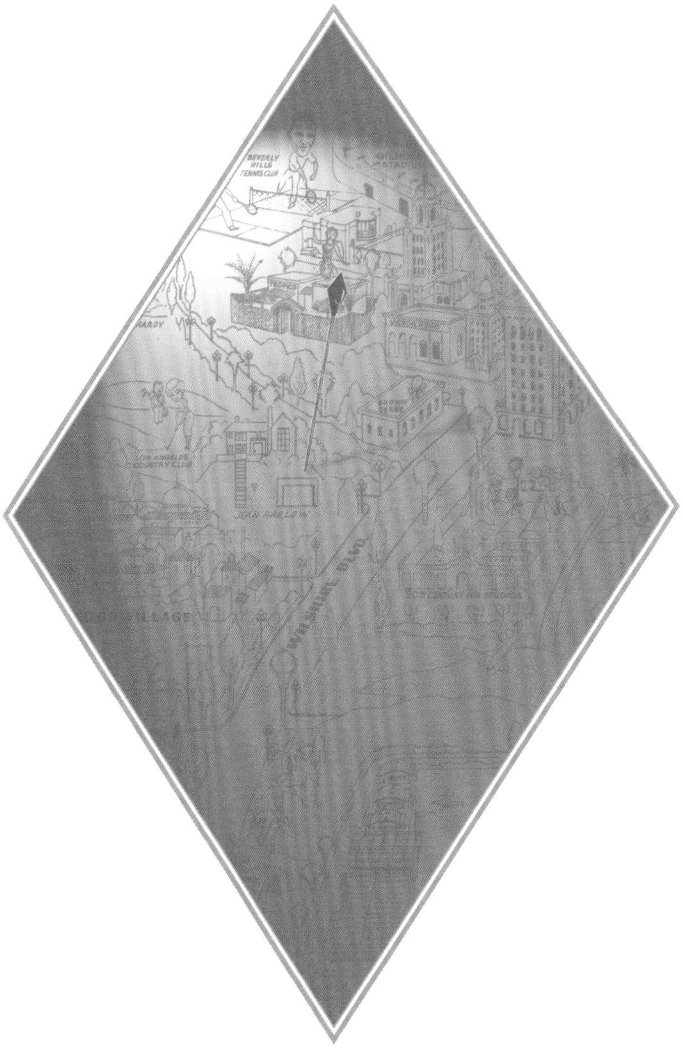

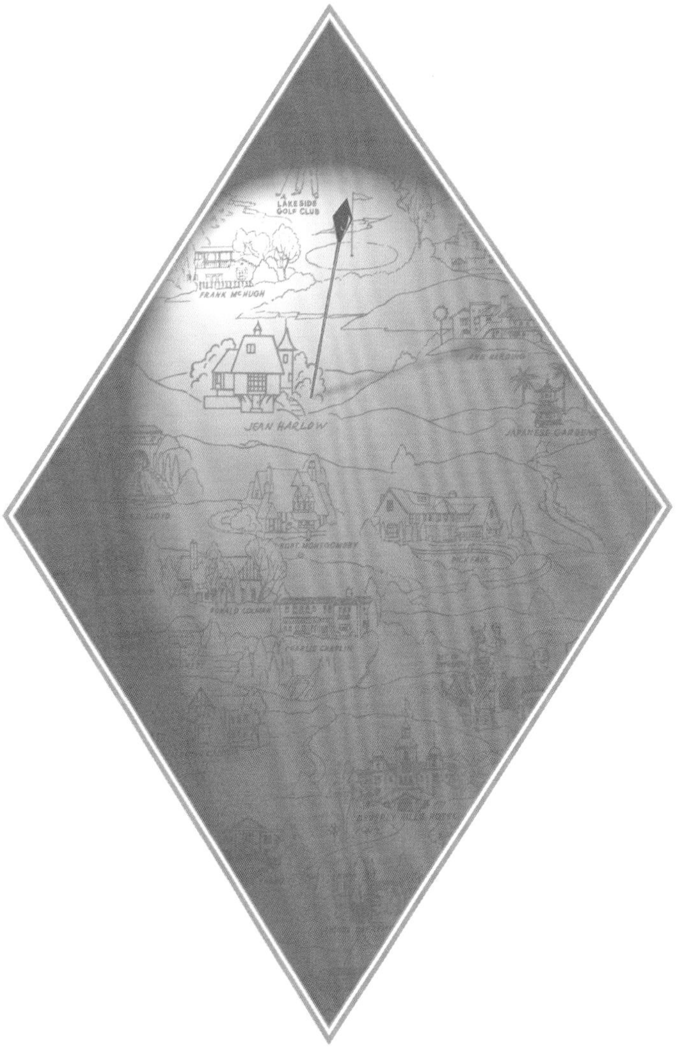

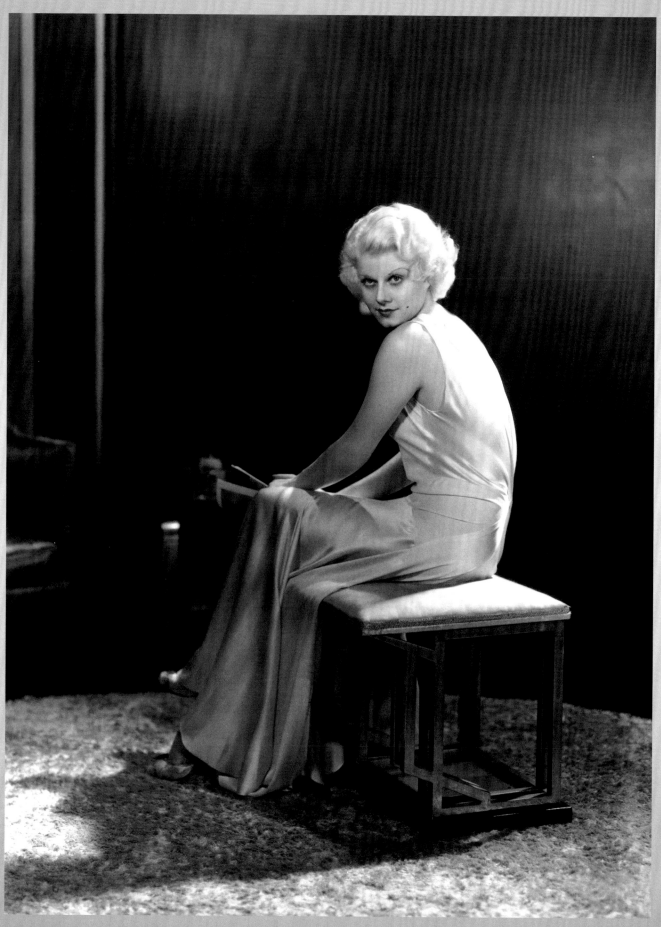

Jean Harlow's second film for M-G-M was Charles' Brabin's *The Beast of the City*.
The unit stills photographer shot this wardrobe test on the set.

• Club View Drive to Culver City •

After three years in Hollywood, Jean Harlow had worked at all the major studios—Paramount, Fox Film, Warner Bros., Universal, and Columbia. The studio that had taken the most care in casting her was the mighty Metro-Goldwyn-Mayer. It wasn't that Metro had the biggest acreage (like Universal), the biggest theater chain (like Fox), or the best directors (like Paramount). It had the best writers, the most stars, and a production head whose intuition was almost infallible. Irving G. Thalberg had the uncanny ability to make screen fare that was both compelling and profitable. Working with company president Louis B. Mayer, himself a management genius, Thalberg had in seven years made M-G-M the most successful film company in the world. Meanwhile, America was in the grip of a depression, though neither Harlow nor the Bellos acknowledged it. Twelve million Americans were out of work. In the span of two years, weekly movie attendance had dropped from ninety million to fifty million, but while every other studio was operating in the red, M-G-M was reaping an eight-million-dollar annual profit. If Harlow's fans were growing tired of her, M-G-M could renew their interest.

The City Sentinel was a project generated by Cosmopolitan Pictures, the production company maintained on the M-G-M lot by William Randolph Hearst, the most powerful publisher in the world. Hearst liked the story of a policeman who fights the influence of the underworld, even hauling in his younger brother, a rogue cop. Harlow was playing the gang girl who corrupts the brother. "I'm another bad woman," she wrote pen pal Stanley Brown on her first day of shooting. "I'm so tired, too tired to fight them any longer. They treat you just like a puppet. This is a game, Stanley, that one keeps fighting every minute, but I'm going to whip it—before I quit." In caste-conscious Hollywood, Harlow's friendships were unorthodox. She partied with young wives from "old money" families in Los Angeles. She was devoted to Bobbe Brown, even though the studio considered the girl a mere secretary.

Jean also formed lasting friendships with a number of fans like Stanley Brown, a middle-aged Chicago copywriter. He had given her a free handwriting analysis, so she began corresponding with him, calling him her "Safety Valve." Why would a cheerful post-adolescent need a safety valve? She was still tethered to Howard Hughes, and he was still farming her out for sex-vulture roles. Marino and Jean Bello, for all their machinations, had not been able to break the contract. Harlow had liked her Columbia films because they gave her "the first opportunity I've ever had to play sympathetic roles." The other roles were making it difficult for her to enjoy herself in public. "I've heard the terrible things that men say about me without even meeting me," she complained. Women were no less opprobrious. "One night we went to a café," said Ruth Hamp. "No sooner were we seated than the women at the next table began expressing their opinions of Jean. Two or three times it's been all I could do to keep from slapping some woman who has deliberately snubbed her."

Harlow wrote to Hughes, appealing for better roles. He did not respond. When she tried to see him, she was told that he was out of town. One day she went to Caddo unannounced. She was made to wait for hours. Finally, she burst into his inner office. "Mr. Hughes was sitting alone," she recalled. "He certainly looked surprised to see me. I begged him to either release me from my contract or give me good pictures. I paced the floor, crying one minute, storming the next. Suddenly I stopped and noticed his smile. It was the kind of smile that patient parents give exasperating children. That did it. I lost my head. I grabbed the phone from his desk, and I threw it at him."

For the first time, Harlow seriously considered quitting the business. Marino and Jean Bello could not countenance this possibility. She was their sole source of income, and they were spending her salary liberally, if not lavishly. Harlow's sometime agent Arthur Landau did some research in the fine print of her contract. There was nothing to prevent him and the Bellos from creating a three-thousand-dollar-a-week Harlow tour. Better yet, she did not have to share her earnings—at least not with Hughes. Hughes heard this and sent a conciliatory check for $8500. Before the Bellos could cash it, Harlow returned it. In December of 1931, the Bellos packed Harlow off for the East Coast. She made appearances in Detroit, Philadelphia, and Pittsburgh, where she caught intestinal influenza. Her mother brought in a doctor and then pushed her back onto the stage. Harlow's Ferry Hall schoolmate Helen Fieger came to congratulate her. Harlow was typically modest. "I'm not an Ethel Barrymore," she said, "but I'm trying terribly hard."

Acting was not the reason crowds came to see her wherever she appeared. Her magnetism came across the footlights, proving her appeal was genuine, not a trick of lights and lenses. In Culver City, Paul Bern pointed this out to his colleagues. Harlow was breaking Loew's box-office records in New York. "These personal appearances caused Metro to sit up and take notice," said Landau. "The casting director in Culver City, Ben Piazza, and the head of the Loew's office in New York, J. Robert Rubin, got these reports." Harlow met with Rubin between shows. He was not encouraging. "We don't think you can act," he told her, "but we can't get around the record you've made on this tour."

Thalberg had recently released *The City Sentinel*, now renamed *Beast of the City* (1932). It was doing good business, and—surprise—Harlow was getting positive reviews. Sitting in a New York dressing room, Harlow was incredulous to receive a letter from the executive vice-president of M-G-M. "We had no idea when we gave you the role," wrote Thalberg, "that you were capable of giving the truly excellent performance you have given." "I'm going to have it framed!" Harlow squealed.

This was the opportunity for which Bern had been waiting. Thalberg had resisted the idea of signing Harlow. Now he was willing. But there was the Caddo contract. Bern began to exert pressure on Hughes, who asked director Lewis Milestone for advice. "She hasn't the slightest idea about acting," answered Milestone. "She has a wonderful body, a ridiculous head, and sixty thousand dollars is much more than you have a right to expect for her contract. Sell it." Meanwhile, Landau and the Bellos began negotiating Harlow's contract with M-G-M studio manager Eddie Mannix. "I asked him for $1500 a week for the first year," Landau recalled. "Then two thousand dollars the second year. I finally settled for $1250 for the first year and $1750 the second because they agreed to pay fifty-two weeks instead of forty. Of course, Hughes had to be bought off." Harlow's contract was abrogated for the tidy sum of thirty thousand dollars. On March 3, 1932, her twenty-first birthday, Harlow received a transcontinental call from Bern telling her that a contract was waiting for her in Culver City. She officially arrived on April 20.

It wasn't only Bern's enthusiasm for Harlow, her in-person popularity, or even her improved acting skills that occasioned the contract. Thalberg was making a new kind of film. "I want to show Will Hays and the Studio Relations Committee (SRC) that M-G-M can make sex entertaining, not offensive," said Thalberg. The vehicle he had in mind for this potent mixture of sex and humor was an unfinished *Saturday Evening Post* serial by the popular author Katharine Brush. *Red-Headed Woman* (1932) was the earthy tale of Lil Andrews, a gold-digging secretary. Director Jack Conway was worried it would get the

The Beast of the City let Harlow create a characterization. Her scenes with Wallace Ford were both sexy and funny.

The Corinthian columns at 10202 Washington Boulevard in Culver City supported the façade of Metro-Goldwyn-Mayer, Hollywood's most prosperous studio.

wrong kind of laughs. "I'll shoot this if you insist," he said to Thalberg and writer Anita Loos, "but I want to tell you right now, people are going to laugh at it." Thalberg turned to Harlow and asked her: "Do you think you can make an audience laugh?"

"With me or at me?"

"At you."

"Why not?" asked Harlow. "People have been laughing at me all my life." When Harlow left Thalberg's office, she paused at the door and gave her trademark farewell nod. Loos made a note of it. It would appear several times in *Red-Headed Woman*.

Numerous actresses had auditioned for or been offered *Red-Headed Woman*, including Clara Bow, Jeanette MacDonald, Nancy Carroll, and Dorothy Mackaill. Before Harlow could step into the role, she had to test in a red wig made by the Max Factor Company. She credited the wig. "It's a symbol of the first chance I ever had to do something in pictures other than rotate my hips," she said. Hips or no hips, the SRC tried to stop the film from going into production. "This is in my mind the most awful script I have ever read," SRC staffer Lamar Trotti cabled his boss Will Hays on April 27, the day before filming was to start. "Thalberg, of course, is a man of persuasive powers. His contention is that the audience will laugh at the situations as broad comedy. Maybe so; but that isn't in the script."

Also not in the script was the red-hot presence of Jean Harlow. Even crew members were affected by her when she came to work on Stage Nine. Workers from adjacent stages crept onto catwalks to watch her, and she inflamed male temperaments by unexpectedly showing her naked body during the shooting of a scene. "She has no inhibitions," said Bern, by way of explanation. Her unique blend of sexuality, innocence, and humor became the talk of the studio.

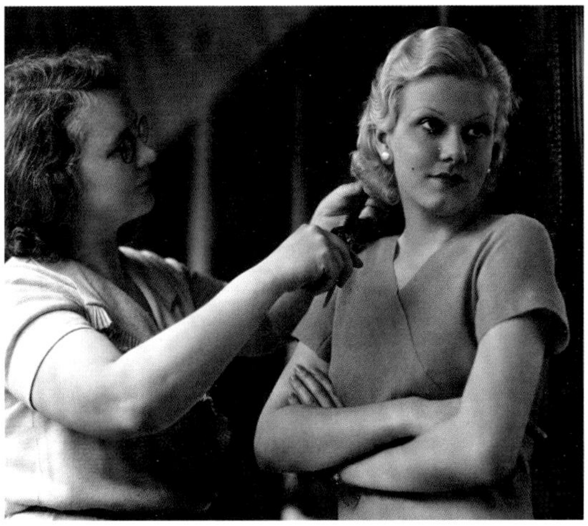

On April 12, 1932, Harlow signed a five-year contract with M-G-M and was promptly subjected to a makeover, including the ministrations of hairdresser Edith Hubner.

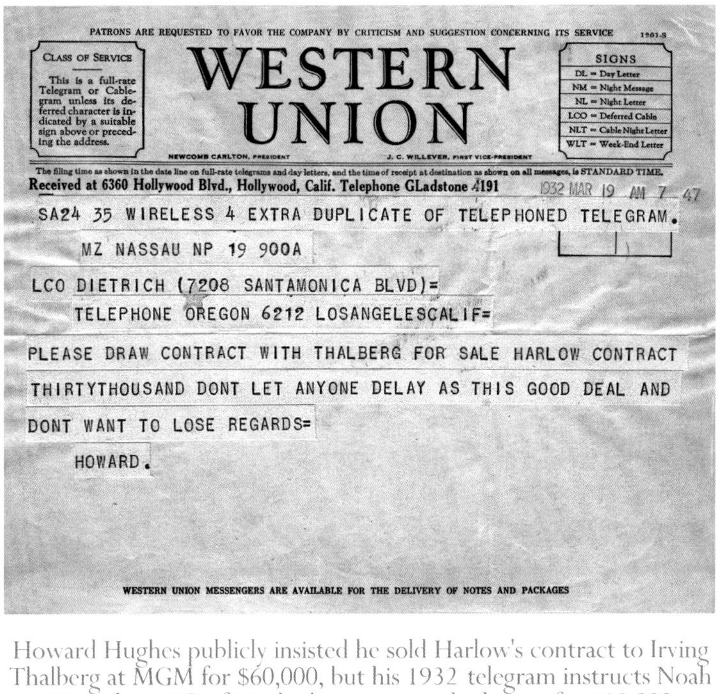

PATRONS ARE REQUESTED TO FAVOR THE COMPANY BY CRITICISM AND SUGGESTION CONCERNING ITS SERVICE 1201-S

CLASS OF SERVICE
This is a full-rate Telegram or Cablegram unless its deferred character is indicated by a suitable sign above or preceding the address.

WESTERN UNION

NEWCOMB CARLTON, PRESIDENT J. C. WILLEVER, FIRST VICE-PRESIDENT

SIGNS
DL = Day Letter
NM = Night Message
NL = Night Letter
LCO = Deferred Cable
NLT = Cable Night Letter
WLT = Week-End Letter

The filing time as shown in the date line on full-rate telegrams and day letters, and the time of receipt at destination as shown on all messages, is STANDARD TIME.

Received at 6360 Hollywood Blvd., Hollywood, Calif. Telephone GLadstone 4191 1932 MAR 19 AM 7 47

SA24 35 WIRELESS 4 EXTRA DUPLICATE OF TELEPHONED TELEGRAM.

MZ NASSAU NP 19 900A

LCO DIETRICH (7208 SANTAMONICA BLVD)=

TELEPHONE OREGON 6212 LOSANGELESCALIF=

PLEASE DRAW CONTRACT WITH THALBERG FOR SALE HARLOW CONTRACT THIRTYTHOUSAND DONT LET ANYONE DELAY AS THIS GOOD DEAL AND DONT WANT TO LOSE REGARDS=

HOWARD.

WESTERN UNION MESSENGERS ARE AVAILABLE FOR THE DELIVERY OF NOTES AND PACKAGES

Howard Hughes publicly insisted he sold Harlow's contract to Irving Thalberg at MGM for $60,000, but his 1932 telegram instructs Noah Dietrich—CEO of Hughes's empire—to let her go for $30,000.

M-G-M's publicity department was the most powerful—and thorough—in Hollywood. Every aspect of Harlow's arrival was disseminated to fan magazines—even the photo she received after a session with M-G-M portrait photographer George Hurrell, who remarked that the cleft in her chin made her face symmetrical. See a larger version of the image at right on page nine.

Clarence Bull, M-G-M's other portraitist, began working with Jean on a regular basis in the spring of 1932. Harlow and her mother both signed this photo.

On April 29, Bern attended the Grauman's Chinese premiere of Thalberg's first all-star film, *Grand Hotel* (1932). Following stars such as Marlene Dietrich, Constance Bennett, Joan Crawford, and Douglas Fairbanks, Jr., Bern walked the red carpet. Fans in the bleachers strained to identify the redhead on his arm, and then screamed with delight. It was Harlow—wearing a red wig.

Harlow's first contracted film at M-G-M went well, despite minor makeup poisoning and a sore jaw caused by too many takes of the shot in which Chester Morris slaps her. "I'd very much wanted Clara Bow for the part," said Conway. When he saw how Harlow's sexy persona improved with the addition of humor, he amended his opinion. "She was a decided contrast to what I'd anticipated." On completing the film, Harlow sent a happy letter to Stanley Brown. "Last night we finished the picture," wrote Harlow. "Hurray! Hurray! King Thalberg said 'great.' Now what he means by 'great' remains to be seen. I got beaten, fired a gun, and delivered a long speech in FRENCH. Other than that, I did nothing but work, so, as I said before, my dear Safety Valve, if it's rotten, tell me. And if it's good, please tell me, I beg you. My love and appreciation. Me."

Red-Headed Woman's first sneak preview was held on June 2 at the Alexander Theatre in Glendale. Harlow was too nervous to go, and rightly so. The audience was unsure whether to laugh at it, with it, or at all. Loos wrote a new prologue making Harlow an insouciant joker. Thalberg tested it in Pasadena. "That did it!" recalled Loos. "Laughs began at once and never ceased." Harlow saw the film at its June 24 premiere at Loew's State Theatre in downtown Los Angeles. "I was scared to death," she admitted, "but halfway through this picture I started to laugh at myself. For the first time since I appeared in pictures, I really enjoyed looking at myself. And I didn't have any particular feeling that it was me."

Harlow's disconnection from her image may have been the result of seeing the first real characterization that she had achieved, or it may have been that she was looking for the first time at Jean Harlow the M-G-M Star. In any case, she had reason to be happy. Thalberg's latest brainstorm had created a new hit and a new star. Bern had begun to show more than a professional interest in her. With any luck, 1932 would be a triumphant year for Jean Harlow.

Bull achieved this intimate shot of Harlow by setting his tripod inside her closet; its door is visible on the right.

Bull made this image of Harlow in her living room on April 25, 1932.

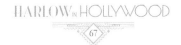

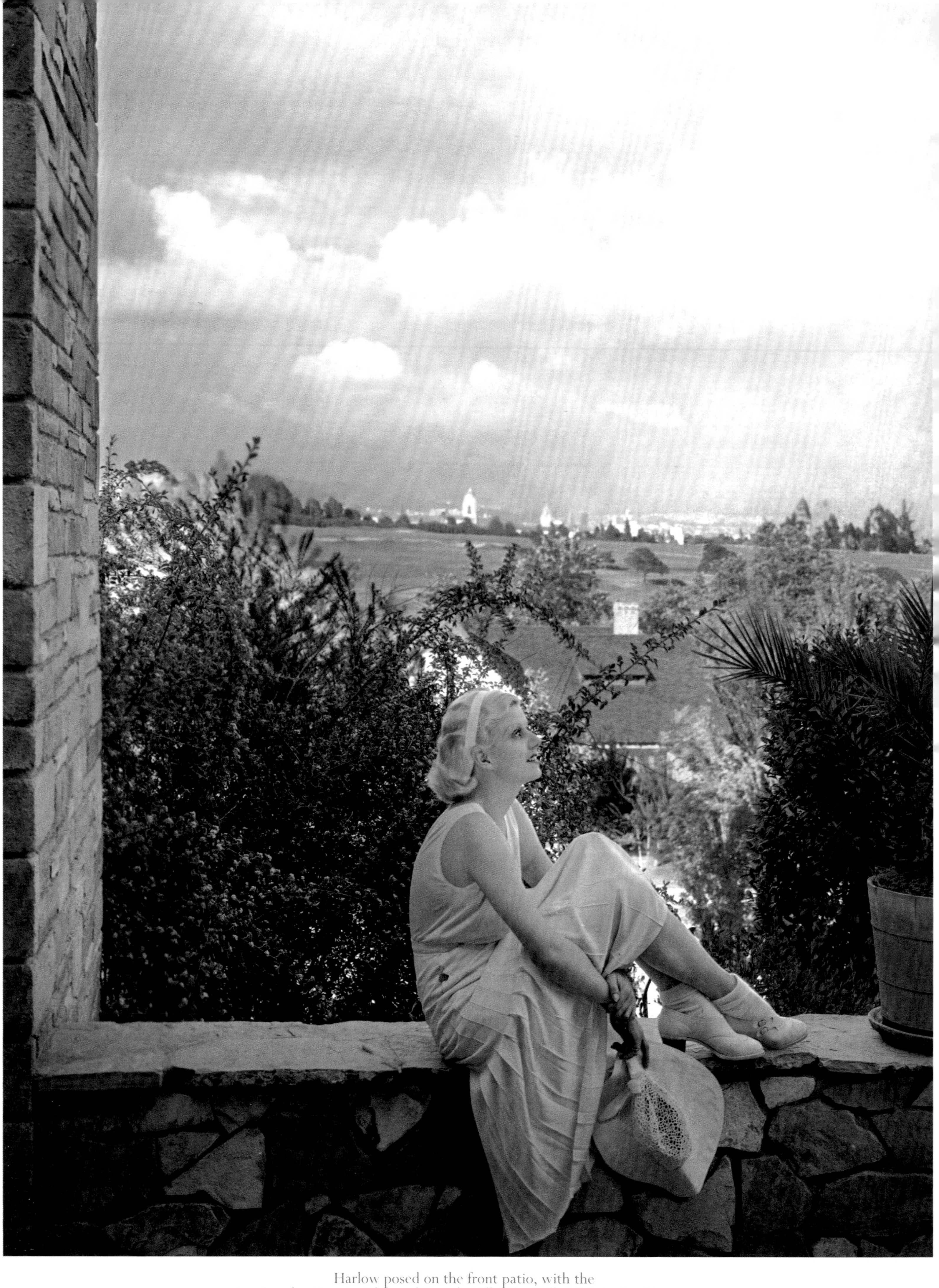

Harlow posed on the front patio, with the
Los Angeles Country Club and Beverly Hills City Hall visible in the distance.

Wearing a red wig, Harlow attended the Grauman's Chinese premiere of M-G-M's *Grand Hotel* on April 29, 1932, with its producer, Paul Bern. Jean Harlow didn't sign with her usual childlike scrawl, explaining "I can't write with gloves on."

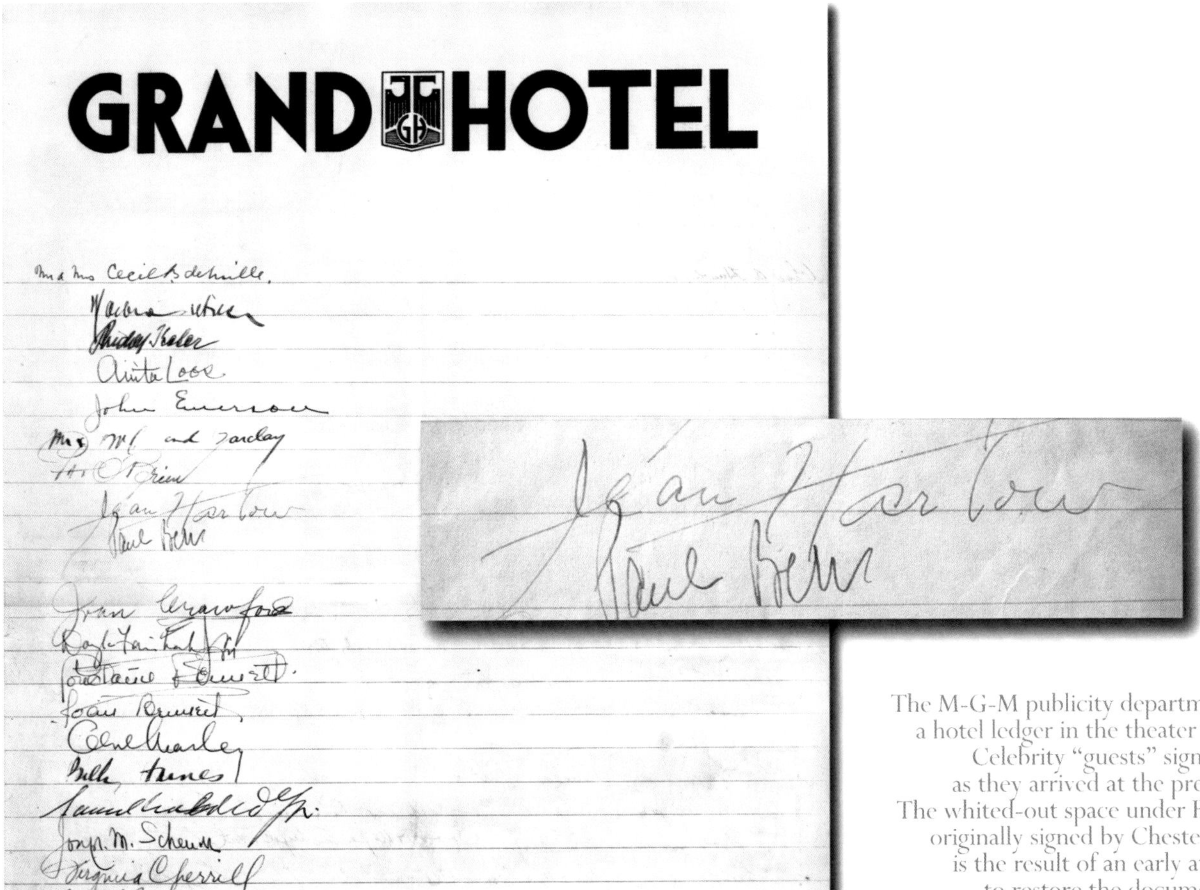

The M-G-M publicity department installed a hotel ledger in the theater forecourt. Celebrity "guests" signed it as they arrived at the premiere. The whited-out space under Bern's name, originally signed by Chester Morris, is the result of an early attempt to restore the document.

Harlow was photographed by several artists while making *Red-Headed Woman,* and she conveyed a range of moods. Hurrell made this kittenish shot, a departure from the sexy poses that had made him famous.

Clarence Bull made this surprisingly soft, accessible portrait.

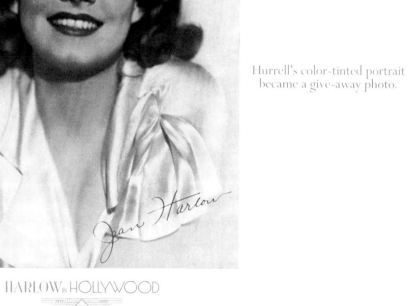

Hurrell's color-tinted portrait became a give-away photo.

Harlow posed for this "gag shot" with screenwriter Anita Loos, who had written the definitive gold digger novel, *Gentlemen Prefer Blondes*.

In *Red-Headed Woman*, Harlow played an amoral-but-funny secretary who ensnares her humorless boss, Chester Morris.

Red-Headed Woman gave Harlow all the accoutrements of the nouveau riche.

[TOP] M-G-M publicity reminded the world that the girl playing the wicked character was really a homebody.

[BOTTOM] Bull shot this portrait of Harlow and her mother perusing a *Hell's Angels* scrapbook on May 16, 1932.

[TOP] Thanks to M-G-M, Harlow was receiving more fan mail, so her friend Bobbe Brown continued as her secretary.

[BOTTOM] Harlow appeared for a week at Loew's State Theatre in downtown Los Angeles to promote *Red-Headed Woman*.

Bull's portraits of Harlow emphasized both her gentleness and her intelligence.

• Tragedy on Easton Drive •

THE HISTORY OF HOLLYWOOD IS REPLETE WITH FORTUNATE marriages and fashionable addresses. Silent star Norma Talmadge married United Artists executive Joseph Schenck and eventually moved to the Santa Monica Gold Coast. Silent star Norma Shearer married M-G-M production head Irving Thalberg and moved to Beverly Hills. In each case, the woman was already a star, but the marriage—and the address—enhanced her status. Movie stars were America's royalty, and Los Angeles had room for palaces. Benedict Canyon runs north from Beverly Hills up through the Santa Monica Mountains. In the late 1920s, the canyon became a destination. Comedy star Harold Lloyd bought fifteen acres and built the ultimate Hollywood palace, a forty-four-room Mediterranean mansion. In 1930, Paul Bern bought five acres and built a three-story home. He was born in Germany, so he modeled 9820 Easton Drive after a Bavarian hunting lodge.

One evening in the spring of 1932, Bern brought Jean Harlow there. Since he had arranged for her to have both an M-G-M contract and a coveted role, Harlow thought it might be time to pay him back. Bern sat her down and poured glasses of wine. Harlow waited for the inevitable advance. Instead, Bern told her about the origins of the wine, describing the importance of the grapes. "He's different," Harlow told a friend. "He explains things. He lets me know I have a brain." For once she was able to forge a friendship with a man. "He's the first guy who ever took me out who didn't reach inside my dress."

Howard Strickling, M-G-M's publicity director, observed that Harlow's screen persona was still at odds with her personality. "While Jean came across as a very sexy woman on the screen," recalled Strickling, "in life I would say that she was undersexed." In truth, she was not. Her marriage (and subsequent affairs) had given her a taste for smoky nightclubs, tart gin, and virile men, yet she was essentially naïve—and totally dependent on her mother. Jean Bello was puzzled when she saw her daughter spending more and more time with Bern. A romance with him would be advantageous were it not so unseemly. Harlow was twenty-one. Bern was forty-two. He was paunchy, balding, and had never married. Jean Bello could overlook these deficiencies because Bern was a power in Hollywood. He had recently supervised *Grand Hotel* (1932), the year's biggest hit. He was known as an intellectual in a community where producers read neither screenplays nor books. When he expounded on Schopenhauer, Nietzsche, and Freud, Thalberg listened attentively.

Bern was also known for generosity. He helped those who had fallen off the Hollywood treadmill, failed stars like Olive Borden and Jetta Goudal. He supported both Mabel Normand and Barbara La Marr when drugs destroyed them. He was known, too, at the Café Montmarte and the Cocoanut Grove. "Bern loved to take out sexy broads," recalled Strickling, "but it wasn't enough for them to be gorgeous dishes. They had to be in trouble." When he was seen with Joan Crawford, it was because the starlet needed help. Harry Rapf had just dumped her. The married supervisor had brought her to M-G-M, kept her as a mistress, and then lost interest. Bern took up her cause, persuading Thalberg to give her better roles. When Bern took her to a play, he introduced her to Hollywood royalty, Douglas Fairbanks, Jr., whom she eventually married.

By 1932, Paul Bern was known as "Hollywood's Father Confessor," the man of whom no one spoke ill. If his acts of kindness were somewhat self-conscious and very well publicized, he could be excused; he was helping the desperate. His interest in Harlow was therefore unexpected. She did not fit the profile of

[OPPOSITE] The location of Paul Bern's Benedict Canyon hideaway at 9820 Easton Drive was purposely remote. "I love solitude," he told story editor Samuel Marx. "I've always been self-sufficient, you know. And when a man isn't married at forty, well, he isn't likely to be."

his female friends. She was not needy. She was on the ascendant, the newest star at the biggest studio. And yet, by Jean Bello's logic, an auspicious marriage would not only ensure her daughter's place at M-G-M; it would also put her on a level with Norma Shearer, the "First Lady of M-G-M." But Bern, the unmarried philanthropist, would never break his pattern. It was too much to hope for. And yet he continued romancing Harlow; it was odd. "Jean Bello worried about it," recalled Marcella Rabwin, assistant to David O. Selznick. "She was a shrewd dame and she knew this man was a phony." The idea of Bern marrying Harlow was too good to be true. But Jean Bello continued to hope.

On June 20, startled newspaper reporters got word to go to City Hall. Jean Harlow and Paul Bern were there—at the marriage license bureau—filing a three-day notice of their intention to marry. The oily, ubiquitous Marino Bello was with them, smiling for photographers. Harlow and Bern then went to the studio and formally announced their engagement. It was all the more incredible because Strickling had recently overheard Thalberg tell Bern not to marry Harlow. "Thalberg never accepted Harlow," recalled Strickling. "He didn't approve of that marriage." Thalberg was not the only one. While Bern was respected by producers, directors, and writers, there was one contingent that found his altruism dubious—M-G-M's female writers. Salka Viertel thought he was "devoted to Thalberg, but arrogant and pretentious with me." Lenore Coffee found his kindness condescending. Frances Marion thought his intellectualism perverted. Anita Loos called him a "German psycho." Adela Rogers St. Johns said he was "interested in abnormality and complexes, in inhibitions, perversions, suicide, and death." And she knew why.

Years earlier, Barbara La Marr had confided that she could not marry Bern. No woman could. St. Johns asked why. Was he an invert? A pervert? Already married? La Marr, with "the direct, uninhibited honesty of a child, had been graphic, technical and explicit." Bern had undersized genitals. Now an ambitious mother and venal stepfather were pushing an unknowing girl into a sham marriage with a middle-aged eunuch. St. Johns decided to tell Harlow the truth.

On June 20, 1932, photographers found Jean Harlow and Paul Bern at the marriage license bureau with Marino Bello. Bern looked slightly ill-at-ease registering to marry a woman half his age.

The marriage license bureau was located at the City Hall, in downtown Los Angeles.

"You mean Paul loves me for something else?" Harlow asked her. "Then it's true. He loves me as he says he does, for my mind, my spirit, my companionship—for *me*. He's paid me the highest compliment I've ever had. Thank God! I'm sick of sex!"

If Harlow saw Bern as a haven, it was not because she was sick of sex. It was because she was tired of being leered at, propositioned, and fondled. The unwelcome attentions had recently come from the most disturbing place, her home. The evenings of three-handed bridge in the card room on Club View Drive had gained a tense undertone. When Jean Bello's back was turned, Marino Bello was looking at Harlow in a distinctly unfatherly way. "I'm tired of climbing those damned stairs," Harlow told a reporter when standing in front of her home. She was more honest with Loos. "It'll be a relief to get away from the rat before Mom finds him out."

Before she could get away, she had to go through the wedding ceremony, and at Club View Drive. It was scheduled for Saturday, July 2. The reception would be at Bern's home the following day, but Bern did not want reporters or photographers there. Strickling made a deal with the press. If they would stay away from the reception at Bern's, they could cover the wedding at the Bello house.

On the day of the wedding, the second-time bride was more nervous than the first-time groom. She walked into the room where the members of the press were waiting and blurted: "Got a cigarette, boys? I'm so nervous I'm shaking!" A cigarette wasn't enough to calm her. By the time of the ceremony, she was in distress. "I'll never make it," she queasily confided to a friend. "Too nervous." It transpired that she had gone for a solitary drive to the beach that afternoon, missed lunch, and then eaten too many hamburgers. The friend ran to fetch bicarbonate of soda.

Harlow and Bern posed for formal engagement photos outside M-G-M's executive bungalow. The Spanish Revival structure later became the studio schoolhouse and in 2010 was the office of producer John Calley.

The ceremony was intimate, simple, and short, attended by family, friends, and a few prominent film folk. The reception was catered by Leo Gray, the former headwaiter at the Ambassador Hotel. A gathering of fans staged an impromptu celebration in the street below. The party continued until three, when Bern drove his bride and her maid Blanche Williams to Easton Drive. If Harlow's second wedding night was less boozy than her first, it was no less odd. She later confided to Strickling that Bern had sat her down and redefined the facts of life. "Sex is not the most important thing in our lives," he said. "Respect for our bodies is. If you agree to that, we'll have a long life together and a long marriage." Harlow was not undersexed, but she agreed to Bern's proposal. "Paul had completely sold her on this 'respect' business," Strickling recalled.

In the morning, when Bern emerged from the bedroom, he ran into Williams. "The Baby's still a virgin," he told her. Williams was baffled by the remark. "I knew very well she couldn't be a virgin," she said later, "I'm not that dumb. What I think he meant was that he'd had no sexual relations with her." Harlow's naiveté was not confined to relations. At the reception that day, Norma Shearer was dressed in silk, Mary Pickford in chiffon, and Irene Selznick in satin. Harlow wore green flannel pajamas. Her aunt Jetta Belle Chadsey asked her about a honeymoon trip. "I'm so happy here," Harlow answered, "that I don't care to go on a honeymoon." Harlow should have been happy in her new home. Bern had deeded the sixty-thousand-dollar property to her a week earlier as a wedding gift.

In the weeks following the wedding, Harlow spent most of her time at the secluded estate. She dismissed Bern's Russian servants, retaining only John Carmichael, the butler, and his wife Winifred, the cook. Three days after the wedding, Strickling had M-G-M portraitist Clarence Bull make the first of a series of photographs of Harlow at the estate. The Blonde Bombshell had to be reintroduced to the public as Mrs. Paul Bern.

Harlow got along well with photographers and took pleasure in sharing deluxe prints with friends. While waiting for her proofs, she wrote her Ferry Hall schoolmate Helen Fieger. "I thought perhaps you had forgotten all about me," she began.

> Of course, I *would* lose your address, just to prove how dumb I am! For the first time since I started in this here business, I am getting a vacation, and you will never know what a thrill I am getting out of just doing

A press photographer shot this photo of the wedding couple.

> nothing. I just take sunbaths and swim in our pool, and I am as brown as a Mexican...Will send the picture under separate cover. Had some new ones taken and as soon as I get them will see that you get one immediately. There isn't much to tell you except that as usual I am trying to get thin before I start this new picture.

Harlow occasionally had visits from her friends Adela Rogers St. Johns and Anita Loos. Harlow would curl up on the cushions of a window seat and talk about upcoming projects. One day, whacking a pillow for emphasis, she turned to Loos and said: "Nita, you can write comedy like nobody else in the world. For the love of Mike, give me comedy in this new one. I can play comedy. I'm sick of slithering around the screen without any clothes on."

Harlow was referring to *Red Dust*, a project first intended for Greta Garbo and John Gilbert. *Red-Headed Woman* was doing so well that Thalberg decided to put Harlow in Garbo's place. By late July, Gilbert had been replaced by Clark Gable, whose star was rising even faster than Harlow's. But Loos was not to work on *Red Dust.* Supervisor Hunt Stromberg and director Victor Fleming preferred that the earthy jungle tale be written by a man, John Lee Mahin. Luckily for Harlow, Mahin had a wicked sense of humor and invested the script with ripe one-liners. He was also an astute observer. When shooting commenced, he saw Jean and Marino Bello visiting the set. "Jean Harlow's parents were horrible," recalled Mahin. "Big Mama wasn't a bright woman. She was Christian Scientist, devout and crazy. Bello was a bad boy. Very bad. He lived off her, spent all the money that Jean made. Jean just conceded and paid their bills."

Harlow enjoyed working on *Red Dust.* She and Gable were perfectly matched, whether wisecracking, sparring, or striking sexual sparks. As in every M-G-M film, Thalberg and his colleagues were looking for the moment when a performer finds the right combination of story and role. Gable had played sexy villains all through 1931. In this film, he was playing a gruff hero. Harlow had found fame as a sexy slut. Now she was playing an American prostitute working in Saigon. The difference was that she was funny and charming, wearing the proverbial heart of gold on her sleeve. Maybe this would be the formula to bring long-term stardom. *Red Dust* was proceeding on schedule when Labor Day weekend arrived.

The Harlow-Bern marriage was not doing as well. Unbeknownst to Harlow, Bern had serious financial problems. He also had personal problems. For more than a decade he had been

Jean Harlow married Paul Bern in her living room on July 2, 1932.

Harlow cuts the wedding cake for (left to right) Thalberg, Jean Bello, Shearer, Bello, and Bern.

A posed portrait of the wedding party: (left to right) Jetta Belle Chadsey (Harlow's aunt), Jean Bello, Miriam (Mrs. Henry) Bern (Paul's sister-in-law), Friederike Bern Marcus and Henry Bern (Bern's sister and brother), Paul Bern, Jean Harlow, Donald Roberson (Harlow's cousin), and Marino Bello. Photograph by William Grimes

A press photograph of the wedding party: (left to right) Irving Thalberg; Norma Shearer; Donald Roberson; Henry Bern; Arthur Landau (Harlow's agent); Marino Bello; Judge Leon Yankwich; Jean Bello; an unidentified man; Jean Harlow; Paul Bern; John Gilbert, who was the best man; Friederike Marcus; Miriam Bern; Virginia Bruce (Gilbert's fiancée); Irene Selznick; and David O. Selznick.

supporting a mentally unstable woman in New York. He had met Dorothy Millette when they were both students at the American Academy of Dramatic Arts. Bern's mother had threatened to commit suicide if he did not break with Millette. The insecure young woman had lived with him long enough to qualify as a common-law wife and would not be put out. Bern's mother drowned herself, and Millette had a mental breakdown. After her release from an institution, she was allowed to live in the Algonquin Hotel. Bern left her there and went to Hollywood in 1923, but continued to support her. In 1932 Millette came out of the fog long enough to read accounts of Bern's marriage. She checked out of the Algonquin and headed for California. Bern persuaded her to go to San Francisco, where she settled in the Plaza Hotel and planned her next move.

Bern envisioned a scandal. A bigamy conviction could end his career as quickly and effectively as the scandals of the 1920s had ended those of Wallace Reid, Mary Miles Minter, and Roscoe Arbuckle. It could endanger everyone at M-G-M who had sponsored him and everyone he had ever helped. It could summarily end Harlow's career. Suddenly the Father Confessor of Hollywood needed his own counselor, someone to turn to. There was no one. He began to show symptoms of depression, and he started talking about suicide. "If the time comes when I'm no longer useful," he told writer Willis Goldbeck, "I'd do it." Actress Colleen Moore and journalist Sidney Skolsky both saw Bern carrying a gun. When asked why, he tried to make light of it but turned somber. "I intend using it someday," he said.

Harlow had gone from the frying pan to the fire, from a lecherous, opportunistic stepfather to an impotent, disturbed husband. She coped with it by being sociable and cheerful, but Bern grew to resent the very temperament that had attracted him. Instead of letting her buoy his spirits, he tried to squelch her. The gentle teacher grew didactic and caustic. "Honest, Paul makes me feel like I'm sitting at a desk in a classroom," Harlow told Frances Marion. "Or on a stool with a dunce cap on my head." There were scenes at parties. On several occasions, he insulted her. On one occasion, he slapped her. Fortunately for Harlow, her work schedule was so demanding—twelve hours a day, six days a week—that she had little time to socialize.

Visitors to the *Red Dust* set sometimes saw Harlow sitting at a typewriter while her portable phonograph blared Bing Crosby songs. "The only time I really, truly forget myself is when I am hammering away at my typewriter," said Harlow. "I use the hunt-and-miss system of two fingers, but I can go pretty fast. I even

[TOP] On July 8, Clarence Bull photographed Harlow in the master bedroom of her new home.

[BOTTOM] Bull made this photograph of butler John Carmichael bringing Harlow buttermilk, a departure from her Spartan diet.

[TOP] Clarence Bull's photos of Harlow were never overtly sexy, just slightly suggestive.

[BOTTOM] Bull photographed Harlow by her oval pool where she enjoyed swimming and tanning.

write personal letters on the typewriter, which may be bad form, but it's a lot more fun." Because Monday September 5 was Labor Day, Harlow was working on Sunday. She found time to write to her friend Stanley Brown. "Although they started this picture with only thirty pages of dialogue," wrote Harlow, "and keep doling it out a few lines at a time, I'm very much afraid it's going to be a darn good picture. Last night I waded through mud up to my knees for the sake of my art, or what have you." She signed off after writing, "They've just yelled for me to come and emote."

Twenty-four hours later, Harlow did not have to pretend emotion. She was the focal point of a real-life drama. She had been visiting her mother at Club View Drive when Irving Thalberg came to tell her that her husband Paul Bern was dead. The front-page story in the *Los Angeles Times* described the scene that Thalberg had encountered that Labor Day morning. "Bern's nude body, a wound

M-G-M publicity director Howard Strickling felt that more photos were needed to convince the public that Harlow and Bern were happy, so he sent William Grimes to Easton Drive. The resulting images said more than Strickling intended.

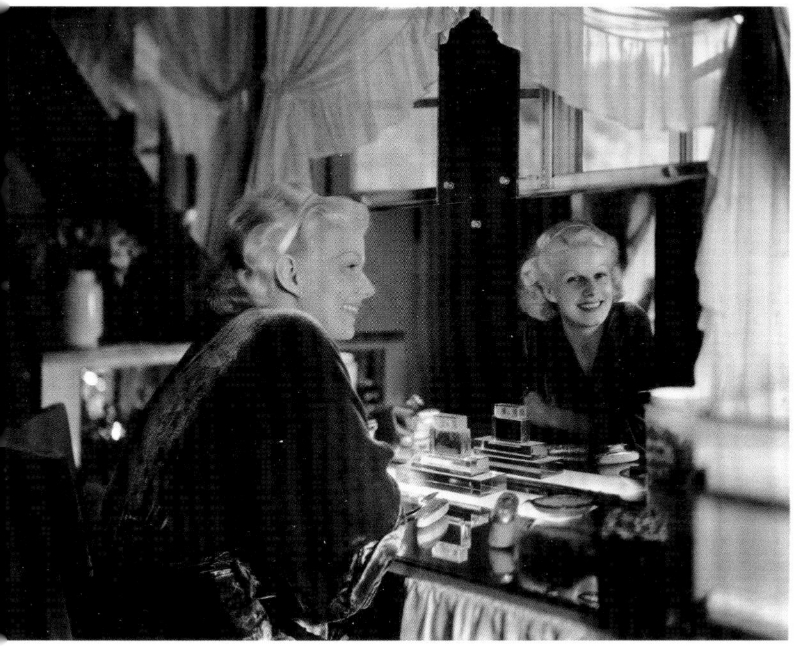

Bern hired the husband-and-wife design team of Harold Grieve and Jetta Goudal to create a mirrored dressing room on the third floor.

in the right temple and a .38-caliber revolver, from which a single shot had been fired, clutched in his right hand, was discovered in the dressing closet off his private bedroom in his rustic mountain home." Harlow was too healthy to faint. She went into restrained hysteria, repeating that she did not understand what Thalberg meant. By the time police arrived, she was pacing the floor of her bedroom, crying: "Isn't this too horrible! Isn't it too terrible! But I mustn't talk about it—I can't." She finally had to be sedated.

Nothing in Harlow's brief, bright flash of stardom had prepared her for the purgatory of a celebrity death. She was still in shock when police began an interrogation, which the doctors soon stopped. Then there were funeral arrangements. Then came the coroner's inquest at the Price-Daniel Mortuary in West Los Angeles on Thursday, September 8. Harlow was excused. The funeral was conducted on Friday, September 9 in the Grace Chapel at the Inglewood Park Cemetery. Louis B. Mayer escorted Harlow to the open casket. She wept openly. Bern's sister Friederike screamed and had to be subdued after seeing the corpse. Conrad Nagel, a Christian Scientist, delivered a eulogy that characterized Bern as "a naïve child in a world of naughty adults."

As Harlow emerged from the chapel, supported by Marino Bello and Willis Goldbeck, she was horrified to see two thousand fans waiting for her. Bello and Goldbeck tried to get her to a limousine but were cut off by the hungry mob. "There were ghastly words and demands for autographs," recalled Harlow. "They seemed heartless. To them I was not a person. I was an institution. I had no more personality than a corporation."

The corporation for which Harlow worked tried to insulate her from scandal. A scenario was written. An official version was decided. Money changed hands. The coroner's inquest ruled Bern's death a suicide. Depression due to impotence was cited as the motive. The press accepted it, even after learning that Dorothy Millette had been at Easton Drive that weekend. Reporters tracked her to San Francisco, where she disappeared after boarding a ferryboat. On Sunday, September 11, Harlow telephoned Thalberg. "This staying home is driving me crazy," she said. "I've got to get busy—to forget." She returned to the studio the next

day via a side entrance, accompanied by Bello and a private nurse.

The *Red Dust* company had been working around Harlow since September 7. The first scene to be shot was a comically bawdy one in which she taunts Gable by plopping herself into a rain barrel—nude. "Being a trouper, she went through with it," recounted Fleming. "She didn't want to inconvenience the rest of us." Harlow managed to get through the day but when Stromberg and Fleming viewed the film the following afternoon, they saw that her eyes could not disguise her pain. Mary Astor, who was playing a supporting role in *Red Dust*, spoke to Harlow: "The only thing to do, Jean, is to pick up where you left off." Harlow concentrated on her work. "She went on working, trying not to hold us up," said Gable. "Then all of a sudden, she crumpled on the floor in a dead faint. Went down like a prize fighter that's been hit right on the button. Scared me to death."

[TOP] Bern commissioned the Russian painter V. Ignatieff to paint a mural of his friends at a Renaissance banquet. The subjects depicted are (from left to right) Douglas Fairbanks, Jr.; Willis Goldbeck; Ben Lyon; director Edmund Goulding; producer B.P. Fineman; David O. Selznick; Norma Shearer; Joan Crawford; Irving Thalberg; Jean Harlow; Irene Selznick; writer Carey Wilson; John Gilbert; opera star Lawrence Tibbett; Bebe Daniels (Mrs. Ben Lyon); writer Gene Markey; and Bern's secretary Irene Harrison.

[RIGHT] The Ignatieff mural was about to be discarded in 1933 by the next owner of the Easton Drive house. The painting contractor asked if he could save it. The mural currently resides with his family.

On September 14, Dorothy Millette's body was found in the Sacramento River, an apparent suicide. Harlow continued working. "I was with my friends," she said, "people who understood. Everyone acted as if nothing had happened. They helped me to pick up the broken threads."

Harlow paid for Millette's burial. The gesture went unreported, but public opinion was already in Harlow's favor. The M-G-M mailroom was swamped with letters of sympathy and support. Though she had spent three years playing brassy, often distasteful characters, it was not her platinum exterior that had won a following, but her inner warmth.

Against Jean Bello's wishes, Harlow had maintained contact with her father Mont Carpenter. At this time he offered to come to her. She declined, but wrote him about her work on the rewritten film, describing the effort it took to memorize pages of new dialogue on short notice. She complained that the experience was almost maddening, but that she was determined to get through it and make good.

Now that she was an M-G-M star, Harlow had to be constantly available for photographs, even at home. Harlow was photographed by Bull for a fashion layout on July 5, 1932.

Red-Headed Woman had created a furor with women's clubs and church groups because the film condoned the character's "immoral" behavior. Although it was earning a sizable profit, it was nonetheless being censored in various parts of the country. Hoping to avoid this problem, Thalberg reworked much of *Red Dust*. On October 9, he attended a sneak preview with industry censor Jason Joy at the Alexander Theatre in Glendale. Harlow was also there, hiding in the back of the auditorium with her mother.

A paraphrased chord from Beethoven's *Coriolan Overture* introduced the film. There was a tense pause as Harlow's name appeared on the screen. The M-G-M contingent jumped in unison as the entire audience burst into applause that lasted two minutes. After the film ended, Joy congratulated Thalberg. The lights came up, and Harlow waited for a quiet moment to escape unnoticed. She could not. Well-wishers mobbed her before she could reach the street. Jean Harlow had become the first star in the fourteen-year history of Hollywood to survive a scandal.

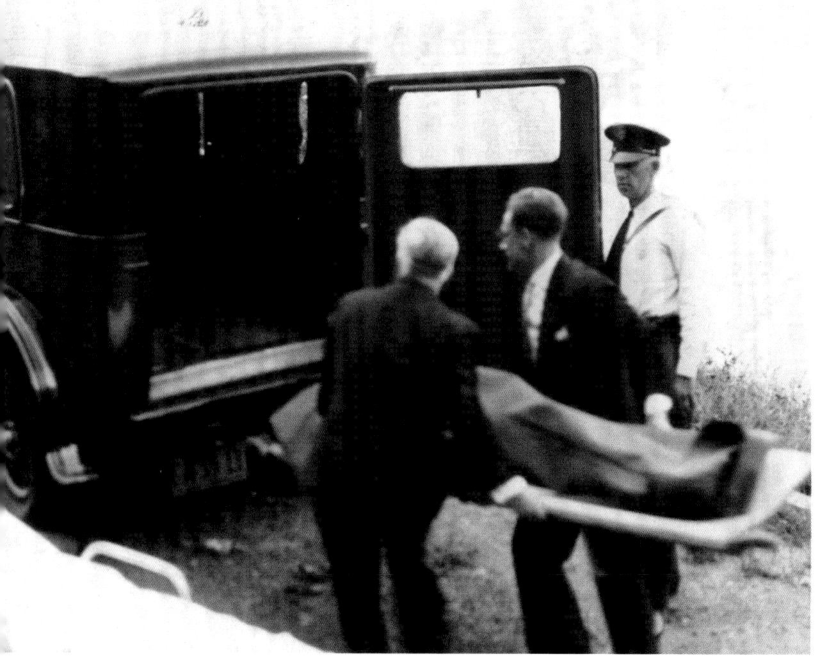

[TOP] On Monday, September 5, Paul Bern was found dead in a small room off the second-floor bedroom. The open bedroom windows are visible in this press photo, which was taken that afternoon.

[BOTTOM] Another press photo shows Bern's body being removed from his home.

Bern's funeral was held on September 9. This press photo shows Harlow descending the steps of her home on Club View Drive with Marino Bello (at left) and Willis Goldbeck.

[TOP] Bern's funeral was conducted at Grace Chapel in Inglewood Park Cemetery.

[ABOVE] The funeral was attended by family members and industry colleagues. It was noted in the press that floral displays had cost $25,000.

Shortly after Harlow was escorted from Grace Chapel, a mob of fans surrounded her.

Harlow's first public appearance after the funeral was at City Hall on October 19. Sitting in the private chambers of Judge May D. Lahey, she signed the probate papers that made her sole executrix of Bern's will.

[OPPOSITE] A few days after the funeral, Harlow told Thalberg that she wanted desperately to return to work. On September 12, she was back on the *Red Dust* set, sitting in a rain barrel. Clark Gable marveled at her ability to rebound. "She has more guts than most men," he said. "Work has been my salvation," Harlow said later. "Believe me—it has kept me from going mad."

Harlow's first scene in *Red Dust* had been shot in July. Even for a 1932 film, her costume was daringly low-cut. After Bern's death, sexy shots of his widow were in questionable taste.

The scene was reshot in late September with a new costume.

Red Dust was released on October 20.

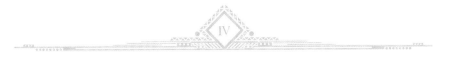

IV

The Blonde Bombshell

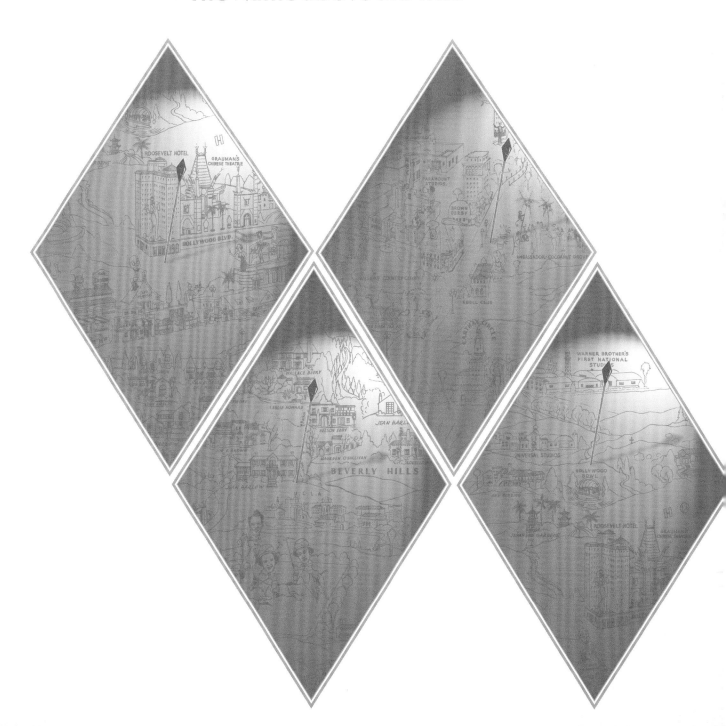

- A Star among Stars
- Holding a Man
- A Bombshell in Beverly Glen
- The Name above the Title

• A Star among Stars •

In late 1932, Jean Harlow was secure in her status as M-G-M's newest star. Six months earlier she had attended the premiere of *Grand Hotel*, the studio's first "all-star" film. Now she was big enough to be included in its second, *Dinner at Eight* (1933). Ironically, Paul Bern, who had made this possible, did not live to see it. Although Harlow had worked on *Red Dust* after his funeral, she was officially in mourning. The studio and Jean Bello agreed that Harlow should honor that custom. She would not work on a new film or make personal appearances for six months. This stricture did not include legal appointments.

When Harlow appeared in court to become executrix of Bern's estate, she learned that he had mortgaged the Easton Drive property to the extent of thirty-four thousand dollars, and owed sixteen thousand dollars in back taxes. The vaunted wedding gift now looked like a hollow piñata. Harlow was forced to sell Bern's 1930 Cord Cabriolet (at an embarrassing loss) and, ultimately, the home. Marino and Jean Bello handled the arrangements but found the task an odious one, since Bern's gutted estate could not underwrite their next extravagance. They had purchased a plot of land on Beverly Glen Boulevard and wanted to build a mansion on it. To complete their project, they had to find funding, so they turned to Harlow's salary, which was already paying off Bern's debts. Although Harlow would later avow genuine affection for Bern, her short involvement with him left a distasteful legacy. She had to fight claims against his estate and testify at hearings when District Attorney Buron Fitts reopened the case. The Bern estate would not be settled and his case would not be put to rest for four years. In that time, all files pertaining to Paul Bern would disappear from M-G-M.

Harlow's mourning period did not preclude posing for photos that would be published when it ended. Harlow was trotted to golf courses and tennis courts in mid-October to pose, not in widow's weeds, but in sporty outfits. She soon found that she enjoyed the sport at which she was posing. "Still playing golf every day," she wrote her friend Carroll Hayes. "Feel marvelous. No story found as yet for my next picture. Isn't that terrible? Wish they would hurry. Must close, as I am due at the club, for my golf game." By the end of the year, Harlow was doing charity work and going to private parties. She was also developing a fondness for gin.

On December 24, Harlow attended the studio Christmas party. M-G-M was ending the worst year of the Depression with a profit of eight million dollars. Every other studio was bankrupt or in receivership, so M-G-M's gates were shut, and bootleg bottles were opened. "There was no shortage of alcohol, just glasses," recalled story editor Sam Marx. "Stars and laborers, executives and secretaries shared drinks, paraded the streets, singing, embracing, kissing." After a few hours of partying, script clerk Willard Sheldon was heading home. Sauntering between sound stages, he almost stepped on a girl who was lying on the ground. He looked more closely at the inert drunk and recognized Harlow. "People were just passing by," recalled Sheldon, "so I picked her up and helped her inside."

Marino and Jean Bello made sure to bring Harlow along when they went to the Agua Caliente Casino and Hotel in Tijuana for New Year's Eve. While visiting the casino, Harlow acquired another vice: shooting craps. She eventually held the unofficial house record of twenty-four straight passes. While golfing in Agua Caliente, she made the acquaintance of Paramount Pictures founder Jesse Lasky, who had recently been deposed in a studio coup. With him was his twenty-two-year-old son, Jesse Jr., a low-level writer at Fox Film. Harlow was still fighting grief and

[OPPOSITE] The talented-but-erratic Harvey White was one of several photographers who made portraits of Jean Harlow after Hurrell left M-G-M in July 1932. White made this one on April 4, 1933.

depression, but no one could tell, least of all young Jesse. "I never saw a star with more personal magnetism," he wrote later. "Many had it on screen, brought to life only by the camera. Not so Jean Harlow. Her stardom was of the immediate moment—of her presence, of her stunning good looks, of her unbounded vitality." Harlow customarily sought the company of much older men but made an exception for the callow-but-earnest Jesse. She dated him into early 1933, using their dates to gradually return to public life. Lunching at Sardi's restaurant or dancing at the Cocoanut Grove, she amused herself with Jesse, distractedly answering his questions. "I like everything," she said while scanning the dance floor. "Every dance. Every drink. Every role. Well, almost. I didn't fancy those sex vulture roles."

The platonic romance ended when Jesse failed to recognize a cue. Harlow was sprawled on her bed in a peach-colored negligee, feigning a mild headache. Instead of massaging her temples, Jesse brought her two aspirin and offered to read to her. "Be a good boy, and go home," Harlow said with a sigh.

Jesse's father was not the only Hollywood executive unseated in early 1933. Irving Thalberg, who had been instrumental in Harlow's stardom, found himself without a position when his business partners Nicholas Schenck and Louis B. Mayer used his latest illness as an excuse to eliminate the post of production chief. Thalberg's absence might have slowed Harlow's career, since Mayer could not see past her screen persona. But Mayer's son-in-law David O. Selznick had come to M-G-M to produce, and his first film had a role for Harlow. *Dinner at Eight* was a hit on Broadway, a cynical look at the lives of the rich. As written by Edna Ferber and George S. Kaufman, the play showed the effects of the Depression on the guests invited to an auspicious Park Avenue dinner. Selznick offered Harlow the role of a former hatcheck girl married to a wealthy stock swindler (to be played by Wallace Beery). This film, like *Grand Hotel*, was a tale of mingled destinies, with each role substantial enough for a star; the cast would include Edmund Lowe, Lee Tracy, John and Lionel Barrymore, and Marie Dressler.

Selznick's reputation was on the line with *Dinner at Eight*. If he failed, Hollywood would say that he was a poor successor to Thalberg, hired only for reasons of nepotism. Accordingly, Selznick focused his native intensity on the film, assigning M-G-M's most distinguished artists to it—writers Frances Marion and Herman Mankiewicz, cameraman William Daniels, and a new art director, Hobart Erwin. In a bid to outdo the sensational lobby of *Grand Hotel*, Selznick had Erwin make Harlow's bedroom a paragon of style, a visual knockout. It would be the first time in the short history of the motion picture that a movie set would be white. Not eggshell white or powder blue or pale yellow to photograph as white. A true white. When Harlow reported to the studio for rehearsal, she was wearing her usual white blouse and blue slacks, her hair windblown from a drive in a convertible. She entered the white-on-white bedroom set and did what was known as a "takem." She stopped in her tracks, looked, and looked again. There were ten shades of white. She turned to Erwin and said: "Why can't people's houses be as really swell as this?"

The director chosen by Selznick was new to M-G-M but not to the producer. George Cukor had directed Selznick's RKO films *A Bill of Divorcement* and *Little Women*, making a star of Katharine Hepburn. Harlow could not have hoped for a more sympathetic craftsman. Before Cukor became known as a skilled woman's director, he was famous for the care he lavished on each actor, whether veteran or neophyte. M-G-M contract player

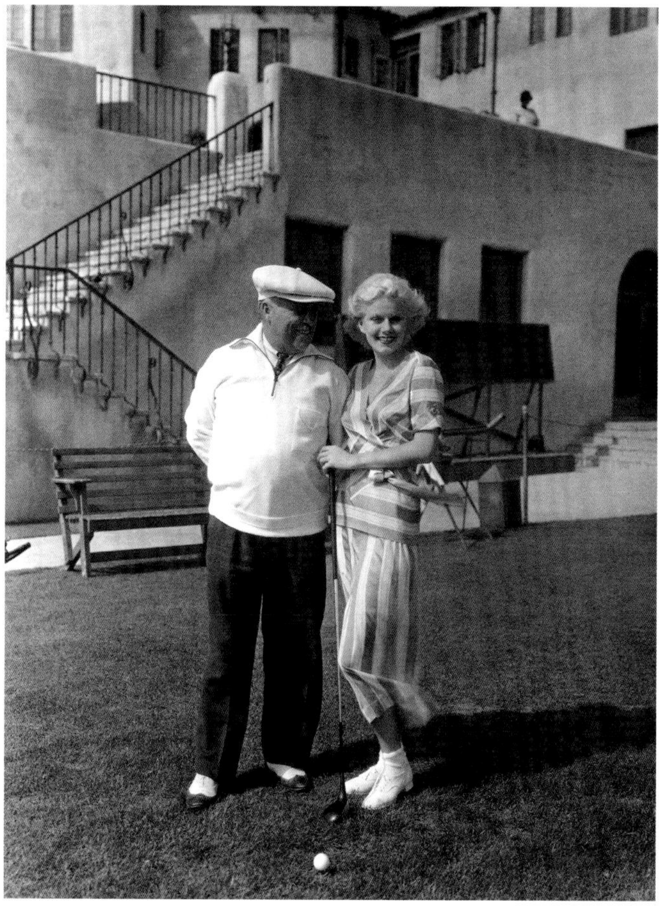

Mourning or not, Harlow was under contract to M-G-M and was expected to work. On October 14, 1932, she posed for photographs at the Riviera Country Club in Pacific Palisades.

The Beverly Hills Hotel, designed by architect Elmer Grey, opened on Sunset Boulevard in 1912. By 1933, its pink gravel driveways and cozy bungalows were famous.

Maureen O'Sullivan later said of Cukor that he showed her "the intimacy of the camera, what it shows, what it picks up." This was especially important for Harlow, whose appearance alone was startling. Cukor sensed this and subdued her, giving her clever bits of business to perform in silence—sampling chocolates and then putting them back into the box, for example. No one had taken so much care with a Harlow performance. It was demanding, but she enjoyed it. "We have started work," she wrote her friend Helen Fieger, "and I am kept in a constant whirl. But I love it. You have no idea how much I've missed my work."

While working on *Dinner at Eight*, Harlow ended her mourning period. On Sunday, April 2, along with Johnny Weissmuller, Anna May Wong, and a host of other celebrities, Harlow helped director W.S. Van Dyke celebrate the completion of his latest production, *Eskimo* (1933). Also present was the Danish naturalist Peter Freuchen. *Eskimo* was based on his books and he had acted in the film. Harlow's introduction to Freuchen nearly ended her mourning period with a bang, as Freuchen related to film historian Richard Griffith in the 1950s. "Jean was as small as I'm big—I'm six foot six, you know—and she was pretty drunk that night." Harlow was impressed by Freuchen's build, but felt the need to tease the explorer, who had lost a leg to frostbite some years earlier. "Aw, big boy," she cooed, "I'll bet you're not as strong as you look." Freuchen took the dare. He put his huge hands around Harlow's waist and raised her to the ceiling of Van Dyke's Brentwood living room. Her silk Jean Patou gown flared open. Flashbulbs popped.

"The next morning," said Freuchen, "I got a message to get my ass over to Louis B. Mayer's office on the double. When I went in, I found him sitting at his desk crying. That was the first time I ever saw a man cry at ten o'clock in the morning. He reached under his blotter and brought out a photographic negative and some prints. They showed Jean in my arms, and they showed all Jean had." The upshot was that Mayer had paid—personally, he said—five thousand dollars for the negative. Freuchen apologized, reimbursed Mayer, and left. Outside Mayer's office he encountered Harlow.

"Did you get it?" she asked.

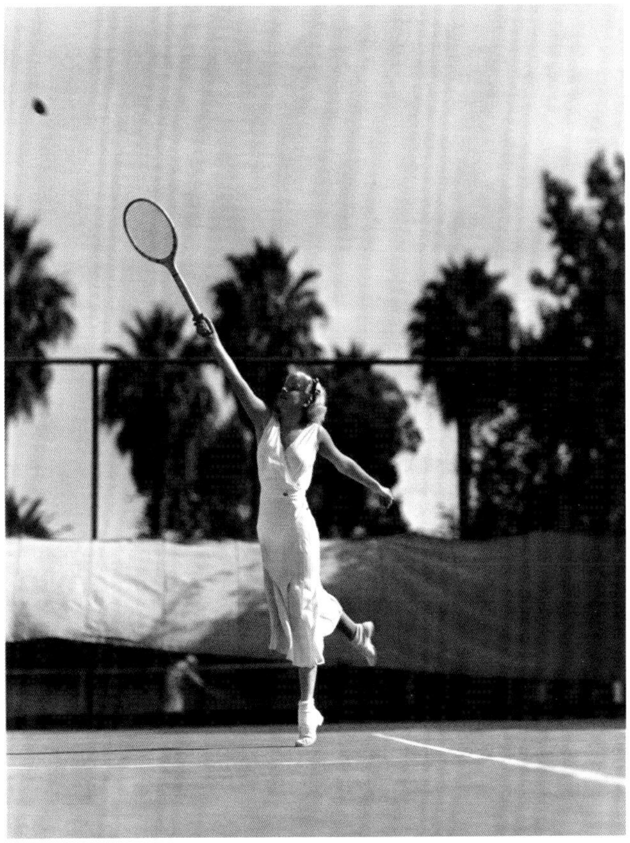

Harlow posed for more photos in October 1932 at the tennis courts at the Beverly Hills Hotel.

Harlow helped the Charity Assistance League in Hollywood by reading stories to needy children on Christmas Eve of 1932. The League and its gift shop are still located at 5604 De Longpre Avenue in Hollywood.

"I got it," said Freuchen.

"Wait here," said Harlow. "I'll tell you how I made out." She assumed "an expression of penitence worthy of Mary Magdalene" and went into Mayer's office. After a few minutes, she emerged, no longer penitent. "The son of a bitch," she said. "The son of a bitch."

"What happened?"

"Well," she said, "Louis went into his crying act, of course. So I went into my crying act and offered to pay the studio—no, him personally—for the photograph. I wrote a check to his name for five thousand dollars and handed it to him, he took it and gave me the prints. But when I reached for the negative, he grabbed it away from me. 'Oh no you don't,' he said, and put it in his drawer and locked it. Now he's got me for life."

Harlow went back to the set of *Dinner at Eight*, where she was working with Cukor to polish each line reading. There was a scene in which Harlow tells Beery "You're gonna pay for it with everything you got." In the first take, Harlow phrased it "with *every thing you* got." In the second take, which is in the finished film, Harlow said "with everything *ya got!*" Few directors would take the time to elicit such subtle shadings. Cukor did.

The result was a performance that made Harlow's previous films look as if they had been acted by a different woman. And yet Cukor had been uncertain. "I'd seen her in *Public Enemy* and *Hell's Angels*," said Cukor, "where she was so bad and self-conscious it was comic. She got big laughs when she didn't want them. Then I saw *Red Dust*. And there she was, suddenly marvelous in comedy." The girl who had been laughed at all her life was honing her comic skills, and, with Cukor's help, creating a character. He was frank with her. "You know, dear, when I first saw you I thought, there goes a hopeless girl." But he was also encouraging and supportive, because she was prone to self-criticism.

Harlow blossomed under Cukor's tutelage. "She was extremely disciplined," recalled Cukor. "A skillful actress. She spoke comedy lines as though she didn't quite understand them. She did it in a marvelous manner, made all these common sounds." Kitty Packard was a distillation of all the sexy tarts

Jean and Marino Bello wanted a mansion, so Harlow got into the spirit of it, reviewing blueprints with Bello at the Beverly Glen construction site.

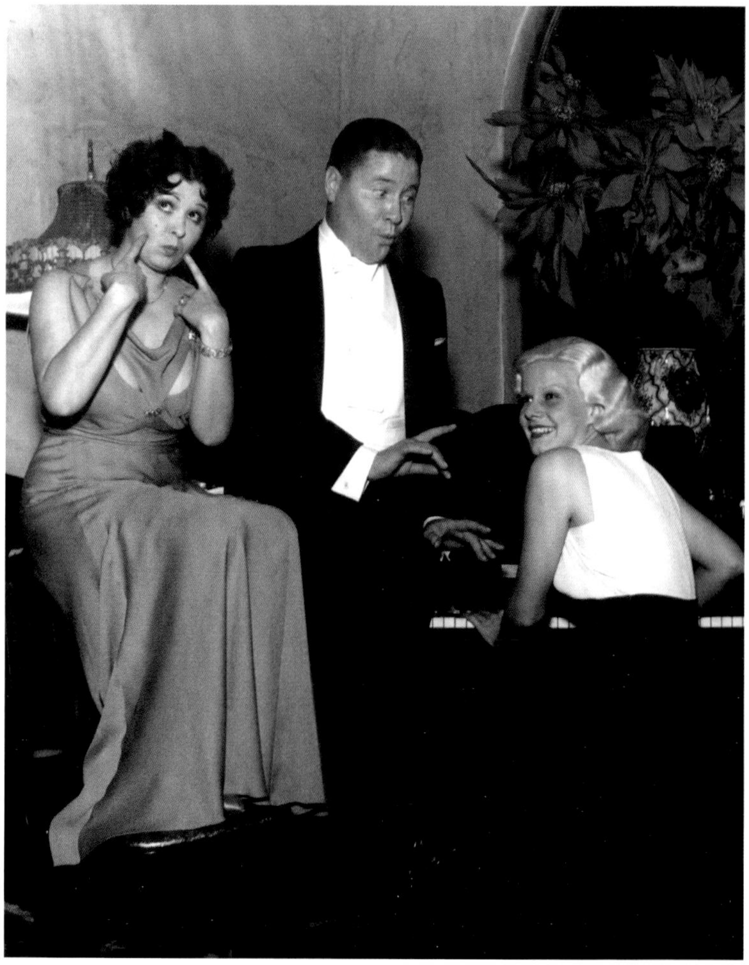

Harlow returned to public life gradually. During the 1932 holiday season, she attended a party given by the Stu Erwins and singer Helen Kane, pictured here with Harlow and Jack Oakie.

Harlow had essayed, but with a difference. She had heart, and she had humor. She knew she was sexy and dumb. But she demanded respect—and affection—both from Beery's character and from the audience.

Cukor completed principal photography on *Dinner at Eight* in a brisk twenty-four days. Harlow had no scenes with John Barrymore, but she did have one exchange with Marie Dressler, so she spent time on the set with the veteran actress. Dressler had been a star of vaudeville and early silent films when her fortunes changed, leaving her almost destitute. Screenwriter Frances Marion took pity on Dressler and suggested her to Thalberg. Within a few years, Dressler had made a brilliant comeback. At age sixty-two, she was the biggest box-office draw in the world. Chatting with Harlow, she sensed the young woman's ambivalence. Harlow confirmed it. "I can't imagine being old," Harlow said quietly. "I don't want to get old."

The Agua Caliente Casino and Hotel Resort in Tijuana was opened in 1928 by Los Angeles hotelier Baron Long and three other investors. It offered gambling and alcohol to Americans suffering through Prohibition.

"Don't be silly," said Dressler. "It isn't fun 'til you're forty."

The scene Harlow and Dressler played at the film's finale was written by Donald Ogden Stewart, who had also written Harlow's closing scenes in *Red Dust*. This proved to be the quintessentially hilarious moment in a funny, touching film. Dressler and Harlow amble toward the Park Avenue dining room, the odd pairing of a frizzy-haired veteran in dark velvet and a porcelain doll dressed in a bias-cut white satin gown.

"I was reading a book the other day," says Harlow out of nowhere.

"Reading a book?" asks Dressler, barely concealing her disbelief.

Harlow spent New Year's Eve of 1932 in Agua Caliente with Jean and Marino Bello.

"Yes. All about civilization or something. A nutty kind of a book. Do you know that the guy says that machinery is going to take the place of every profession?"

"Oh my dear," chortles Dressler, scanning Harlow's bias-cut curves. "That's something *you* need never worry about."

Dinner at Eight premiered on Tuesday, August 29, 1933, at Grauman's Chinese Theatre. Harlow prepared for her big night by having her hair waved. She was still enduring the ritual bleaching at Jim's Beauty Salon. On one occasion, while being shampooed, she heard two girls arguing. One insisted that Harlow's hair was a wig. She pulled away from her hairdresser, stuck her soapy head through a curtain, and said: "Pardon me, but did I leave my wig in here?"

On her way home from Jim's, Harlow dropped in on Bobbe Brown, who was frantically preparing a meal for out-of-town guests. "Jean laughed at my predicament and put on a bungalow apron and set to work," reported Brown. "Inside of forty-five minutes she had everything cooked and ready, correct to the smallest detail. While I worried a lot about the heat from the oven ruining her wave, she didn't. She thought it was a real lark."

The premiere was not of the magnitude of *Hell's Angels* or even *Grand Hotel*. There was still a depression going on (the film—unlike the play—dared to name it), but the streets around Grauman's were so clogged with pedestrians that *Los Angeles Times* columnist Lee Shippey was unable to get to the theater. Radio station KFI was broadcasting the event, and Harlow was able to say a few words. "This may sound sentimental," Harlow said, "but I want to express my thanks to my father and mother, who are responsible for me being here."

Inside the theater, a live stage show preceded the evening's film, which finally started at 9:15. For the first time, Harlow had the experience previously reserved for Greta Garbo, Norma Shearer, and King Kong. At the conclusion of the brawl between Kitty Packard and her husband, when the scene fades out on a telling close-up of Harlow, the Grauman's audience broke into a spontaneous, thunderous applause. As the reviews rolled in, incredulous executives at M-G-M read the same thing over and over. *Dinner at Eight*'s all-star ensemble had been upended by the twenty-two-year-old sex symbol who was suddenly a triple-threat comedienne.

Agua Caliente's attractions included this racetrack.

Harlow and Bello attended the Agua Caliente horse races in early January 1933.

Harlow played golf in Agua Caliente with pioneer producer Jesse Lasky, but it was his son who piqued her interest.

Robert H. Cobb and Herbert Somborn opened the Brown Derby Café, 1628 North Vine Street, in January 1929, to capitalize on the success of the original Brown Derby, 3427 Wilshire Boulevard, which they had opened in 1926.

In March 1933, Marino Bello poured apricot brandy in a secret bar for Harlow, Jean Bello, and Ruth and Johnny Hamp.

Harlow signed this Brown Derby caricature to the artist Vitch in 1933.

In early 1933, Harlow lunched at the Brown Derby Café with Robert H. Cobb, at far left, and her agent Arthur Landau.

While Will Hays was warning the studios not to make sexy movies, Harvey White was making sexy photos of Harlow.

[OPPOSITE] Jean Harlow posed for this unusually somber George Hurrell portrait in the spring of 1932. It was released during her mourning period; sexy poses from the session were held back. The photo caption described her black onyx cross as "a present from her late husband, Paul Bern."

Harlow, photographed here with Hilda Vaughn by Frank Tanner, was acknowledged as a skilled comedienne in *Dinner at Eight* (1933), producer David O. Selznick's first film at M-G-M.

Dinner At Eight was also director George Cukor's first M-G-M film. Thanks to him, Harlow was able to refine her comic talents. Her scenes with Wallace Beery were tart and comical.

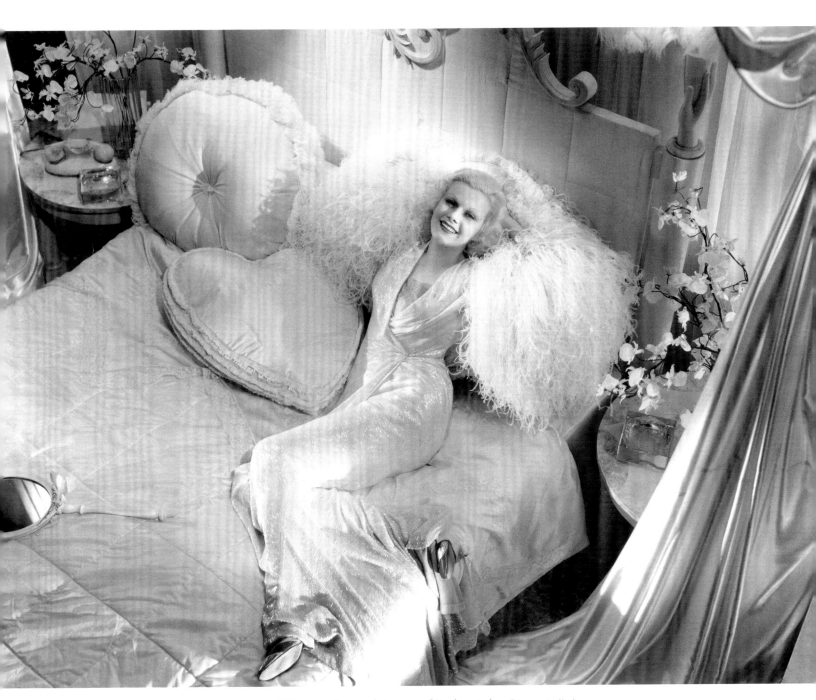

Harvey White made superb images of Harlow in her *Dinner At Eight* bedroom, the first all-white set in film history.

"There are ten shades of white in that set," said Hobe Erwin. "Flesh-white chiffon for the glass curtains, oyster-white satin for the over-curtains, lacquer-white ornamented in dead chalk-white in the wardrobe, cream-white velvet on the walls, translucent alabaster-white in the pilasters, milk-white for the chenille rug, metallic-white and warm-white on the chaise lounge, and ivory-white in the taffeta bedspread with the monogram."

Unit still photographer Frank Tanner snapped Harlow walking from Selznick's bungalow to the *Dinner at Eight* soundstage.

The Ambassador Hotel, designed by Myron Hunt, opened at 3400 Wilshire Boulevard in 1921. By 1933, one of its chief attractions was a nightclub called the Cocoanut Grove.

Harlow visited the Cocoanut Grove in March 1933 to hear Johnny Hamp's orchestra. Seated with her are, from left, Johnny Hamp, Ruth Hamp, actor Dick Powell, band vocalist June McCloy, and Jack Campbell.

Harlow was one of numerous celebrities broadcasting to South America from KNX Radio in Hollywood on April 2, 1933. With her are Ramon Novarro and Claudette Colbert.

The Hollywood Roosevelt Hotel, named for Theodore Roosevelt, opened on May 15, 1927.

Harlow and director W.S. ("Woody") Van Dyke were photographed with band leader Jay Whidden in the Roosevelt's Blossom Room in April of 1933.

A scandal nearly resulted when Harlow met explorer Peter Freuchen at a party given by "Woody" Van Dyke on April 2. Harlow, wearing a new Jean Patou gown, gave Freuchen a challenge he could not resist.

Harlow joined Walter Huston at the L.A. Brewing Company on April 6 to help executives Robert Mentier and Charles J. Lick celebrate the repeal of Prohibition.

The depression was hurting business, so Harlow got a good deal from the Thompson Motor Company of Beverly Hills on this 1932 Deluxe Eight 903 Sport Phaeton. She took delivery and posed for photos on April 15, 1933.

Harlow's favorite pet in 1933 was a ginger Pomeranian named Oscar.

[OPPOSITE]
Dinner at Eight was such an important film that Selznick commissioned a second portrait sitting of Harlow. Hurrell shot it in June on sets from the film that were still standing.

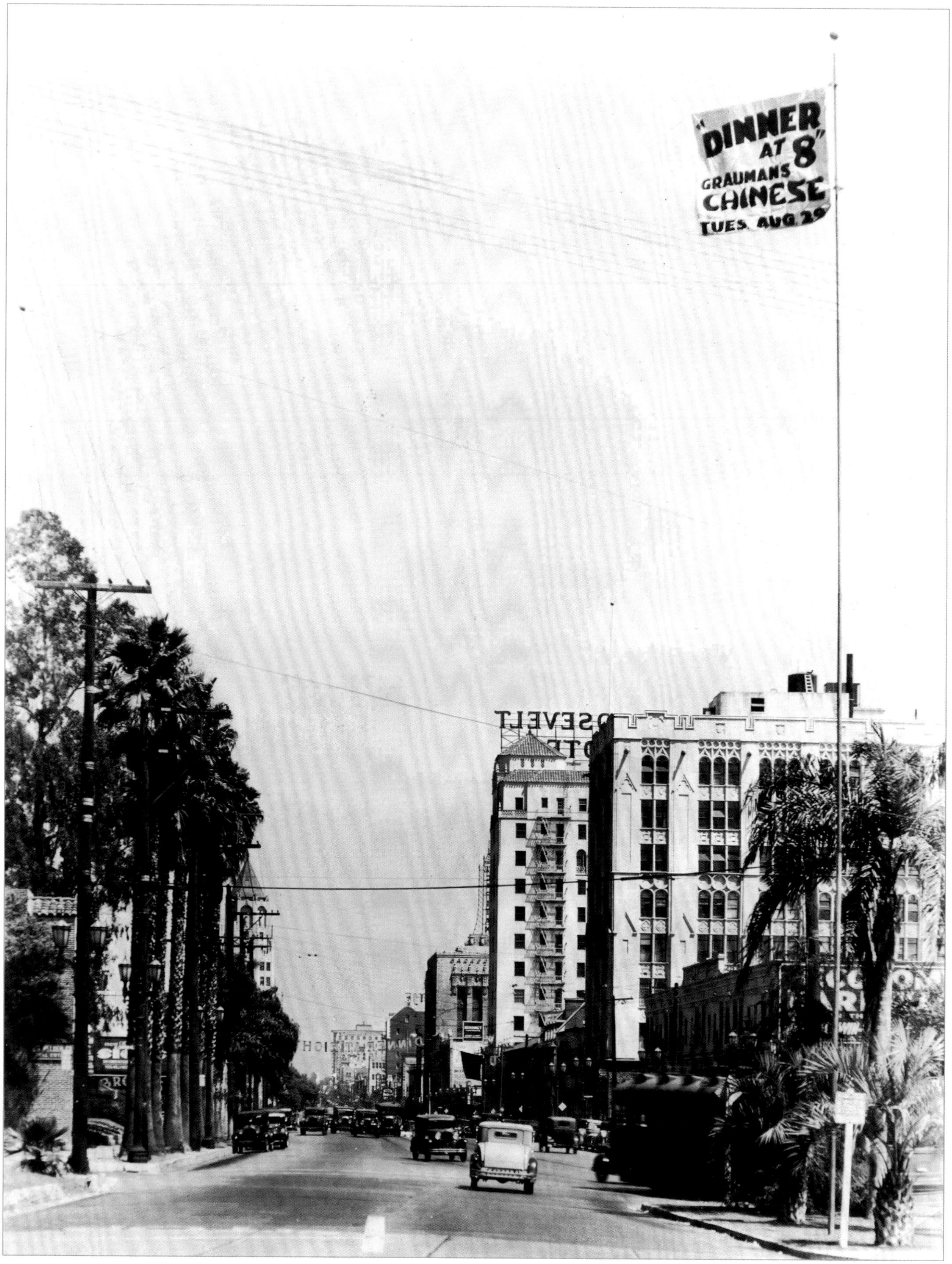

The premiere of *Dinner at Eight* took place at Grauman's Chinese Theatre on Tuesday, August 29, 1933. Harlow had attended the premiere of *King Kong* there in March, but did not expect that her scenes in *Dinner at Eight* would elicit as much enthusiasm.

Hurrell was not averse to Harlow's drinking gin during their photo session; Harlow was not averse to disrobing. Her burnished skin tone was the result, not of makeup (which Hurrell discouraged), but of tanning sessions at her pool.

• Holding a Man •

In the spring of 1933, it looked as if Hollywood might close down. There was an economic crisis, an earthquake, and the threat of federal censorship. Jean Harlow was not worried. She was insulated from these concerns. She had her work and her mother's solicitude. Jean Bello was managing, controlling, and pushing. The young woman did not mind; she doted on her mother.

When the so-called Long Beach Earthquake (actually centered in Huntington Beach) shook M-G-M on Friday, March 10, at 5:55 in the evening, Harlow's first thought was for her mother's safety. Jean Bello was in no danger. She was in Holmby Hills, decorating a new home. Years earlier, little Harlean had admired a white colonial mansion. Now she had one. Her M-G-M earnings had built the "Whitest House in Hollywood," a Georgian-style mansion at 214 South Beverly Glen Boulevard. But she had little to do with it. Jean and Marino Bello, her de facto managers, had diverted her salary to the project. Jean Bello's new hobby was convenient; she was an antique collector. Harlow indulged her mother but found much of the house pretentious, especially her own bedroom. "Get a load of this," Harlow giggled as she showed the over-decorated room to actress Anita Page. Harlow's favorite area was the swimming pool. Everyone she talked to was invited for a swim.

One indication of Harlow's prominence was the volume of her fan mail. Although she enjoyed typing and threatened to "write the Great American Novel," she and Bobbe Brown together could not handle her correspondence. A stenographer named Maydelle Jewell was hired to type letters. Harlow kept in touch with her friends from school, but her letters began to sound as if she were dictating them to a secretary, which she was.

The Cocoanut Grove, though located in Los Angeles, was the hub of Hollywood nightlife in 1933. When the Ambassador Hotel was razed in 2006, the shell of the Grove was spared. It became the auditorium of the Robert F. Kennedy Community Schools; the learning center opened in September of 2010.

Harlow poses in the Grove with visiting orchestra leader Guy Lombardo.

[OPPOSITE] Jean Harlow posed outside the Cocoanut Grove with Hal Rosson, left, Johnny Weissmuller, and Irene Jones, the couturier who later became the costume designer known simply as Irene.

"Dear Helen: I just have time for a wee note," she began a letter to Helen Fieger.

> I am in my dressing room with full make-up on, waiting for a call. It surely was grand hearing from you so soon, and such a nice newsy letter. . . . The house is finished but we are still "camping," as most of the furniture has not arrived from the factory. It is a lovely place. I went for my first swim in the pool last Sunday, and surely enjoyed myself. I will stop now dear, as I had better read my lines over.

The film on which Harlow was working was *Hold Your Man* (1933). Sam Wood was directing from a script by Harlow's friend Anita Loos. Harlow had wanted a comedy. The film had funny situations, but it was essentially a sex melodrama meant to capitalize on *Red Dust*. Clark Gable was co-starring with Harlow. A hot new team was in prospect. Charles Farrell and Janet Gaynor had been box-office champions for Fox since 1928, the most exemplary screen team. Greta Garbo and John Gilbert had brought M-G-M as much publicity as box office with their onscreen chemistry (and off-screen romance), but there had been no team at Metro since they parted in 1929.

Abe Lyman led the Cocoanut Grove house orchestra from 1922 to 1927. Harlow and director Sam Wood posed with him on June 4, 1933.

Harlow and Gable generated excitement on screen, but not because of mutual attraction. Gable regarded Harlow as something of a tomboy, and Harlow thought of Gable as an overgrown kid. Instead of passion, there was genuine fondness, expressed in teasing and practical jokes. One day on the *Hold Your Man* stage, Harlow and Gable were rigidly posed for a close shot of a kiss. There was quiet on the set as the soundman made his adjustments. The microphone hung overhead, and the potentiometers in the sound booth were cranked up. A visiting journalist eavesdropped on the two stars. "Rhea and I had dinner with Helen Hayes and Charlie MacArthur last night," said Gable. "Swell people." (Rhea was Mrs. Gable. His last film *The White Sister* (1933), had co-starred Hayes.)

"Yes," said Harlow. "Grand."

"Okay, ready!" yelled Wood.

"Quiet!" the assistant director shouted.

"They're turning," announced the soundman from his booth. Cameraman Hal Rosson was about to call "Speed," when Gable whispered: "Jean, wait. You've got your eyebrows on upside down." Of course, this broke everyone up, which is what he wanted. The time wasted in getting back into character was offset by the authentic warmth of the scene.

Visitors to the *Hold Your Man* set observed that Harlow enjoyed her work and was liked by her co-workers. She started a large jigsaw puzzle and then left it on a table for the cast and crew to work on. She was affectionate with Loos, who was on the set to rewrite lines, and with Rosson, who was shooting his third Harlow film. Although not as celebrated for his glamour lighting as Lee Garmes or William Daniels, Rosson was one

George Hurrell made this portrait of Harlow with Ruth and Johnny Hamp in 1933.

Harlow was seen dancing at the Miramar on June 27, 1933, with architect and sometime actor Jack Donovan.

Clark Gable was recuperating from appendicitis at his Brentwood home. Harlow lugged a portable 35mm projector there so he could see the Marie Dressler film *Tugboat Annie* (1933).

The Miramar Hotel, built in Santa Monica in 1925, also had a popular ballroom.

Harlow dined with actor Walter Huston on August 8 on the patio rooftop of the Hollywood Roosevelt.

of Hollywood's top ten cinematographers. His photography had done as much to make Harlow a star as M-G-M's drama coaches and makeup artists. Her close-ups in *Red Dust* were more than flattering; they were transcendent.

The third act of *Hold Your Man* had Harlow in a women's prison—and pregnant. This was a risky plot element, even with a lax Production Code. One day a prop window resisted her. "Who the hell fixed this window blind?" Harlow asked in mock rage. "Every time I swing up this gadget, a piece of canvas hits me in the head. Is that a nice way to treat an expectant mother?" Harlow's only real complaint about her work was being inside for twelve hours a day. "I miss being out of doors," she said. Most stars were driven in a limousine from their dressing rooms to the soundstage; not Harlow. She preferred to walk in the fragrant spring air. "That's my only grouse against studio work," she said. "I live in the fresh air when my time is my own." But her time was not her own.

Harlow was expected to be available for studio work whenever it occurred. She was usually good-natured about post-production retakes, but when they jeopardized a trip to Chicago, she was not happy. She had planned to visit the Century of Progress International Exposition with her pen pal Stanley Brown.

"Stan, I was to leave Monday for the Fair," she wrote Brown.

> This morning I get a call from the studio. So I go out. And guess what! The studio heads decided I should have a stepfather in the picture for the protection of my honor. The picture has been previewed and I can't figure for the life of me where there's a spot where they can get a stepfather in and then get him out again. So that means no trip for me to Chicago or at least my stay will be cut down something fearful. So, I ask you, what's the use?

Harlow's next film was *Hold Your Man*. It was shot by Rosson, far left, directed by Wood, seated under camera, and co-starred Gable.

The scenes in question had Guy Kibbee as an errant stepfather who causes Harlow's character to lead a wayward life. She canceled her June 6 departure and dutifully made the new scenes. On June 10 she departed Los Angeles for the first time in more than a year. Her return to the Midwest was a triumph. There was Jean Harlow Day in Chicago on June 12, and Jean Harlow Day at the Exposition the next day. She toured it with Brown, signing scores of autographs along the way. At one point she craved a hot dog. "You're not going to get mustard all over that cute white dress," protested Brown.

"Stan, won't you let me be *natural*?" She had just bitten into her hot dog when the autograph hounds showed up again. They crowded in and would not take no for an answer. "Stan, get me *out* of here!" The throng turned into a crowd. Harlow's walk turned into a run. A hundred people began chasing her. She became frightened. Brown tried to help her escape, but there was nowhere to hide. Police finally intervened but she was genuinely shaken.

Harlow stayed at the LaSalle Hotel and at the Lakeshore, the guest of Johnny and Ruth Hamp. She visited Skip and Ella Harlow in Kansas City, posing for pictures with neighborhood children. The only sour note was a snub from the *Kansas City Kansan*, which refused to cover her visit because it objected to her "image." Back in Hollywood, she learned that the urgently needed new scenes were not being used. *Hold Your Man* was released in early July, and, despite a certain lack of consistency—it turned mushy in the third act—it soon surpassed *Red Dust*'s profits. The Depression notwithstanding, people were paying to see Harlow.

The publicity department mandated this *Hold Your Man* gag shot; left to right, Sam Wood, Clark Gable, in back of car; producer Bernard Hyman, writer Howard Emmett Rogers, Harlow, and Anita Loos.

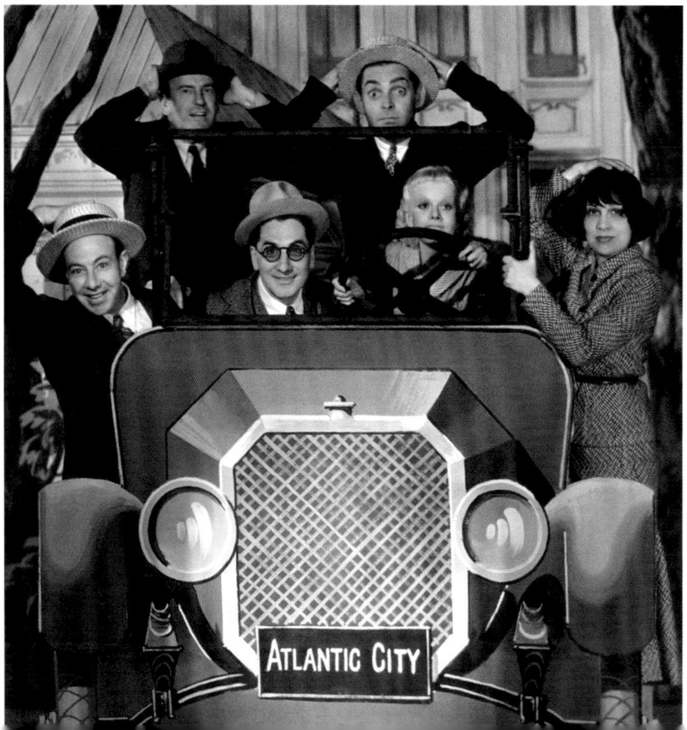

When Harlow sat on Rosson's lap, no one thought it significant.

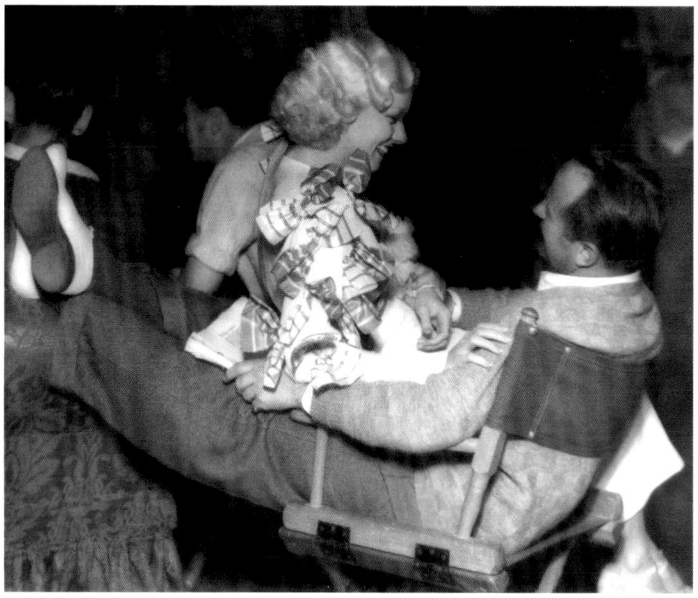

After making two films back to back, Harlow had some leisure time. She spent her days with friends, having lunch at the Ambassador Hotel and then cruising Beverly Hills in her new Packard convertible. "She drives herself," said her friend Phyllis Clare, "with the wireless set going full blast. Then we drop in at a gramophone shop and listen to records. Any that Jean buys are duplicated. She gives the duplicate set to whichever friend is with her at the time. My record collection just grew and grew and grew." Harlow's collection of pets was also growing. She had brought her Great Dane Bleak from Club View Drive. She adopted Oscar, the Pomeranian. Then she found eight ducklings. Then she acquired one of Rin-Tin-Tin, Jr.'s puppies, a platinum blonde named Duncie. Then a Norwegian husky called Nudger. Plus two alley cats, Nip and Tuck, and Erbert, the goldfish. "Now if the

[TOP] More than thirty percent of M-G-M's box office came from foreign countries, so it was politic to show Harlow reading the Argentine publication *La Nacion*.

[ABOVE] Harlow had to delay a vacation to shoot new scenes for *Hold Your Man*. Guy Kibbee was borrowed from Warner Bros. to play her no-good stepfather.

June 13, 1933, was Jean Harlow Day at Chicago's Century of Progress International Exposition.

In *Hold Your Man*, Harlow was sexy, funny, and lovable.

picture industry goes on the rocks, or if I do," wrote Harlow, "I am surely going to start a circus. How does that sound? Oh, yes. I'm a white girl again instead of a brown girl. Lost my tan. Anyway, I'm not going to be any good for the rest of the day and I appreciate it. I started out not wanting to be good for anything but a nice glass of beer. Oh, all right then. Four or five."

The beer reference was one of several in recent letters and interviews. "When they legalized beer they ruined my figure," she said in Chicago. "I'm crazy about beer." A journalist asked her how she could go to a party after a long day of work. "Oh, a bath and a highball," Harlow answered, "and I'll be ready to go again." Drinking continued to be a habit. Jean Bello tried to put a stop to it, but this was one area that Harlow kept off limits. Stanley Brown was her distant safety valve. Her local one was a bottle, preferably Graves Distilled Superior Dry Gin. "Jean would have her favorite, Graves Gin, delivered to our house," recalled Bobbe Brown, "so her mother wouldn't know how much she drank." Writer Leonard Mosley attended a party at Harlow's house. He was standing with Cary Grant, Bruce Cabot, and Charles Laughton when Harlow came up to him. She was obviously intoxicated. "D'you know the only man in the world I'd like to be my lover?" she asked, and then pointed to another party guest, the very unpleasant Wallace Beery.

"You can't mean it," said Mosley.

"Beery hates me," said Harlow, bursting into tears. "Why does anyone hate me?"

Beery did not hate Harlow any more than he hated Marie Dressler or Jackie Cooper, whom he also treated with contempt. Harlow assumed that his meanness was her fault. Marcella Rabwin, David O. Selznick's assistant, thought that Harlow had a "severe inferiority complex." The girl desired by a nation of men could not hold a man. This was evidenced by a series of brief affairs.

There was writer Thomas Wolfe, visiting M-G-M. There was director Howard Hawks, who was married to Norma Shearer's sister. In August of 1933, there was heavyweight contender Max Baer, making his film debut in *The Prizefighter and the Lady* (1933). Baer saw Harlow in the commissary and asked her out. They were already involved when he invited her to visit the set where he was filming a fight scene with heavyweight champion Primo Carnera on Sunday, September 3. "There must have been about a thousand people there," said Harlow. "Sports writers, old-guard fighters, hundreds of extras." She found a safe spot and watched the so-called "Jewish Adonis." An item appeared in the newspapers: "Jean Harlow was a very interested spectator on Max Baer's set yesterday." Knowing she was being set up, Harlow commented: "Yeah, Jean Harlow and a thousand other people." Whether she liked it or not, the word was out. And Baer was married.

Louis B. Mayer ordered Howard Strickling to speak to the Bellos. They warned Harlow. She was intractable, fascinated by Baer. He, on the other hand, was bored. When he ignored her calls, she took to sitting outside his house in her car. Baer was indifferent. "He said that the person she was in the movies wasn't her at all," according to his son, Max Baer, Jr. "She wasn't flashy," said Rabwin. "She was shy." The girl who signed her letters "Just Me" could not get a man to see who "Me" was.

Harlow poses next to a Pitcairn Autogyro. With her is Lieutenant Tito Falconi of the Royal Italian Air Service, who had recently set a world record for flying upside down.

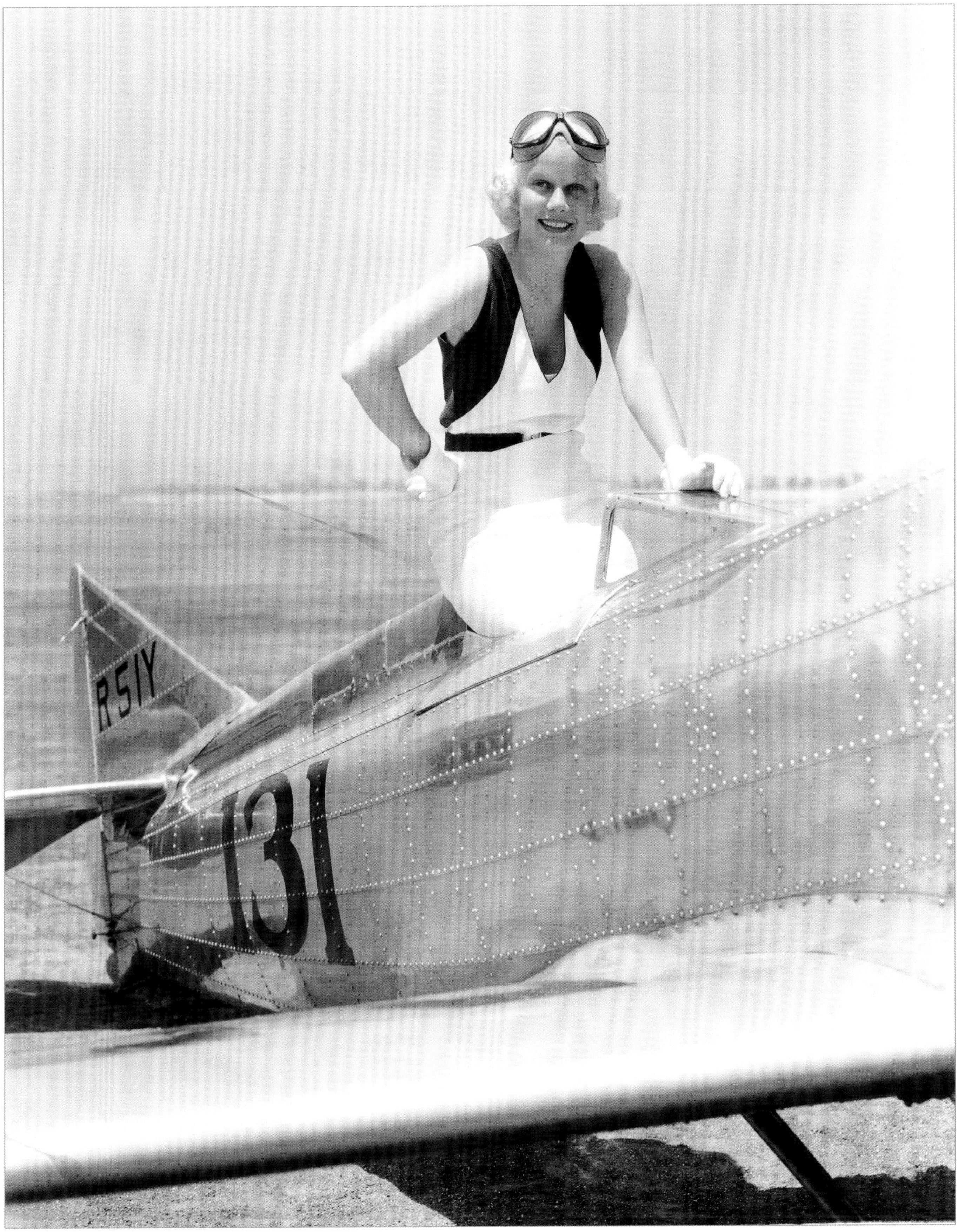

Harlow was at Mines Field on July 1 to lead the Grand Parade at the 1933 National Air Races. In this M-G-M photo, she poses in the cockpit of the racing plane "San Francisco." (Mines Field became Los Angeles International Airport in 1946.)

[OVERLEAF] Looking aerodynamic herself, Harlow poses with an Auburn speedster, the "San Francisco." Standing in apposite awe is Cliff Henderson, National Air Race director.

San Fr

R51Y
PRESS

• A Bombshell in Beverly Glen •

Jean Harlow had come so far so fast that M-G-M was contemplating a film based on her life. The story department had purchased an unproduced play called *Bombshell*, the humorless tale of a long-suffering actress whose family so exploits her that she finally kills herself. The team that made *Red Dust*—producer Hunt Stromberg, director Victor Fleming, and writer John Lee Mahin—considered various ways of adapting the play to fit Harlow, who was anything but humorless. "She was a pretty happy-go-lucky girl, except when her mother and father gave her fits," recalled Mahin.

"Let's turn this into a comedy," he said to Stromberg and Fleming. "It's funny. Vic, you must have known people like this in the early days."

"I know one right now," Fleming responded. "Clara Bow. Her place is a madhouse. Leeches, drunks, hangers-on. Spilling highballs, leaving cigarette burns on the furniture. You come into the living room—there's a beautiful Oriental rug with coffee stains and dog shit all over it. And her father comes in drunk."

"That's enough," Stromberg cut in. "We've got it." The plot was changed so that Harlow could portray a put-upon young sex symbol named Lola Burns. Her father is a mountebank, her brother a lush, her secretary an embezzler, and her sheepdogs wild. Her studio publicist—the only person she relates to—is a con artist who implicates her in one scandal after another. Stromberg let Mahin run wilder than the dogs and the result was some of the funniest dialogue recorded at M-G-M that year. The most quoted line was spoken by Franchot Tone, playing yet another *Bombshell* poseur. "Your hair is like a field of silver daisies," Gifford Middleton tells Lola. "I'd like to run barefoot through your hair."

"Not even Norma Shearer or Helen Hayes in their nicest pictures was ever spoken to like that," says the quixotic Lola. Harlow was not smart enough to pry loose her own parasites, but neither was she a "Dumb Dora." She was, first of all, an avid reader, finishing two to four books a week. Her tastes ran from S.S. Van Dine to John Galsworthy. "I re-read the *Forsyte Saga* every year or so," she said. "And I've just finished Romain Rolland's *Jean Christophe*. I read not only for pleasure but also for style and characterization. I think Wasserman's *The World's Illusion* has meant more to me than any book I've ever read. I've read it five times and feel a sixth creeping up on me. I'm especially fond, too, of Sigrid Undset's *Kristin Lavransdatter*." Not surprisingly, she was more articulate than the average film actress. She was also a quick study. "She never ran lines," recalled Bobbe Brown. "I'd have lunch with her every day, and not once would she rehearse. She'd look over the script, then come out of her dressing room and do it perfectly, take after take. And I'd wonder, 'When does she learn her dialogue?'"

There was plenty of it to learn in *Bombshell*, page after page of rat-a-tat exchanges. For a performer with absolutely no stage training, Harlow was delivering a remarkable performance. She credited her experience at Hal Roach Studios. "Don't rush your laughs," Stan Laurel had told her. "Time each action. Build to a climax." There were also the lingering effects of *Dinner at Eight*. George Cukor had taken the time to work with her and teach her technique. "Nobody could direct a dialogue scene like Cukor," said Fleming, who took Harlow aside and told her how much she had improved. She was disbelieving. "When Vic told me I'd improved so much and asked me what had happened, I was completely surprised," said Harlow. "All I feel is a little more sure of myself."

If the *Bombshell* production was going well, Harlow's affair with Max Baer was not. "We are working night and day," she wrote to Helen Fieger on September 7. "We leave for Arizona tomorrow,

[Opposite] Russell Ball made this portrait of Jean Harlow in September of 1933 to publicize Victor Fleming's *Bombshell*.

to be on location for a few days. It will be a change, and I feel badly in need of one." In the desert outside Yuma, crew members worried about her moodiness. "All the stagehands, all the crews liked her," said Mahin. One member of the crew was sweet on her, cameraman Hal Rosson. "After about the second week on the picture," Harlow told a journalist, "I began to notice a subtle change in Hal's attitude. At first I thought that I was imagining it. There was just a trace of formality in his free-and-easy manner. And, one day, to my surprise, I found that I was feeling self-conscious with him."

Harlow was not too self-conscious to propose marriage to the thirty-eight-year-old Rosson, who said yes without stopping to think that a marriage between a star and a technician would be frowned upon by caste-conscious Hollywood. Nor did he stop to consider the prospect of Jean and Marino Bello as in-laws. Rosson had golfed with Marino and taken Harlow out on occasion, but nothing had prepared him for her proposal. He could not know that Baer's wife was threatening to name Harlow as co-respondent in a divorce suit. M-G-M executives had ordered Harlow to marry someone—or else. So she chose a respectable, available guy. Rosson also happened to be older, reserved, and mustachioed; in other words, a lookalike for her over-attentive, tyrannical grandfather.

The Bullocks Wilshire specialty store, which opened in 1929 at 3050 Wilshire Boulevard, drew numerous clients from Hollywood.

Harlow wore this Irene gown in a fashion shot by Hurrell in Bullocks Wilshire. The garment was made of dark green sauvage velvet and soon became part of Harlow's wardrobe.

Harlow posed for George Hurrell several times in Bullocks Wilshire salons.

The only clue to Harlow's Electra complex was disclosed forty years later by David Lewis, a young producer in whom she uncharacteristically confided family secrets during evening walks along Sunset Boulevard; perhaps it was because Lewis was her first homosexual friend. "On these walks she told me of an unhappy childhood," Lewis wrote in 1979. "At some time as a child, perhaps nine or ten, she had been raped by a close relative, and it left her with a terrible fear of sex. Jean married very young to someone from a socially prominent family, a gentle young man. This had appealed to Jean, but the marriage was broken up. She never mentioned by whom or why. Each of Jean's marriages after that had been to older men."

On September 14, the *Bombshell* company returned to Culver City. Its premiere was scheduled for September 29. Shooting ended on September 17. On that evening Harlow and Hal Rosson dined at the Colony Club. "If someone should ask me what I ate, I couldn't tell them," Harlow said later. "And I've proved that a girl can keep a secret. We met several people whom we knew in the club where we had dinner and it took every ounce of will power

Harlow poses with director Howard Hawks and boxer Max Baer, both of whom were her intimate friends.

On September 3, Harlow paid a visit to the set of W.S. Van Dyke's *The Prizefighter and the Lady*. She posed with heavyweight champion Primo Carnera but was more interested in the contender.

Harlow bicycled around the M-G-M lot, wearing her trademark sweater and slacks.

I possessed to keep from bursting forth with my big news. I was sure that people would guess from the look on our faces and our nervousness." Harlow and Rosson then chartered a plane and flew to Yuma, Arizona. At 4:30 A.M. they were married by Justice of the Peace Earl A. Freeman. Pilot Allen Russell and airport manager John Redondo acted as witnesses. "When the ceremony ended," said Harlow, "I looked down and saw a run in my stocking. It was too early for the stores to be open, so I did the next best thing. I took the stockings off and returned home barelegged."

Harlow was nothing if not unorthodox. She went for almost two days on a minimum of sleep while she and a flagging Rosson caught the full glare of Hollywood publicity. Rosson had grown up with the industry. All his siblings were employed in it, but mostly behind the cameras. None of them had known the assault of hungry journalists. A Rosson eloping with a sex symbol was news. As the newlyweds stepped off the plane at United Airport in Burbank at 9:00 A.M., they were surrounded by reporters. Rosson grew quiet. "My new husband can't take it," Harlow teased as she posed for photographers. "We decided last night on a swift airplane elopement," she laughed. "And here we are." Rosson had nothing to add. As he and Harlow walked to a waiting car, she said, "Now we must see Mother and Father."

Clarence Bull photographed Harlow on July 19 in her freshly decorated dressing room. It was located in the wood-frame structure known as Washington Row.

In Kansas City, Ella Harlow was as surprised as anyone in Hollywood. "I can't believe it yet," she told reporters. "Jean made no mention of her approaching marriage. I never heard her discuss any man, and if she was interested in a man she would have told me."

Skip Harlow was terse. "The youngster doesn't take up those delicate matters with a grandfather," he snapped.

By 11 A.M., Harlow and Rosson were at the Beverly Glen mansion, eating a hastily prepared wedding breakfast. Reporters were served sandwiches and beer. A press conference was convened on the manicured lawn in the garden. "It's pretty hard to say when we fell in love," Harlow said, trying to answer the obvious question, and then faltering. "Looks like I'm on the well-known spot, doesn't it? Why I can't answer that question, I don't know." Rosson was asked if he thought Harlow was the most beautiful actress at M-G-M. "She's the only beautiful actress at the studio," he said. "I fell in love with everything about her. I loved her from the start."

"Oh, darling," exclaimed Jean. "Did you? I didn't know it was as bad as all that. I'm afraid I'll have to feel sorry for you." The abashed Rosson turned to the reporters and said, "Wouldn't you like to play a game of ping-pong or something?" The real game was being played elsewhere. When Max Baer's wife filed for divorce a week later, she withheld Harlow's name from her suit. Rosson had been working with Harlow for a year. If he

Harlow's dressing room was decorated in white, with pastel accents.

Harlow's makeup table was mostly for show, since M-G-M's artists applied it elsewhere. Harlow did, however, enjoy her dressing room. Greta Garbo's dressing room was nearby; she was known to comment on the happy sounds coming from Harlow's gramophone.

hadn't figured out what drove Harlow's world, he soon did.

Jean Bello fully expected that the newlyweds would live in the white house. Rosson, who earned a thousand dollars a week, had a home of his own, but was renting it to friends. Home or no, he had no intention of becoming an adjunct to the Bello scene. As usual, Harlow was put on the "well-known spot." A compromise was reached. She agreed to move with Rosson to an apartment in the elegant Sunset Boulevard hotel, the Chateau

As a teenager, Harlow had admired a Georgian mansion in Michigan. "I want to be rich so I can have a home like that," she told her friend Virginia Woodbridge. In mid-1933 she moved into 214 South Beverly Glen Boulevard.

Marmont. The Bellos wasted no time. On September 25, they had Harlean Bern sign over the deed for 214 South Beverly Glen Boulevard. On the same day, in front of a paid audience, Harlow put her footprints in a block of wet cement on the stage of Grauman's Chinese Theatre. When the block was lifted, it broke in pieces, necessitating a repeat of the ceremony. This took place on September 29, just hours before the premiere of *Bombshell*. Harlow put three pennies in the cement for good luck.

Bombshell was well received, a nonstop laugh fest. According to Jean Bello, "The audience was wild!" She complained in a letter to Arthur Landau that Louis B. Mayer had slighted her daughter. "God, Tracy has great lines," said Mayer.

"If I had NOT heard it," wrote Jean Bello, "I could not have believed that. Not even, 'Jean, your work was nice.' Not one word except JUST what I have told you. Can you imagine such a fool as to think he could intimidate three people like us with such childish tactics?" It was known that Mayer did not care for Harlow's image and made no effort to know the real woman. "He thought she was cheap," said Mahin. "And she had the spunk to stand up to him. She was even-tempered, but she'd always defend herself. It took a lot to get her riled up."

Harlow suppressed her anger when the Bellos made Rosson sign a postnuptial agreement waiving his right to community property. Continually suppressing anger can lead to illness. On Saturday, October 15, after attending a USC football game at the Los Angeles Coliseum and dinner at the Bellos, Harlow complained of stomach pain. In the wee hours of the morning, she was rushed to Good Samaritan Hospital. An emergency appendectomy was performed. This was a serious operation. A ruptured appendix could lead to peritonitis, which had killed both Rudolph Valentino and Robert Williams (who worked with Harlow in *Platinum Blonde*). Clark

The staircase of Washington Row became a *Bombshell* location.

[TOP] Harlow and Lee Tracy filmed scenes for Victor Fleming's *Bombshell* at the Ambassador Hotel, but only in the Cocoanut Grove; this photo shows them relaxing on the grounds.

[BOTTOM] Harlow and Victor Fleming were an effective team in *Bombshell*.

[TOP] In *Bombshell,* Harlow plays a movie star who yearns for a child. The star's visit to an orphanage tickled Harlow. "Oh, I'm going to love doing the baby sequence," she told a friend.

[BOTTOM] Jean and Marino Bello visited Harlow at the Pasadena Langham Hotel, where she was filming *Bombshell*.

Gable had recently had an appendectomy, too.

After two weeks of recuperation, it was time for Harlow to go home and regain her strength. But which home? As Rosson later told his family, his wife was spirited away from the hospital by her "greedy, voracious prison keepers." She was installed at Beverly Glen; he fumed at the Chateau Marmont. While Jean Bello nursed her daughter, Marino Bello began hammering at them. He pointed out the grosses earned by Harlow's last four films—more than three million dollars. Crawford, Shearer, and Garbo were each earning ten thousand a week. She was as popular as they were. Why was she earning only $1500 a week?

In truth, the Harlow fan clubs had gained many new members since her foray into comedy. She was also getting critical approval. Journalists who had sneered at her were praising her. Richard Watts, Jr., of the *New York Herald Tribune* had been her foremost detractor. Now he wrote: "*Bombshell* is chiefly important for the fact that it provides the first full-length portrait of this amazing young woman's increasing acting talent. Miss Harlow reveals again the amalgamation of sophisticated sex comedy with curiously honest innocence which is the secret of her individuality. There can be no doubt that she is a distinguished performer."

Harlow poses with Fleming, at right, and *Bombshell* screenwriter John Lee Mahin.

Bello marched into Mayer's office and demanded a salary increase for Harlow. Mayer and his studio manager Eddie Mannix countered that she had a contract; it had to be honored. Bello was not interested in details. Harlow had grown more popular than the contract had anticipated. If she didn't get more money, she was going on strike. Fine, said Mayer. On November 13, M-G-M put Harlow on suspension. Industry insiders knew that Bello was to blame, but the suspension made Harlow look bad, not Bello, whom she called the "Sicilian pimp." The Depression was far from over. It was considered bad form to grub for millions when a third of the nation was out of work. "If Marino Bello has made mistakes in handling Jean's hectic career," wrote Adela Rogers St. Johns, "Jean knows it is because he is overzealous where her welfare is concerned." The industry laughed at this jaundiced comment. Harlow was furious.

In early December, Hal Roach celebrated twenty years as a producer. Harlow was a featured guest at his party, along with Laurel and Hardy, Thelma Todd, and Harold Lloyd. The press

Bombshell began as a thinly veiled satire on Clara Bow's life, but began to reflect the life of its star. Harlow's blustering father was played with great aplomb by Frank Morgan, in his first comic role at M-G-M.

was quick to spot Harlow sitting at Louis B. Mayer's table. "There has been no fight between the studio and myself," explained Harlow. "You can't fight with your friends. And Louis B. Mayer is the best friend any girl in the world could have." When asked about her husband, Harlow stated that he was working late on a picture. "Whenever Hal is busy, and whenever a business friend invites me to dine, I shall continue to do this—in spite of [sic] Hollywood's interpretation." In truth, Rosson was tired of competing with Jean Bello for Harlow's time. Harlow and Rosson attended the *Bowery* party at the Café Vendome to celebrate the first film made by Darryl F. Zanuck's newly formed Twentieth Century Pictures. The party was at its height when Rosson turned to Harlow. "Let's go home," he said. Not the type to leave a party early, she nonetheless complied.

Harlow had fully recovered, but she spent less and less time at the Chateau Marmont. She devoted herself to her pets and a new toy, a model train set. "We start work on *Living in a Big Way,* the new picture teaming Marie Dressler and myself, in about four weeks," Harlow wrote a friend, knowing full well that her suspension precluded any film work—indefinitely.

In early December, both Harlow and Rosson denied rumors of marital discord. "I hate being in a position of having to defend our happiness," Harlow told columnist Dorothy Manners. The couple went on short trips to Big Bear and San Francisco. Still, Harlow could not stay away from her mother for any length of time. Rosson accompanied her to Beverly Glen but grew impatient with her submissiveness. On December 31, during a holiday party at Beverly Glen, Rosson refused to help Harlow and her parents welcome the New Year. "He remained upstairs until about 11:45," said Harlow later. "I had to exert considerable persuasion to get him to come down and bid our guests a happy New Year. When he did appear he made sarcastic remarks." *Bombshell*'s wacky denouement had not offered any real solution to Lola Burns's family problems. She would just have to live with them. As 1934 arrived, Harlow's life was equally unresolved.

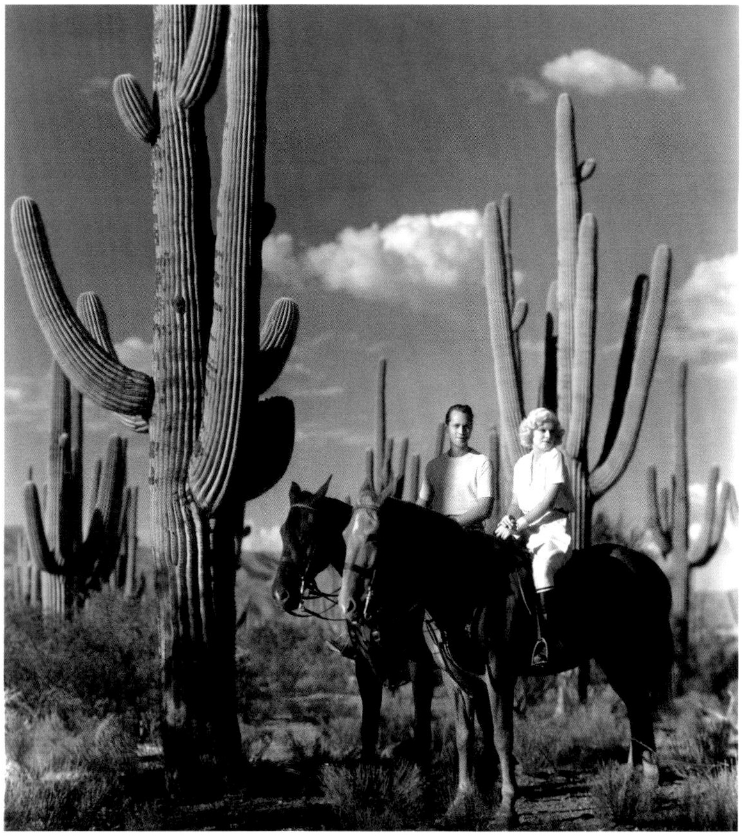

Bombshell took Harlow and Franchot Tone on location to Tucson, Arizona.

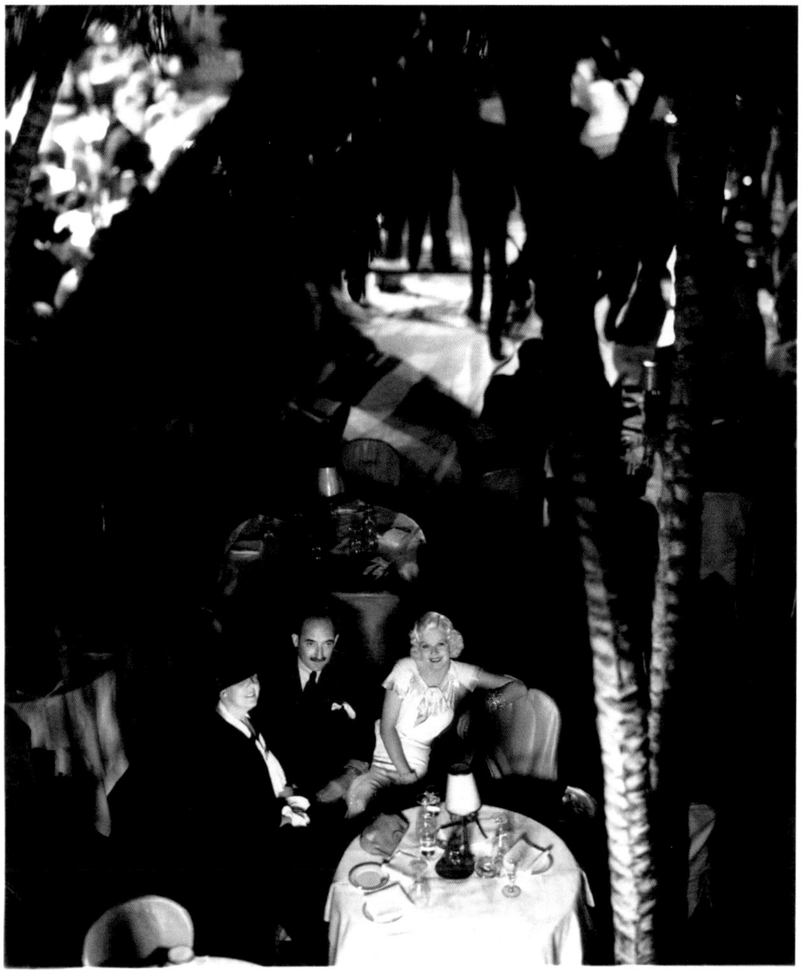

When Harlow filmed scenes for *Bombshell* at the Cocoanut Grove, Jean and Marino Bello appeared on the set. "Bello was on the set with a stopwatch, timing my dialogue," recalled Lee Tracy. "I said I couldn't work under such circumstances. I asked Jean why she didn't make him go. She said she couldn't do that. If she did, all hell would break loose at home."

This behind-the-scenes photograph shows Fleming directing Harlow and Tracy. Watching from behind the silver M-G-M camera blimp is Hal Rosson. *Bombshell* was his fourth film with Harlow.

After completing *Bombshell,* Harlow eloped with Rosson. Here they emerge from a chartered plane at United Airport in Burbank on September 18, after their wedding.

[TOP] Reporters and photographers mass around the newlyweds in the Beverly Glen garden.

[LEFT] The Chateau Marmont is located at 8221 Sunset Boulevard in West Hollywood.

Rosson has just told the Bellos that he and Harlow will be living at the Chateau Marmont. Marino Bello cannot disguise his anger. Jean Bello, the consummate actress, strikes a pose.

Harlow sat with Irving Thalberg on October 6 at a Warner Bros. luncheon honoring visiting members of the United States Naval Affairs Committee. Harlow was one of the few M-G-M stars with whom Thalberg could have discussed John Galsworthy's *The Forsyte Saga*. She had read it several times.

On October 13, Harlow and Rosson attended a Gay Nineties party at the Café Vendome in honor of Darryl Zanuck's *The Bowery*. Harlow is seen here with George Raft and Arline Judge.

Hal Roach celebrated twenty years as a producer with a party on December 9. He is flanked here by: left to right, Harold Lloyd, Harlow, Stan Laurel, journalist Warren Stockes, and Oliver Hardy.

On September 25, Jean Klossner and Sid Grauman helped Harlow make an impression in cement for a paying audience at Grauman's Chinese Theater.

Grauman's Chinese Theatre usherette Evelyn True snapped this photograph of Jean Harlow signing in wet cement in the repeated ceremony of September 29, 1933.

Harlow positioned three pennies for good luck.

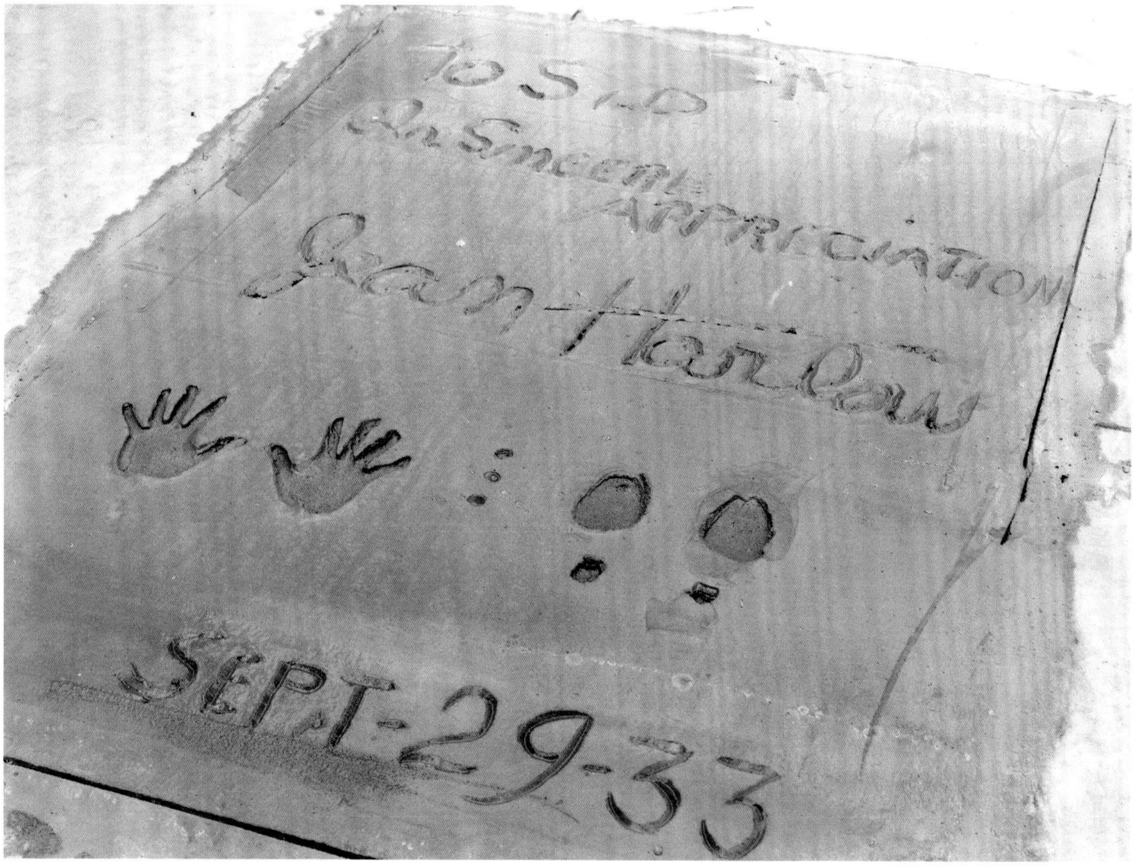

The block was in place for the *Bombshell* premiere that evening.

Hurrell also made glamour portraits of Harlow for *Bombshell* publicity.
He remembered her as a "big, healthy, happy girl."

Jean HARLOW
Born to be Kissed
WITH
LIONEL
BARRYMORE
FRANCHOT TONE
LEWIS STONE
Directed by
JACK
CONWAY
PRODUCED BY
BERNARD H. HYMAN
A
Metro-
Goldwyn-
Mayer
PICTURE

The Name above the Title

New ad art was prepared when *Born To Be Kissed* was shut down, reshot, and retitled *The Girl from Missouri.* Harlow was one of numerous scapegoats in the 1934 campaign against "immoral" movies.

On January 6, 1934, the influential *Motion Picture Herald* reported that Jean Harlow had placed Number Five in 1933 box-office grosses. This was ammunition for Marino Bello. Harlow did not need Clark Gable as a co-star. She could carry a picture on her own. She could be the "name above the title." What was working against Bello was his stupid, naked greed. There was no chance in Hades that Louis B. Mayer was going to raise Harlow's salary from $1500 a week to five thousand dollars a week. As the deadlock continued, and Harlow's suspension moved into its third month, Bello came to see her at the Chateau Marmont. She refused to admit him.

The Bellos kept on spending. In late November, they had taken out a $22,500 chattel mortgage on the Beverly Glen estate, and even though Harlow's income had ceased, the bills had not. On January 26, disregarding the Bellos, Harlow reported to M-G-M for work. "I am going to forget what I have been told and advised I am worth," conceded Harlow, "and go on to fulfill the terms of the contract to which I signed my name before my alleged 'walk out.' I believe that the executives who have been my close friends in every trouble, especially during the time of my great trouble, Paul Bern's death, will make the adjustment fairly and squarely." Harlow agreed to fulfill her contract until May, at which time she would sign a new seven-year contract—with a salary hike to three thousand dollars a week. Bello had accomplished something, but at what cost?

In late January, Harlow's marriage reached an impasse. Rosson could not compete with a filial obsession. "I would rather be with my mother," stated Harlow, "than with any other living being I know. She offers me the only true understanding and companionship I have ever known." On February 4, Harlow quietly moved her belongings out of the Chateau Marmont. Until legalities were resolved, however, the studio required that the Rossons appear together in public. Mayer, as much as Jean Bello, ran Harlow's life, and not always to her liking.

"I'm sore," Harlow wrote to Stanley Brown in February. "Here I was all set to do *Living in a Big Way.* Then it was decided I was not to make it. Then *Red-Headed Woman in Paris.* And now I am not to make that. Then *Repeal* and I have not heard one word further about what is what. So maybe they'll take that away from me. So what shall I say? Or will you say it?" No one needed to say it. As Rudolph Valentino had once lamented, when you are a movie star, you don't live your life. It lives you.

In early March, Harlow began her first film as a star, an Anita Loos sex comedy called *Eadie Was a Lady.* Harlow was overjoyed. "I can't keep away from pictures," she said. "I am lost without my work. You don't know how impatient I am to be back, making another picture again. I want to get back in

[Opposite] Jean Harlow's first film after her four-month salary strike was the sex comedy *Born to be Kissed.* The film was still in production when this advertising art was prepared.

makeup, to hear the sound technicians call 'turn 'em over.' In ten weeks I've missed that more than I can tell you."

While Harlow was on suspension, she had gotten an urge. Without encouragement from anyone, the avid reader decided to write her own book. She described its inception as "an idea that came to me in the middle of the night about eight months ago, rousing me out of a deep sleep." *Today is Tonight* was a story of young married couple. The husband temporarily loses his vision. The wife discovers that she can support them better in a nightclub job than in a day job. She moves her daytime chores to nighttime to shield her husband from the truth. Will he find out? Will she resist temptation? Will he sustain their love?

Harlow first wrote character sketches and script pages, then asked Carey Wilson to help her convert the story into a novel. "Don't write obviously," he counseled her. "Remember that when a person is unhappy, he doesn't let anyone know. Don't make your characters behave like robots. Write about what you know." Harlow was excited by the challenge and set to work. Following Wilson's advice, she gave the main character her own voice.

> If you talk fast enough, and about human psychology, you always sound very important. It would be very easy to write a book about philosophy. It wouldn't be good philosophy but it would be philosophy. All you have to do is begin every eighth sentence with the words, "All men are" or "Every woman will" and all men or all women will think you are saying something important. If I had a stenographer to take down what I am thinking, it would be an awful lesson to George Bernard Shaw.

Harlow and Hal Rosson were living apart in early 1934, but the studio required that they attend M-G-M's belated Hollywood premiere of *Queen Christina* (1933) at Grauman's Chinese Theatre on February 12. Harlow enjoyed the film, later saying that its final shot of Garbo was her favorite movie scene.

When Harlow began *Born To Be Kissed,* Rosson, at far left, was her cameraman, but not for long. This production still shows Harlow with Lewis Stone, and Anita Loos sitting next to director Sam Wood.

Harlow visited another soundstage—and a new acquaintance—on March 26. William Powell was working with Clark Gable and Myrna Loy in W.S. Van Dyke's *Manhattan Melodrama* (1934).

Harlow caused a furor at the May 6 wedding of Carey Wilson and Carmelita Geraghty.

The insecure young woman completed her project without pressure from anyone. "I did it all by myself," she beamed. "It was the hardest work I ever attempted. It required unflagging patience, but the thrill of having created something in a new field is my reward."

Harlow had visions of a sale to M-G-M. "I've written a script of the story and I'd like very much to play the girl," Harlow told journalist Harrison Carroll. "It would be more of a straight part than I've done yet and would carry more sympathy." When *Cosmopolitan* magazine expressed interest in publishing rights, Marino Bello elbowed his way in. Hedging his bets, he paid an untried publicist named Tony Beacon a paltry five hundred dollars to write a seventy-thousand-word text from Harlow's manuscript.

Carrying this "hot property" under his arm, Bello was an unwelcome visitor to the M-G-M story department. "It was submitted to me," said story editor Sam Marx, "and proved to be a rather trashy sex novel. It was embarrassing to Mayer and Thalberg." The book was no worse than any of the other properties that became M-G-M films. The real problem was its main character. Obviously based on Harlow, she had an unrepentant yen for sexual release and binge drinking. "I'll just take a little one," says her alter ego.

> But that's silly, too. There's no such thing as a little drink. If it's a drink, it's a drink! People who say they want only a little drink are pretending it isn't a drink at all. So I'll pour myself a medium-sized drink, and then I can't kid myself that it's only a little drink. It's a drink. I'm only going to take this one. No. That's kidding myself, too. I'll be honest. I'm taking this

Jean Bello spent a year (and a great deal of Harlow's money) decorating the house in Beverly Glen. The polar bear rug had been in Harlow's bedroom in her previous home.

Harlow poses in the sunroom of the "Whitest House in the World."

Harlow was an accomplished cook, making frequent use of her barbecue pit.

Dick Powell brought Mary Carlisle to Harlow's home during the Fourth of July weekend. "It was a different time, a charming time," said Carlisle in 2010. "Everybody knew everybody else."

medium-sized drink because I want it very badly and I think I need it and I won't make any promises about not taking another. I know I will take another.

Whatever publicity a Harlow novel could generate, there would be no way to excuse such lurid scenes in print and no way to put them on the screen, especially in the face of a grassroots movement against adult-themed films. Marx's solution was to avoid responding.

Undeterred, Harlow sent him another copy. "Carey tells me you didn't get a copy of my story," she wrote. "A sociological error, Sam, because I sent a copy via Marino to you—the first copy out except for the one sent to Mannix. Apparently your office received it instead of yourself. I'm sorry. Would you like to call me at your convenience and tell me what you think of the yarn?" Harlow was left to figure it out for herself.

Eadie Was a Lady was in trouble. The Catholic Legion of Decency had gained momentum in its campaign against "immoral movies." Churchmen and clubwomen called the Production Code of 1930 an industry fraud, a do-nothing document meant to smokescreen the sale of salacious fare. Norma Shearer, Mae West, and Jean Harlow were denounced as corrupting influences. Boycotts followed. Harlow was distressed, but she defended herself. "The clean-up campaign in films doesn't hurt me a bit," she said. "I never did vulgar or over-sexy acts in my film roles. It was chiefly my figure and sometimes my clothes which were considered objectionable. It wasn't Jean Harlow herself that was objected to." A militant Catholic censor

Marion Davies loved the sea air, so William Randolph Hearst built her a mansion on the "Gold Coast" of Santa Monica Beach.

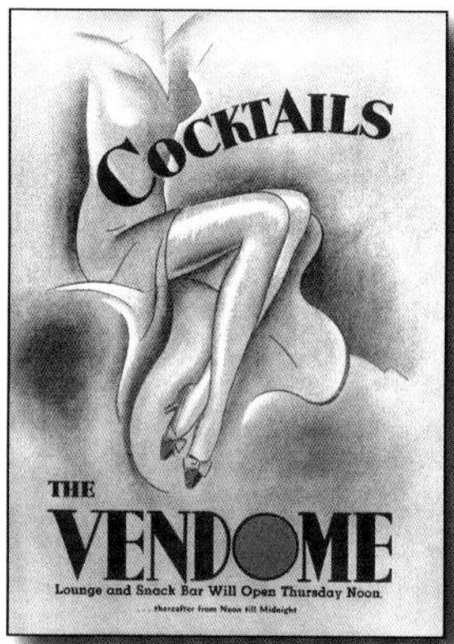

Eye-catching advertising was one reason for Wilkerson's success.

The Café Vendome opened in May 1933 at 6666 Sunset Boulevard as a gourmet shop. In 1934, Billy Wilkerson, who was both the publisher of the *Hollywood Reporter* and a wildly successful entrepreneur, transformed it into an elegant lunch spot.

Harlow attended the Tyrolean party Marion Davies gave at her beachfront mansion on September 27, 1934. With Harlow are: from left, Gloria Swanson, Davies, and Constance Bennett.

Harlow came with William Powell to Wilkerson's Café Vendome party for Richard Barthelmess and his wife. Harlow posed with Barthelmess and Clark Gable but would not allow photos of herself and Powell. She was loath to feed the rumor mill.

named Joseph I. Breen was in charge of the Studio Relations Committee and was enforcing the Code. He required that every script be submitted to and approved by the SRC. He rejected *Eadie Was a Lady*. The script was rewritten, and the film went into production, first as *100% Pure*, then as *Born to Be Kissed*.

"The heat is *really* turned on the industry," Harlow wrote Stanley Brown.

> But it isn't turned on where it *should* be turned on. A lot of it has been turned on *me*. I have been receiving some pretty hot letters about my type, and so on. It's too bad the public can't understand the way we are cast. The general opinion seems that we write our story as we want it and act it as we feel it. You know that is not the case, but try to tell the public that. I have had a lot of parts that I was not in sympathy with at all and did not believe in, but what to do about it? As long as the same public will pay to see certain pictures, you can bet your collection of ancient coins that they are going to get those pictures.

During the break in filming, Rosson withdrew as cameraman. The studio denied there was friction between

On September 17, 1934, Jean Harlow and William Powell were at the Hollywood Bowl for the opening of the most spectacular Shakespeare presentation in history, Max Reinhardt's *A Midsummer Night's Dream*.

Harlow posed with both British and Hollywood royalty at the Ambassador Hotel in September when Louella Parsons feted Admiral Sir Roger Keyes, M.P., and Lady Keyes. In this photo are: left to right, Lord Keyes, Harlow, Marlene Dietrich, Lady Keyes, Norma Shearer, and Rouben Mamoulian.

The Hollywood Bowl, the world's largest natural amphitheater, officially opened on July 11, 1922. Its signature shell was designed in 1926 by Allied Architects, refined by Lloyd Wright, and completed in 1929 by the engineering firm of Elliott, Bowen, and Walz.

Harlow celebrated her twenty-third birthday in an odd way. She bought a V12 Cadillac Town Car—for her mother.

The production code administration passed this scene of Harlow and Lionel Barrymore in *The Girl from Missouri* (1934), most likely because the film was already bowdlerized beyond recognition.

Not every pose made by Clarence Bull during a portrait sitting was released by the M-G-M publicity department. This one was rejected because Harlow was showing too much cleavage.

Harlow and her husband, but rumors of divorce were rampant. As usual, Harlow took a passive role.

"My marriage to Hal Rosson is almost finished," Harlow confided to columnist Sonia Lee. "We can't possibly go on together. He would like to put me in a golden cage and throw the key away." On May 5, there was a nasty quarrel. Rosson moved to the Hollywood Athletic Club (HAC). His decision was final. The next day he and Harlow were supposed to attend the wedding of Carey Wilson and Carmelita Geraghty, which was being held at the Bel-Air home of agent Phil Berg and his wife Leila Hyams. Harlow had been chosen matron of honor. She considered not going, but at the last minute decided to honor her commitment.

On May 6, five hundred guests assembled for the wedding. Harlow was in the wedding party, front and center. Rosson was absent. After vows were exchanged and group photos taken, Harlow walked away from the dais. She was immediately accosted by the press and asked about Rosson, who had been seen at the HAC. "Get a lot of close-ups, boys," Harlow smiled gamely. "You'll need them." Why? Harlow revealed that she and Rosson had separated. Chaos ensued. A score of men raced from the dais, past wedding guests, and into the house, looking for telephones. "I am sorry that the news of our separation became known when it did," Harlow apologized. "Hal and I had planned to say nothing about it for a few days. But Hal was seen at the club."

Rosson made no public statement but privately called Harlow "a captive daughter." As usual, she avoided the issue. "Hal is a normal man," she explained. "He wants his wife to belong to him utterly and completely. But I can't belong to anyone, not even to myself. I am in bondage, in slavery, to a career." Harlow's enslavement was not only to her career, but also—and more profoundly—to her mother. The needy young woman was unable to admit it, least of all to herself. Instead, she posed as a fatalist. "I've learned to accept whatever happens placidly and passively," she said. "I am passive, and I am swept along."

Thanks to the implacable Breen, Harlow's film *Born to Be Kissed* (now known as *The Girl from Missouri*) went through weeks of retakes. Hollywood had barely recovered from an economic crisis; now it faced a moral crisis. The "Catholic Bishops' Revolt" and the Legion of Decency campaign had effected a damaging boycott. First exhibition and then production were affected. *The Girl From Missouri* was one of several films (*Cleopatra*, *Madame Du Barry*, *Belle of the Nineties*) caught in the teeth of the Summer 1934 crisis. "Everybody is under a terrific strain with this

Bull usually emphasized Harlow's thoughtful side, as in this February 1934 portrait.

campaign," Harlow wrote Stanley Brown. "Ready to cut each other's throats any minute. I'm going to hate for you to see *Eadie Was a Lady, 100% Pure, Born to be Kissed, It Pays to be Good*— and now *Girl from Missouri.* I'm all in, Stan. I'm tired and weary, mentally and physically." After weeks of empty theaters, Hollywood capitulated. Breen was authorized to establish a new Production Code Administration. A reconstituted Code went into effect on July 1. Films in production were re-evaluated and reshot; hence, Harlow's tribulations.

The Girl from Missouri opened on August 3, 1934. It was a box-office smash. The Sex Symbol was now the Star. "When Jean Harlow first appeared half undressed as the sex-menace in *Hell's*

Angels, it was clear that Hollywood would find a niche for her," wrote *Time* magazine on August 13. "The remarkable thing about her subsequent career is that, instead of becoming

Bull turned Harlow into an Art Deco icon in this 1934 study.

Hollywood's Number One Siren, she has become its Number One Comedienne."

Visiting Clark Gable and director W.S. Van Dyke on the set of *Manhattan Melodrama* (1934) in March, Harlow had chanced to meet the debonair actor William Powell. He was a new addition to M-G-M, one of many players brought there from other studios with the promise of a revitalized career. In his case it happened. While Harlow was filming her multi-titled saga, Powell was making *The Thin Man* (1934) with Van Dyke. It made stars of both him and Myrna Loy. When Powell heard about Harlow's separation, he called to see if it was true. Harlow glumly confirmed. He asked for a date. She accepted.

The date was a Sunday afternoon drive to Santa Barbara. Harlow curled up in the passenger seat and slept all the way there. "I have affected women in many ways," Powell said, "but you are the first I ever lulled to sleep." Harlow liked Powell. They had much in common. Both had grown up in Kansas City, Missouri, and both were recently divorced. (Powell had been married for three years to actress Carole Lombard.) Powell was forty-two, reserved, and mustachioed, something that Harlow could not ignore. Unlike her previous infatuations, he was tight with a dollar and fast with a quip.

On July 31, Harlow and her mother were vacationing at the Del Monte Lodge, a resort on the Monterey peninsula, three hundred miles north of Los Angeles. So was Powell. Harlow called it a coincidence, but they were seen playing golf and walking arm in arm. "We're just good friends," Harlow said when cornered by the press. "And when friends meet, the natural thing is to play a game of golf, isn't it?" Harlow pointed out that she was still technically married. Her claims of platonic friendship with Powell were met with laughter. "We are not romantic friends," Harlow insisted. "We are not engaged. We shall not be married. Like every normal woman, I long for a home and I want to have children. But matrimony has not turned out fortunately for me." She told writer Maude Cheatham: "I'm not thinking of love or marriage right now." Harlow's attempts to convince the public were futile, perhaps because she could not convince herself. Whether she liked it or not, she was falling in love.

Bull could also capture Harlow's provocative side.

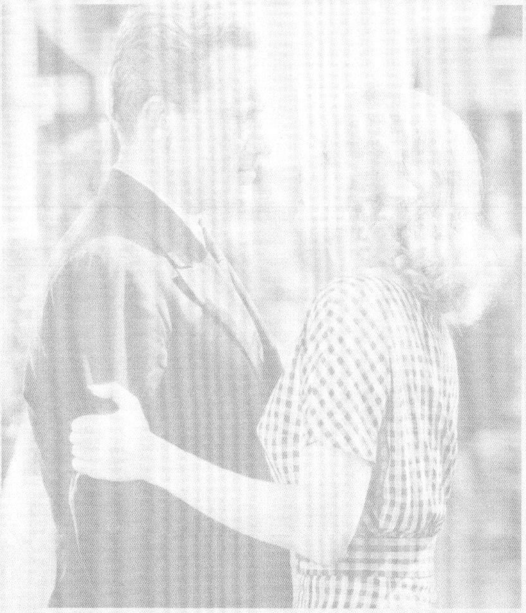

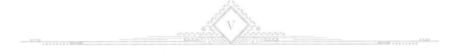

V

The Alabaster Icon

- *Reckless*
- China Doll
- Brownette

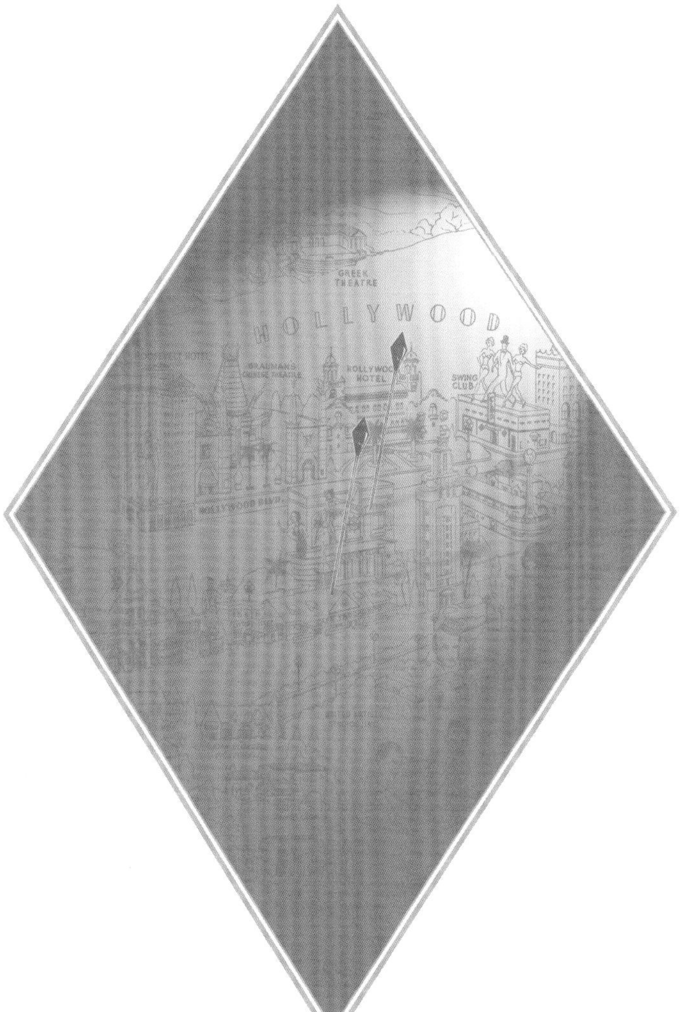

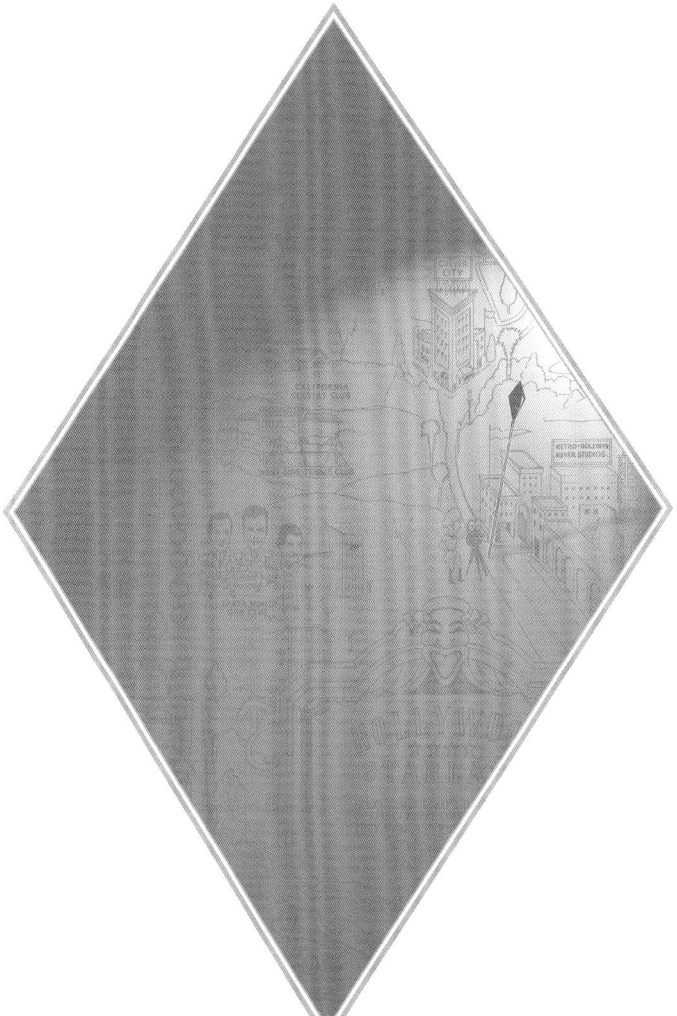

Harlow attended the Academy Awards banquet in the Biltmore Bowl with William Powell on February 27, 1935. That night their friend and co-star Clark Gable won the Best Actor award for *It Happened One Night* (1934).

♦ *Reckless* ♦

In a small town, a new romance is grist for the gossip mill, especially if the woman is married and the man divorced. In 1934 Hollywood, the romance between Jean Harlow and William Powell offered more than titillation. It was an opportunity to make money. Producer David O. Selznick, riding high on his "hundred-percent commercial" musical, *Dancing Lady* (1933), was planning a follow-up for Joan Crawford, tentatively titled *A Woman Called Cheap*. Still, the prospect of teaming Harlow and Powell in a musical was too good to pass up. In December, a week before shooting was to begin, Louis B. Mayer removed Crawford from the project and gave Selznick the hot new couple. The title was changed to the highly appropriate *Reckless*.

Selznick had concocted the tale of a Broadway star who marries an unstable blueblood and then falls from grace when he commits suicide. The story bore an uncomfortable resemblance to the tragedy endured by torch singer Libby Holman; her brief marriage to tobacco heir Zachary Reynolds ended when he drunkenly shot himself. Worse, the story recalled Harlow's own trauma. Both incidents had occurred only two years earlier. Holman threatened to sue for libel, but did not. Harlow was urged by Powell to cooperate and pressured to keep quiet by her mother. She did as she was told.

For Harlow, making a musical meant singing and dancing lessons, and losing weight. Her meals consisted of little more than shredded carrots, pineapple slices, and cottage cheese. The regimen was trying. She sought solace in studio friendships and strength in stolen snacks. "C'mon! Let's get a goody!" she would whisper daily to her new pal Movita Castaneda, who was rehearsing Tahitian dances for *Mutiny on the Bounty* (1935). The two young women would sneak from the rehearsal hall to the commissary, where Harlow would nibble on a slice of pie.

On December 5, 1934, Harlow's lawyer Oscar A. Trippet filed a petition to begin divorce proceedings against Hal Rosson. Since his estrangement from Harlow, he had fallen ill with infantile paralysis (now called polio), recovered, and then gone to work in England. He offered no resistance to the suit. On March 11, 1935, after a weekend of drinking and gambling in Agua Caliente, she returned to Superior Court to get her divorce from Hal Rosson. Judge Elliott Craig required her to take the witness stand and enumerate her claims. Harlow testified that Rosson was morose and sullen, jealous of her time, and belittled her profession. She further claimed that he had interfered with her much-needed beauty sleep by sitting up in bed reading. This revelation, rather than causing shock waves, caused what columnist Ed Sullivan described as "waves of international mirth." Harlow was beginning to sound like the sex symbol who couldn't get sex. "How long can I hide my disappointment under a smile," Harlow asked an interviewer. "I married Hal because I loved him deeply and sincerely. I thought, At last I have found the happiness I always longed for. And now—well, what am I to do?" Harlow walked out of the courtroom, decree in hand, but would not be free to marry for twelve months.

Reckless was directed by Victor Fleming, as odd a choice for a musical as Harlow, but the film was more a melodrama than a musical. Its songs did not advance the plot, and even after weeks of rehearsal, she couldn't sing on key or dance in time. The solution was to use doubles. Virginia Verrill dubbed her voice and Betty Halsey danced her steps in long shots. "I did the singing sequences for Jean Harlow in *Reckless*," Verrill said later. "She realized that I couldn't have credit for my singing, so she went out of her way to give me a hand up whenever she could. If a reporter were around, she'd say something like: 'This is Virginia Verrill. She's working on the set next to me,' so I'd get my name in the paper."

Performing in an unfamiliar idiom was not Harlow's only problem. Her trademark hair was falling out, a result of the brutal bleaching to which it was subjected weekly—peroxide mixed with ammonia, and occasionally with Lux flakes. Simply breathing these chemicals was risky; applying them to the scalp was dangerous. Fearing publicity, the studio secluded Harlow in a bungalow and sent for a dye specialist named Marcel Machu. His prognosis was grim. "If you expect this woman to work today, tomorrow, or the next day, you're crazy," he told Fleming. "Touch her again and she'll have no hair at all." For the duration of *Reckless*, Machu gave Harlow's hair daily olive oil massages. She managed to finish the film without going bald. The long-term solution was one that M-G-M had already found for stars whose hair was less than robust—wigs. *Reckless*, released in April 1935, became the first Jean Harlow film to lose money.

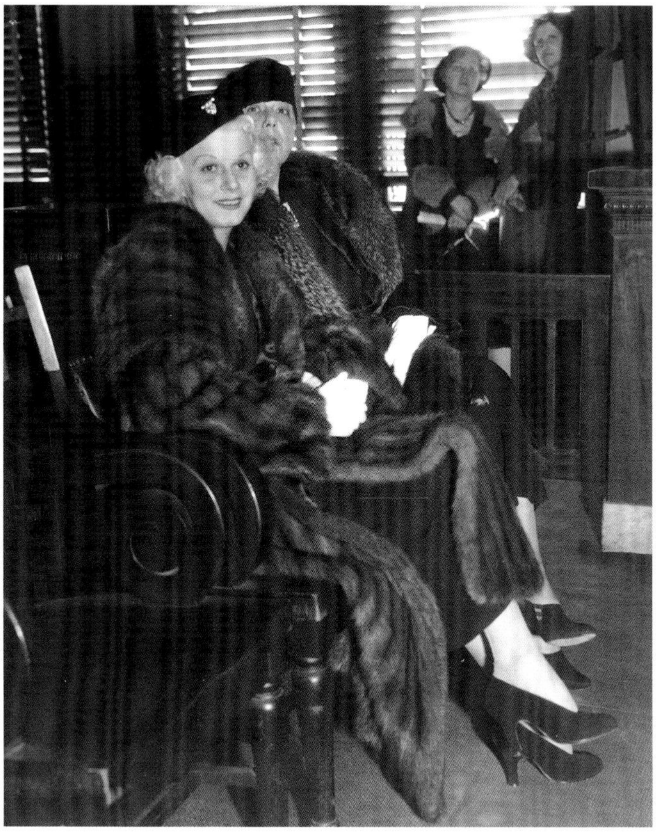

Accompanied by her mother, Harlow went to Los Angeles Superior Court on March 11, 1935, to testify at her divorce hearing.

Leaving a dental appointment in the Equitable Building at the corner of Hollywood and Vine, Harlow posed for Wayne Martin, a teenaged member of the Jean Harlow Fan Club.

Jean Harlow was leaving a Hollywood store in 1935 when a fan approached her and asked a favor. "I believe Hollywood stars owe the fans everything," Harlow said later. "Yes, even the right to ask us to pose for their own cameras."

[ABOVE] In early 1935, Harlow and Powell attended a party at the Café Trocadero for Edith Gwynne Wilkerson, wife of the club's owner Billy Wilkerson. This private photograph shows, from left to right: Edith; Harlow; Powell; Jimmy Shields, standing; Anderson Lawler; unidentified man, standing; William Haines; and Edith's sister, Marge. The presence of Lawler, Haines, and Shields, his longtime companion, confirms that Harlow had gay friends.

[BELOW] The opening of the Café Trocadero at 8610 Sunset Boulevard in September 1934 made West Hollywood a destination. Neighbors on Sunset included the William Haines interior design studio and Adrian's early couture salon.

George Hurrell's portrait studio was at 8706 Sunset Boulevard, a block from Café Trocadero. Both buildings were owned by Francis J. Montgomery, whose properties helped popularize the style known as Hollywood Colonial.

Harlow had worked with Hurrell numerous times in the M-G-M gallery, but after he left the company in July 1932, she usually came to his studio. Its sprayed-stucco wall, painted white, made a lambent background for Hollywood's most famous blonde.

This Hurrell portrait of Harlow shows her modeling a silk-satin gown and Galalith buckle in a Bullocks Wilshire salon.

[opposite] The Franklin Canyon reservoir was a seemingly exotic location for Victor Fleming's *Reckless*. In actuality, it was at the top of Coldwater Canyon, less than an hour's drive from M-G-M.

In this musical sequence from *Reckless* (1935), Harlow's hair is braided around a wiglet to hide a thinning-hair problem discovered during production.

The sets designed by Edwin Willis and Merrill Pye for *Reckless* showed Art Deco's evolution from ziggurat-like angles to streamlined curves.

On a lunch break during the making of *China Seas,* Beery, Harlow, and Gable stroll past stages 4, 5, and 21. Harlow's skin-tight Adrian gown was striking even in daylight. "I call it nude satin," Harlow told an interviewer. "But I guess you'd better call it something different—or the censors will get sore." During a scene in which Beery pushes Harlow against a dresser, two rhinestone-studded straps came loose and slid down her arm, exposing one of her breasts for a few frames. The censors missed it.

• China Doll •

After *Reckless*, Jean Harlow needed a hit. So did the producer who had made her a star. Irving Thalberg was no longer M-G-M's head of production. He was an independent producer, and, if he wanted access to stars such as Jean Harlow, he had to compete with David Selznick and Hunt Stromberg. According to an exhibitors' poll published in *Film Daily* in January 1935, Clark Gable was the second-highest-grossing star in Hollywood (after Fox Film's Will Rogers). Wallace Beery was fourth. Surprisingly, Harlow was not in the top ten. Thalberg was pleased, therefore, when M-G-M schedules allowed him to cast Gable, Beery, and Harlow in an adventure film titled *China Seas*. Thalberg's last film, *No More Ladies* (1935), had not done well. Like many of his previous films, it was a drawing-room comedy based on a Broadway play. He sensed that it was time for a change. "To hell with art," he said. "This time I'm going to produce a picture that will make money."

As written by James Kevin McGuinness and an uncredited John Lee Mahin, *China Seas* was an amusement-park ride of comedy, violence and, if not sex, romance. Harlow was playing an American entertainer known as China Doll. The script implied that she was Gable's mistress. The Production Code Administration warned Thalberg that romance would have to supplant sex. Harlow's screen persona could be brassy, but her sexual antics would have to be as fake as the platinum wig she was wearing. Harlow took it all in stride. When a journalist asked her about *China Seas*, she answered: "Oh, I play another of those darned sex vultures."

On March 21, Harlow and Powell attended a dinner party at Thalberg's home on the Santa Monica Gold Coast. Other guests included Gable, Jeanette MacDonald, Charles Laughton, and his wife Elsa Lanchester. At one point during the evening, Harlow took a stroll on the moonlit beach outside Thalberg's half-timbered mansion. A few minutes later, Lanchester saw Harlow run in, her skirt hiked up. She dropped something silver and wriggling into a flower bowl.

"What is *that*?" asked Lanchester.

"A grunion," replied Harlow.

In this rare image, Harlow, William Powell, and Marion Davies's sister Rose stand in front of William Randolph Hearst's mansion at San Simeon.

Lanchester recalled from a newspaper report that the grunion were running that night. Knowing that grunion are saltwater fish, she pulled the grunion from the bowl and ran outside to return it to the beach. Harlow continued to socialize with Thalberg and his wife Norma Shearer. On April 4, she went with them and Powell to the Biltmore Theatre to see Ethel Waters sing "Suppertime" in the Moss Hart-Irving Berlin play *As Thousands Cheer*. The same foursome attended an Easter party at the home of Cedric Gibbons and Dolores Del Rio. Working in a Thalberg

In 1934, M-G-M moved its stars from the wood-frame dressing rooms to this streamlined structure. Harlow occupied Suite A on the ground floor. Its suites are now used by Sony as private production offices.

production had elevated Harlow to Hollywood's upper ranks.

China Seas was at times a difficult production. Harlow worked in typhoon scenes that required her to be soaked with water. Even though a stunt double performed the dangerous shot in which a giant wave washes over the deck, Harlow fell ill with influenza during filming. There was more than the usual amount of stress on the set. Thalberg had decided to coach the three stars he had made, and without telling director Tay Garnett. One day, in the middle of a rehearsal, Gable said to Garnett: "This is really Jean's scene, so let's play it a little more to her, you know, give it to her." Garnett went to Thalberg's home and confronted him, threatening to quit. Thalberg agreed to leave his players alone. Still, Harlow gave

Harlow is interviewed by writer Gene Hersholt, Jr., at the entrance to the female stars' wing of the dressing-room building.

her best performance to date, making the potentially one-note character of China Doll both believable and sympathetic.

After *China Seas* was completed, Harlow began traveling. First she went with Powell to San Simeon, William Randolph Hearst's castle by the sea, to celebrate the anniversary of their first date. "Jean Harlow came up to San Simeon quite frequently," wrote Marion Davies, who was both the lady of the manor and Hearst's mistress. "She was crazy about Bill Powell. She waited on him hand and foot. I thought they were going to get married." Harlow sent a wire to Mother Jean expressing her state of mind: "DARLING, HAVING DIVINE TIME. NEVER HAPPIER. LOVE TO ALL. ME." In July, Harlow spent a two-week vacation at Wyntoon, Hearst's medieval manor house on the McCloud River in Northern California. At one point, when Hearst was entertaining some visitors from Washington, her revealing gown ran afoul of his unstated dress code.

"Will you please tell Miss Harlow to go back to her room and get dressed?" Hearst asked Davies.

Davies was diplomatic but firm with Harlow. "Do you

Harlow was photographed by the Hungarian photographer Martin Munkácsi during the making of *China Seas* (1935). Visible in the background is the music recording stage. Built in 1929, the acoustically superior facility is still in use, and is known as the Barbra Streisand Scoring Stage.

On Saturday, June 29, 1935, Harlow attended a luncheon for the District Attorneys' Association at M-G-M. Regardless of Harlow's experiences with Buron Fitts, her presence was required. Seated at the head table are, from left: Eileen Percy Ruby, Irving Thalberg, Harlow, Fitts, Louis B. Mayer, Los Angeles Mayor Fred Thomas, Frank Morgan, Eddie Mannix, and an unidentified woman.

Whether vacationing at Yosemite, Lake Arrowhead, or the McCloud River in Northern California, Jean Harlow tried to leave her bombshell image behind. Away from Los Angeles, bothered by no one, she indulged in fishing, hiking, letter writing, and reading.

realize your dress is a little...?"

Harlow went upstairs to her room. A few minutes later, she came down, wearing a coat over the offending dress. She sat down to dinner in it.

When Harlow landed at the Union Air Terminal in Burbank on July 23, Powell was waiting for her. So were a lot of reporters. She deftly fielded their questions about marriage. In Santa Barbara in early August, the couple was spotted buying pots and pans. Did it mean something? "It doesn't mean a thing," said Harlow. "Mr. Powell and I have never discussed marriage, and I can say frankly that we have no such thing in mind."

In private, however, Harlow told a different story. When she went to Louella Parsons' home to rehearse for a *Hollywood Hotel* broadcast of *China Seas*, she broke down and confessed to the motherly gossip columnist. "I love him," said Harlow. "But he feels we shouldn't be married. I've always been crazy about children, and he is the only man I ever thought I would like to marry and settle down with and raise a family. But I suppose he's right. Marriage hasn't panned out for either of us. And perhaps two movie people with careers shouldn't marry."

The much-anticipated *China Seas* was released on August 9, 1935, at the Capitol Theatre in New York. "The walls of the Capitol began to bulge last Friday when 14,885 paid admissions were checked through the turnstiles," reported the *Los Angeles Times*. "On Saturday, the total reached 18,565." The weekend's standing-room-only attendance totaled 53,181. Both Thalberg and Harlow had a

The cast of *China Seas* went to the CBS Studios on Vine Street for Louella Parsons' *Hollywood Hotel* on August 9, 1935. Posed in this photo are, from left to right: Igor Gorin and Frances Langford, who sang on the program; Rosalind Russell; Clark Gable, who had come directly from filming *Mutiny on the Bounty*; Parsons; Harlow; and co-host Dick Powell.

Harlow is torn between co-stars Wallace Beery and Clark Gable in this "poster art" for *China Seas*. The gowns Adrian designed for Harlow were costumes; she never wore in public what she wore on the screen.

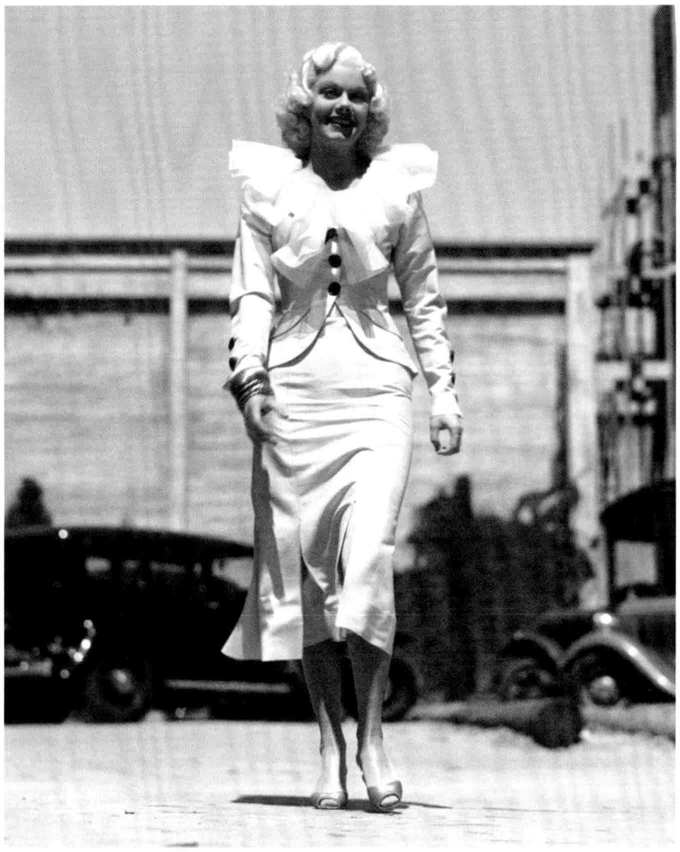

Speed Graphic cameras were set up on M-G-M pathways so that studio photographers could catch stars walking to and from their dressing rooms.

hit. For her there was more recognition. On August 19, 1935, she graced the cover of *Time* magazine, a signal honor.

Harlow's newly enhanced status did not affect her. She became friends with Adela Rogers St. Johns' twelve-year-old daughter Elaine. One day Elaine expressed impatience with her mother. Harlow stopped the child in her tracks. "She took me aside," recalled Elaine, "and verbally tanned my hide, and then she explained to me what mothers were and what they meant." On another occasion, Harlow was asked to make a speech at a birthday party. She stood up and said that she owed everything to her mother and God. John Lee Mahin chuckled and asked her why she had given God second billing. Harlow was not amused. She turned away and did not speak to Mahin for months. Eventually, she approached him and apologized. Still, she was blind to what everyone around her could see, even *Time* magazine. Her mother had sold her to the public. Only William Powell looked at Marino and Jean Bello with a jaundiced eye. The *Time* article mentioned Bello's investments in Mexican gold mines. Emulating the sleuths he portrayed on screen, Powell decided to investigate.

In this scene, which was deleted to shorten the film's running time, China Doll (Harlow) has just insulted a powerful Chinese woman. A dacoit throws a knife at China Doll, who misses being hit because she has bent down to pet the ship's cat. It is amusing to speculate that the pattern on Harlow's dress was inspired by the cat's calico coat.

In this genuinely candid photo, not intended for publication, director Tay Garnett discusses script pages with Gable while Harlow puffs on a cigarette.

This scene still from *China Seas* shows the *Kin Lung* docked in Hong Kong harbor. The scene was staged not in Hong Kong or even San Pedro, but on M-G-M's Lot Two. The wilds of Culver City are visible in the distance.

[OVERLEAF] In *China Seas*, the pitch and yaw of the *Kin Lung* supplies numerous plot points. This production still shows: at right, next to the camera, Tay Garnett, cameraman Ray June, and assistant director Joseph Newman filming Harlow and Beery, who are on a platform built on hydraulic rockers.

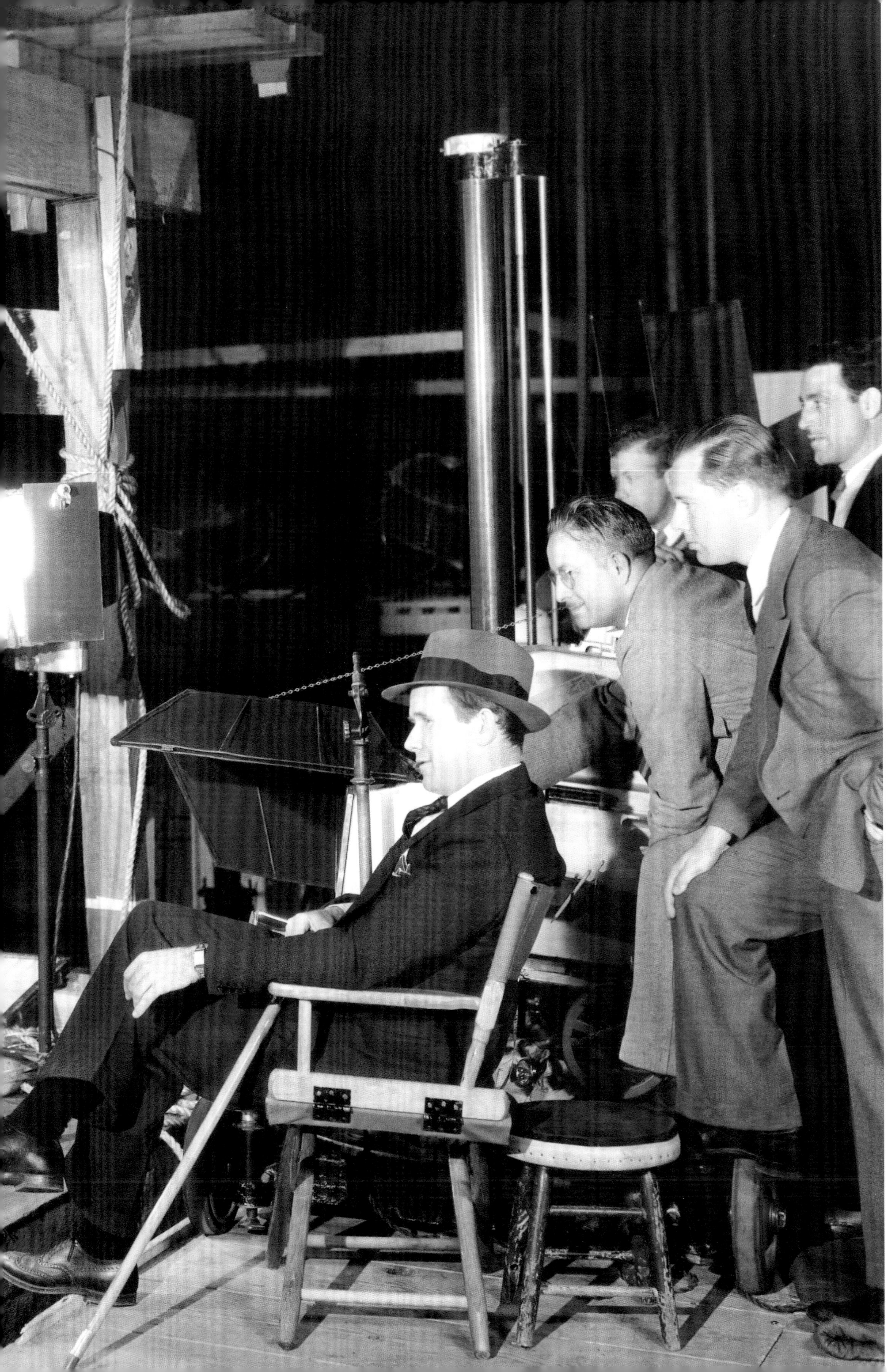

Harlow and William Powell visit on the set of *China Seas*.

[OPPOSITE] Making the cover of *Time* magazine was an achievement in mid-1935. This was only the third time in the 1930s in which a film star was so honored. The previous honorees were Marie Dressler in 1933, and Miriam Hopkins in early 1935. For reasons known only to the supercilious editors of the famed periodical, the photograph chosen was two years old.

FIFTEEN CENTS (IN CANADA, 20c Reason: Tariff) August 19, 1935

TIME

The Weekly Newsmagazine

JEAN HARLOW

Fine feathers make fine fans.

(See CINEMA)

Volume XXVI Number 8

Circulation Office, 350 East 22nd Street, Chicago. (Reg. U. S. Pat. Off.) Editorial and Advertising Offices, 135 East 42nd Street, New York.

movie
MIRROR
JANUARY
10¢
A MACFADDEN PUBLICATION
Combined with
Shadoplay
JEAN HARLOW
The AMAZING
MYRNA LOY
BILL POWELL
LUISE RAINER
TRIANGLE!

• Brownette •

THE SUCCESS OF *CHINA SEAS* AND THE HONOR OF A *TIME* magazine cover should have put Jean Harlow in an unassailable position. Instead she became a target, the last of the "wicked women" who had to be subdued by the Production Code. In the year since its formation, Joseph Breen's Production Code Administration (PCA) had forced Mae West, Norma Shearer, and Marlene Dietrich into less sexy roles, but Harlow had flouted the PCA by playing a tropical trollop. Her time was up. M-G-M had to sanitize her image. Her platinum hair was the obvious place to start. "I always hated my hair," said Harlow, "not only because it limited me as an actress, but also because it limited me as a person. It made me look hard and spectacular. I had to live up to that platinum personality." While Harlow's bleach-damaged hair grew out, tests were made of different-colored wigs. The shade finally chosen was dubbed "Brownette."

"Isn't this a peach of a wig?" Harlow exclaimed when she showed the honey-colored appliance to a visiting journalist. The wig had been manufactured from real human hair sewn onto a lace cap by Max Factor's company. "I'm tired of hearing people whisper that I'm in pictures because I'm an unusual type of blonde," said Harlow. "I'm tired of playing second to a head of hair. I want to be known as an actress." Harlow's new look included her wardrobe. The British designer Dolly Tree, who was more conservative than Adrian, was assigned to Harlow's films. Slinky satin would give way to tailored tweed, but not immediately. Harlow's first brownette outing would be "off the rack."

Since Irving Thalberg had done so well with Harlow's last film, Louis B. Mayer allowed him to cast her in his next production, *Riffraff*, a Frances Marion story about cannery girls and tuna fishermen. Harlow would play a tough but honest factory worker. For her co-star Thalberg chose the newly signed Spencer Tracy, a formidable actor. Could Harlow hold her own in scenes with him? Studio executives said no, but Thalberg kept his own counsel. "I think she needs a crack at a dramatic story," he said, "and this is

This Carbro image by Hurrell graced the cover of the *Illustrated Sunday News* in the fall of 1935.

[OPPOSITE] Hollywood's changing moral climate required Jean Harlow to dim her platinum flash. Her new "brownette" hair color was introduced in late 1935. George Hurrell captured it with the Carbro color process, and the photos were printed on movie-theater giveaways like this one. In case anyone harbored doubts, a caption read: "Authentic Color Photo Shows Actual Shade of Hair."

it." Unfortunately, his renewed prominence meant big productions like *A Night at the Opera* (1935), and he failed to give *Riffraff* the attention it needed, missing story conferences to concentrate on the Marx Brothers. In his absence, he assigned *Riffraff* to David Lewis, a young assistant producer, and Tay Garnett, the director of *China Seas*. By the time Garnett saw the script, it had gone from melodrama to comedy and back again. Harlow's character was ill-defined and incredible. "You're making a terrible mistake to put Harlow in this," Garnett told Thalberg. "You're destroying a star."

"How?" asked Thalberg.

"Harlow is the most famous courtesan in the world," answered Garnett. "People know her as a lovable tramp. Now you're trying to put her in the role of a Madonna."

"I'm not destroying a star," Thalberg said. "I'm giving her a new dimension." Garnett refused to continue on the project. Thalberg replaced him with a B-picture director named J. Walter Ruben.

"It seems rather nice to be back at the studio," Harlow wrote Helen Fieger. "This morning I had my breakfast served at my swimming pool. There was a slight breeze in the garden. The flowers looked so beautiful, nodding their pretty heads, as if to say 'Good morning Jean.' I loved it but I had to leave for work. Or I won't have a garden."

Harlow's concern about money was not misplaced. As William Powell continued visiting, he saw disturbing things. "I spent so many hours with that family," said Powell. "Very soon I was convinced that Marino Bello was a rogue." For one thing, the rich young actress never had any cash on her. Her allowance was supposed to be doled out to her by Bello, but her purse was always empty. Yet the Bellos were on an endless spree—Jean on antiques and Marino on investments. When questioned about her finances, Harlow was sadly ignorant, but even studio employees knew what was going on. "Bello had just ordered an entire new wardrobe of a couple dozen suits," recalled story department executive Kay Mulvey. Script clerk Morris Abrams saw Harlow stuck on a soundstage from six a.m. to mid-evening while the Bellos were out spending her money. "In they'd stroll in the middle of the day, dressed to the nines, riding high. They were parasites."

Powell hired private detectives and used his M-G-M connections to gain access to bank records of international transactions. What he learned about Bello's "investments" was unsettling. "I discovered she was taking an awful rooking from that man," said Powell. "He had a confederate in Mexico who would send him dummied-up reports about a silver mine. He'd show Jean

Harlow learned hemstitching from Rosalind Russell when they worked together in early 1935. By the time Harlow worked on *Riffraff* (1936), she was skilled enough to show her technique to hairdresser Edith Hubner.

The proverbial galaxy of stars attended the opening of Max Factor's Hollywood Make-up Studio at 1666 North Highland Avenue in Hollywood on November 26, 1935.

The Max Factor Studio, designed by S. Charles Lee, featured special rooms where technicians could see color accurately. Claudette Colbert dedicated its Brunette Room, Ginger Rogers the Red-Head Room, and Harlow, here with Max Factor, dedicated the Blonde Room.

these 'reports' and she'd hand over twenty-five percent of her salary. I investigated. There was no mine. It was fiction." While Harlow worked on *Riffraff*, Powell met privately with Jean Bello and presented his findings. There was more than the bogus mine. There was philandering. Jean knew about Marino's affairs with extra girls. What Powell told her was a shock. Bello was keeping a woman in Mexico. On September 10, 1935, Jean Bello filed for divorce.

Harlow had become close friends with David Lewis, even though she knew him to be homosexual. "Contrary to all the talk of the 'tough dame,'" wrote Lewis, "Jean spoke like the perfect lady. Her speech was good, her voice cultured and well modulated. She read a great deal, strange to report, and was intelligent about what she read. I occasionally drove her home. I found her mother to be cold and somewhat hostile to me." Despite Jean Bello's attitude, Harlow confided in Lewis. "Often, in the evenings," wrote Lewis, "Jean would telephone me at home and ask me to come and take a walk with her. On these walks she told me of an unhappy childhood, of a frighteningly ambitious mother who was grooming her at any cost to become a picture star."

Thalberg went to the sneak preview of *Riffraff*, which was held at the Golden Gate Theatre in East Los Angeles, a neighborhood populated by both Jewish and Mexican immigrants. The work print broke numerous times during the preview. This could have been a disaster had the audience not been hooked by a sensitive moment in Harlow's playing. "I can't put my finger on just what it was that she had," wrote Lewis, "but it was something beyond star charisma—a moment of naked truth, perhaps." Thalberg was satisfied that Harlow's acting had matched Tracy's, and the film was released without his customary retakes. It was not a success.

In Irving Thalberg's *Riffraff*, Harlow, at the corner of the balcony, played a cannery worker.

Harlow was working with Spencer Tracy for the first time in four years. Some executives thought her unqualified to work with the gifted actor.

This may have been due to its unattractive setting or Harlow's unglamorous role. *Riffraff* lost $103,000, one of Harlow's few films to show a loss. Her popularity continued unchanged, proving that it was not a function of either her latest film or her hair color. Her fans stayed with her. And she gave as good as she got.

On one occasion, a small group of tourists from the Midwest happened on Harlow as she was walking from her dressing room to the stage. They asked if she would pose with them for one snapshot. She ended up spending ten minutes, posing and signing, until an assistant came to fetch her. On another occasion, Eddie Lawrence, a new publicist, was escorting Harlow to the NBC radio studios. When they arrived, he was alarmed to see a huge crowd of fans. It looked as if he would not be able to get his valuable charge from the car to the studio. "No, wait," Harlow said to him. "I'll handle this." She opened the door and got out. The crowd surged forward. She calmly raised her arms and called for quiet. The crowd calmed. "Listen, everybody," she said. "I have to go in and do the show, so here's what you do. Give your name to my chauffeur. I guarantee that when I get back to the studio, every one of you will get an autographed picture." The crowd parted. She went in. A week later, a couple hundred photos were mailed out. Jean Bello had signed them.

In the fall of 1935, Harlow's brownette portraits were accomplished with wigs.

Harlow wore only one satin gown in *Riffraff*. Perhaps because of its unglamorous setting, the film did not do well at the box office.

VI

The Comedienne

- The Perfect Secretary
- The Lady on Palm Drive
- The Woman in Possession

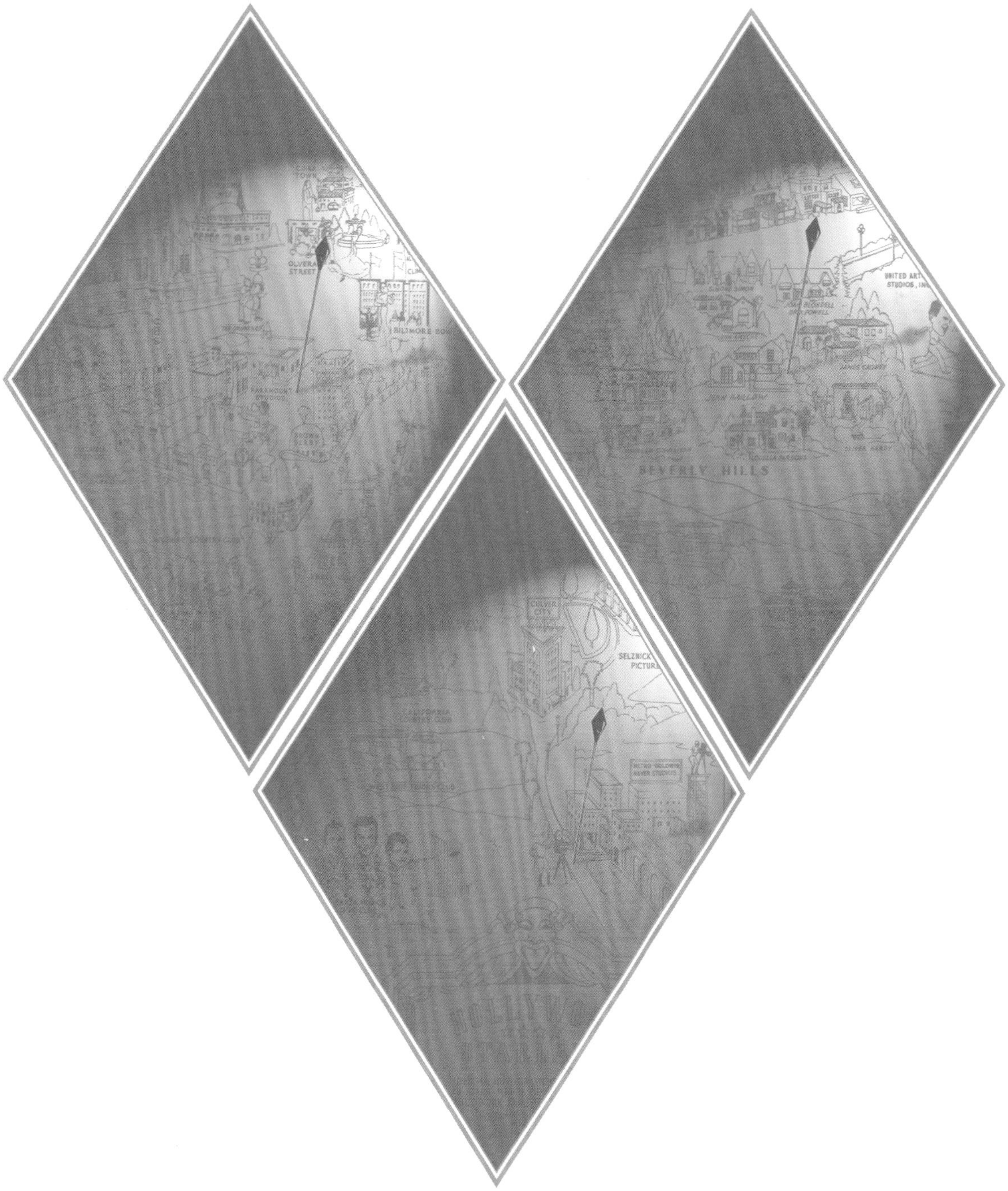

• The Perfect Secretary •

Jean Harlow had been living in Los Angeles for seven years. In that time she had become a world-famous movie star and survived three troubled marriages. The film industry had survived both the transition to sound and an economic depression. As 1935 drew to a close, everyone in Hollywood was doing better. Box office had improved by 15.5 percent, bringing weekly attendance to eighty million. Although Harlow was not among the top ten box-office attractions, she was in her own category. Magazines and newspapers constantly referred to her, whether in terms of fashion, cosmetics, or health. Her advice on romance was frequently sought. She was cited and quoted as few movie stars were. Yet even she knew the lifespan of a star.

One of Harlow's close friends was Colleen Moore, a star of silent comedies who had not made the transition to talkies. In 1932, Thalberg had tried to revive Moore's career by bringing her to M-G-M. In 1934, he had tried the same thing with Gloria Swanson, who was also slipping. By 1935, both actresses were "retired." It was no wonder, then, that Harlow wanted to improve her skills. She turned to producer Hunt Stromberg. Since *Red Dust*, he had made M-G-M stars of William Powell, Myrna Loy, Jeanette MacDonald, and Nelson Eddy. Stromberg came up with *Wife vs. Secretary*, a story that had Loy and Harlow vying for Clark Gable. It had a gimmick. Loy would be sexy, and Harlow would be reserved. What appealed to Harlow was the opportunity to say her lines in a natural tone of voice; in other words, her own.

"I begged and begged for a part in which I wouldn't have to speak bad English and slink up to 'my man,'" said Harlow. When she got the part, she suddenly became afraid. Could she carry it off? She came to director Clarence Brown. "I'm not an actress," she said. "You tell me what to do, and I'll do it." Brown was known for directing the shy Greta Garbo in a whisper. This approach also worked with Harlow. After she researched her role by observing studio secretaries at work, she let Brown lower the pitch of her voice. She still had traces of her regional accent, but her tone was soft and mellow.

After seven years, Harlow was a skilled motion picture actress yet still unsure of herself. She turned to Gable. "I read my lines to him," she said, "and he suggests that I stress this line or emphasize that word. I always do what he tells me. And he's always right." After four films with Gable, Harlow trusted him. "He's just the same today as he was the first day in *The Secret Six*," said Harlow. "He threw hard rolls at me in one of the scenes—and then between scenes, he kept it up. 'Just for fun.'

In Clarence Brown's *Wife vs. Secretary* (1936), Clark Gable played a publisher and Jean Harlow played an administrative assistant.

[OPPOSITE] After several films with William Powell, Myrna Loy had been dubbed the "perfect wife." *Wife vs. Secretary* pitted her against Harlow's "perfect secretary," with Gable as the prize. Critics complained that no real-life secretary could afford a gown like Harlow's.

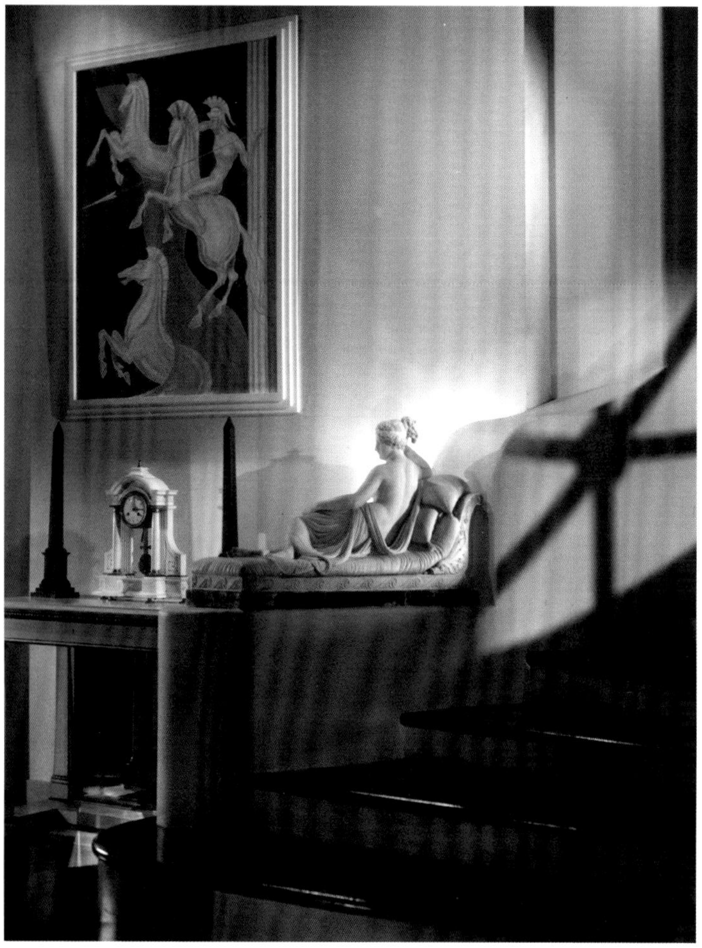

New York critic Norbert Lusk wrote that no real-life publisher "earns enough to afford the sybaritic establishment that houses Mr. Gable and Miss Loy in *Wife vs. Secretary.*" William A. Horning and Edwin B. Willis designed the mansion in question.

Fun! He aimed 'em with deadly precision." In truth, a great deal had changed in five years. "D'you remember, Clark, that funny little dressing room you had, tucked away at the end of nowhere?"

"Just enough room to change my coat and vest."

"We weren't allowed to see the rushes," remembered Harlow.

"And now we don't want to," said Clark.

Harlow had begun watching herself during the production of *Dinner at Eight*. There were still mannerisms that could be improved—the way she nervously knotted her fingers, for instance—but she had come a long way. Like Norma Shearer, she was able to study herself objectively, but there was something more, a disconnection between herself and the person on the screen. "If I could have remained just Harlean Carpenter," said Harlow, "if I could put on the Harlow personality like a mask while I was working and then take it off when the day was done, that would be heaven. I can't ever be myself. I can't develop myself. I spend all my time developing the girls I play on the screen. No sooner am I through with one than I must figure out the characterization of another. I can perfect the parts I play, but I can never perfect the person I am."

"I found her friendly, full of life, but not really happy," recalled James Stewart, a contract player who was cast as Harlow's boyfriend in *Wife vs. Secretary*. What he sensed may have been

Harlow shows actor Freddie Bartholomew her new pet Nosey (later named Adolph, the Flying Dutchman). Harlow had received the pup as a Christmas gift from Paramount producer Walter Wanger after the premature death of her Great Dane Bleak.

her ambivalence. "I never think of 'me' as a star," said Harlow. "I find myself thinking of Garbo and Dietrich and Crawford as big stars. Then the thought comes: 'But you're a star, too.' And it doesn't ring a bell. It doesn't seem to be real."

Stewart had worked on Broadway, but he found Harlow's skills impressive. "She could look at a page of dialogue," he recalled, "and then she would just do it, with every word exactly as written." While they were shooting a scene in a car, Stewart saw another side of the star. "The scene ended with a kiss," recalled Stewart. "In the first rehearsal she took charge of the kissing. It was then I knew that I'd never really been kissed. There were six rehearsals, thank you, and the kissing gained each time in interest and enthusiasm." Harlow was by this time known for her playfulness, spontaneity, and sexiness. She was highly popular with co-workers, whom she was always treating to gifts or teasing. Being laughed with—or at—was more than a way of coping. It was a way of life. She was the class clown.

On December 11, Harlow fainted on the set. She was sent home, reportedly "suffering from fatigue." Jean Bello engaged Dr. Leland Chapman, an unmarried forty-two-year-old internist. Harlow recovered rapidly, but persisted in calling Chapman. One day, she startled him by answering the door in the nude. A romance did not ensue; the doctor was engaged to a highly jealous young woman. Harlow had something else to laugh off.

If Harlow didn't take herself or her career seriously, she took her writing very seriously. The failure to get her novel published had hurt her confidence, but she went back to her typewriter. "I have worked harder at writing than I ever have at anything else in my life," said Harlow. "It's the only way I can really express myself. Acting is more or less dictated by someone else, but writing comes out of my very insides. It's purely creative." Harlow read abstruse works in order to analyze structure and form, and she finished every book she started. Then she discussed it with Carey Wilson and his wife. A visitor to Harlow's dressing room remarked on the selection of books on her table: *The Sheik*, *Slovakia Then and Now*, *Song of the Flesh*, and *The Gay Family*. "Oh, gee!" she said to the journalist. "Don't print that. People will think they're from my library. That Slovakia thing was sent to Bill Powell as a gag. Somebody sent me *The Sheik* with a ribbing that here was something to improve my mind. *Song of the Flesh* is a possible story for me." Significantly, the only book that was hers was the trifle about the happy family.

[TOP] The Santa Anita racetrack, located in Arcadia, opened on December 25, 1934. By 1936, everyone in Hollywood was either buying a racehorse or betting on one.

[BOTTOM] In early 1936, Harlow and Powell followed the crowd to Santa Anita's daily races.

Marion Davies posed with Harlow and Powell in the Santa Anita clubhouse.

On March 7, at her first session with Ted Allan, Harlow pulled down a fishing net that was hanging on the set, wrapped herself in it, and then shed her clothes. "I realized then," said Allan, "that she always needed something personal, that feeling of being liked. It made her feel secure."

Ted Allan's portraits of Harlow emphasized warmth rather than heat.

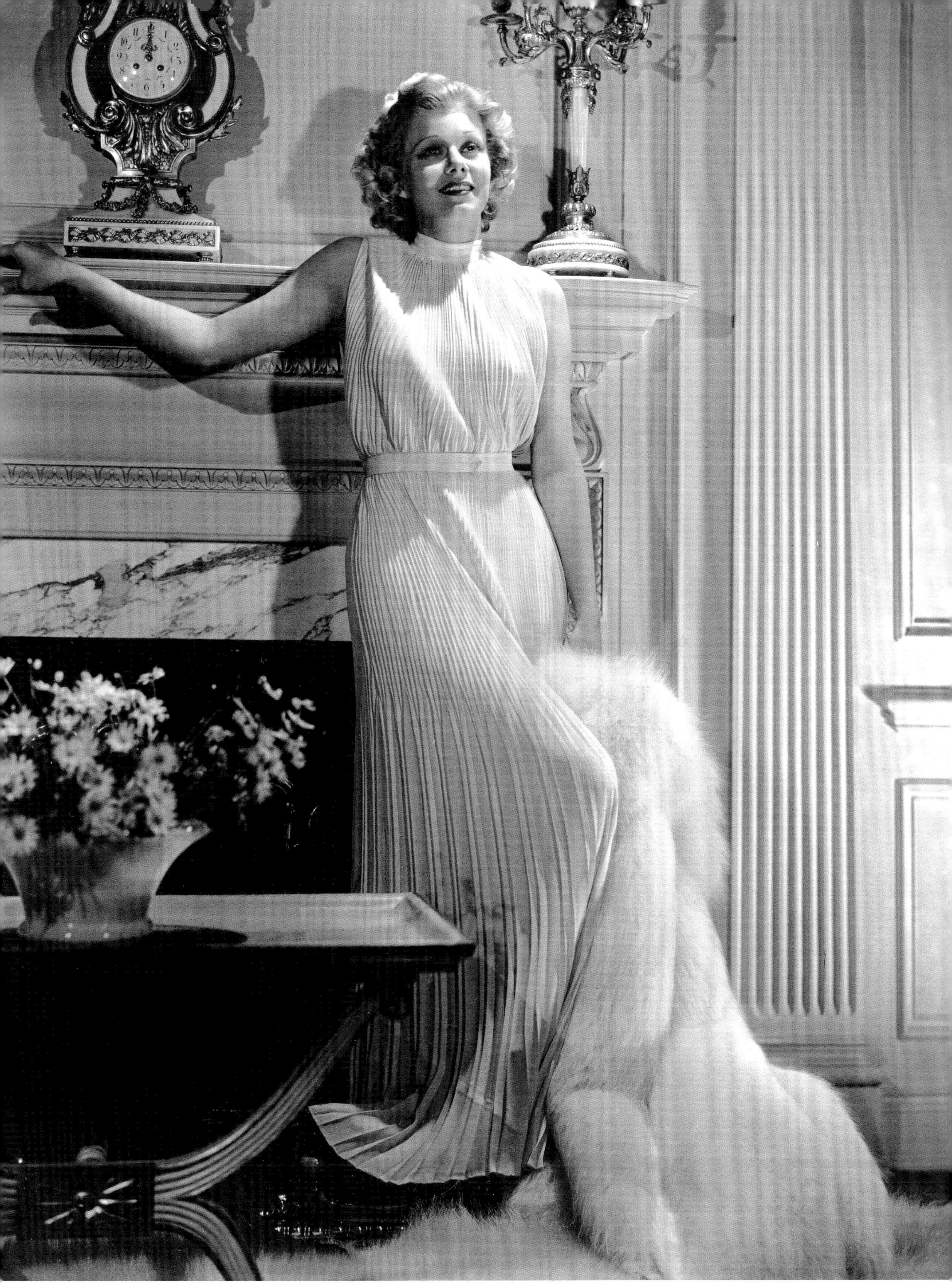

Harlow posed in her living room for Ted Allan on March 18, 1936.

• The Lady on Palm Drive •

In the spring of 1936, Jean Harlow was among the most envied of stars. Her new image was winning more fans and her new roles were earning critical acclaim. No wonder that gossip columns reported a feud between her and Joan Crawford. Crawford's first husband Douglas Fairbanks, Jr., was hard pressed to understand Crawford's "controlled detestation" of Harlow and her fear that Harlow was trying to eclipse her. M-G-M had "more stars than there are in the heavens," but these luminaries were not interchangeable. Harlow could no more play a dancing lady than Crawford could play a bombshell. Still, the two stars avoided one another.

Harlow's current release was odd by anyone's estimation. She was co-starred with Franchot Tone (Crawford's second husband) and Cary Grant (borrowed from Paramount) in a World War I spy story called *Suzy* (1936). Publicity released during its production reinforced Harlow's image as the best-liked star on the lot. "We're not just people who work on her set," said a crew member. "We're real to her. If you're out sick, she's the first one to miss you and find out what's wrong and send flowers or fruit." Harlow endeared herself to the football fans on one crew by telling her director on a Friday afternoon: "Let's work tonight so the boys can get away to the game tomorrow."

Harlow's evenings had settled into a predictable rut. Either she was with her mother or with William Powell; never with both. But her mother came first. "The grip she had on that girl was unbelievable," wrote Myrna Loy. By 1936, Harlow's warm glow had a dark undercurrent. "She was a sad girl, driven by her mother, madly in love with a man who wouldn't marry her," wrote Rosalind Russell. Harlow doted on Powell, acting as if she were his wife, which after two years she was not. He in turn acted like a husband, advising her on business affairs. After Marino Bello's departure, Powell had discovered that Harlow's finances were in a mess. There was little ready cash to deal with her expenses, the most conspicuous of which was her home. Its upkeep was costly and she was not using it to entertain. "Mother

On May 2, 1936, Harlow and Powell attended another William Randolph Hearst birthday party at Marion Davies' beachfront mansion. The party's theme was Mexican Fiesta.

[OPPOSITE] Harlow had wire mesh nailed to her Palm Drive gate to keep her dogs safe inside.

and I have eaten about two meals in the dining room in the past two years," said Harlow. "We eat on trays." Goaded by Powell, she defied her mother and put the house on the market. On May 11, 1936, she signed a deed of sale to Nat Levine, president of Republic Pictures. He paid $125,000, a modest price for the whitest house in Hollywood. Harlow saw her mother's disappointment but, for once, was practical. "It was too large a house for two women," said Harlow. "We rattled around in it. If

George Fitzmaurice's *Suzy* (1936) was Harlow's only film with Cary Grant. It was, unfortunately, a melodrama. A screwball comedy with Grant would have been ideal for Harlow.

Mother happened to be on one side of the place and I on the other, I had to holler my lungs out to make her hear me."

A week later, Harlow leased a two-story hacienda at 512 North Palm Drive in Beverly Hills. The monthly lease payment was three hundred dollars, but the home was beautifully designed and spacious, with a large garden. Powell lived at 801 North Hillcrest Road in Beverly Hills. He had commissioned architect James Dolena to tear down the Spanish-style home built in 1926 by film pioneer Hobart Bosworth and erect a white Regency mansion in its place. Once the home got sufficient publicity, Powell sold it—at a sizable profit. This caused speculation that he would buy a home for himself and Harlow. He chose to rent. The relationship continued unchanged, but unbeknownst to him, Harlow was pregnant with his child.

On May 27 Harlow appeared in Superior Court to formally change her name from Harlean Carpenter Rosson to Jean Harlow. Two days later she checked into Good Samaritan Hospital under the name of Mrs. Jean Carpenter, accompanied by a Mrs. Webb, who was in actuality her mother. Harlow was placed under the care of Dr. Harold Barnard, who had first

When Harlow went to the coastal town of Carpinteria to film scenes for *Suzy*, her portable dressing room was brought on a flatbed truck. "All it needs is a garden," she said when seeing the funny-looking perch for the first time. The next time she saw it, the film's crew had festooned the deck with shrubs and flowers.

Harlow called her employees "My Gang." They are, from top left: her assistant Bobbe Brown; her makeup artist Violet Denoyer; her maid Blanche Williams, bottom left; and her hairdresser Edith Hubner.

[TOP] In May 1936, Harlow sold her Beverly Glen mansion and rented a house at 512 North Palm Drive in Beverly Hills.

[ABOVE] This rare photo of Harlow at Palm Drive shows her collection of autographed photos, including one from California novelist Jack London.

treated her in 1932 for an episode of makeup poisoning. (Dr. Leland Chapman, although fond of Harlow, was not able to continue as her physician. His pathologically jealous wife had forbidden him to see Harlow.) Dr. Barnard performed an unspecified procedure on "Mrs. Carpenter." The notation on her chart read simply: "Accomplished purpose."

Three weeks later, Harlow did retakes on *Suzy*. She was weak. "Jean had to rest between takes with ice packs over her eyes," reported Dorothy Manners, "to be able to finish the picture." When Crawford heard that Harlow was ill, she waited until the set was cleared and then came to Harlow's dressing room. Harlow looked up to see Crawford in her doorway. "Jean, may I come in?" Crawford asked hesitantly. "May I help?" Thus ended the feud.

Harlow had submitted to her second abortion without telling Powell. There was no point. He was not going to marry her. His vanity had been hurt by his marriage to the incandescent Carole Lombard. He had no intention of marrying another sex symbol, which was unfair to Harlow. She was doing everything she could to shed that image. It was not enough. Powell played on her insecurities, characterizing her as dim and common. She was hurt, but too passive to complain, except to the occasional sob sister. "This I have never said before," she told writer Sonia Lee. "I do love Bill Powell."

Other than work, Harlow's only release from frustration—when neither Powell nor her mother could see—was Graves Gin. She would sneak out to visit her Aunt Jetty and Cousin Donald, whom Jean Bello had banned from their home. "Mrs. Graves calling" was the code for an impending visit. Harlow would show up with her bottle and then drink until she oozed maudlin regrets about her lost love, Chuck McGrew, and her inability to have a normal life. She would also speak of a recurring pain in her lower back.

On the brighter side, Harlow was cast with Powell in a film that looked like a sure-fire hit. *Libeled Lady* also starred Myrna Loy and Spencer Tracy. The four-star comedy was directed by Jack Conway, who had done *Red-Headed Woman*. Skip Harlow wrote to his granddaughter that he had seen the film and enjoyed Powell. Harlow was disappointed until Ella told her that Skip saw all her films at least four times each. He was not the only one. *Libeled Lady* was a spectacular success, grossing $2.7 million. Powell's next film was *After the Thin Man* (1936). He and Loy had to travel to San Francisco for one sequence. Harlow followed him. The movie-struck management at the Hotel St.

Artist James Montgomery Flagg made a portrait of Harlow in her garden for *Photoplay* magazine.

Harlow's susceptibility to sunburn caused work delays.

The bedroom community of Pacific Palisades, although adjacent to Santa Monica, is a district of Los Angeles.

Harlow's confidantes included publicist Kay Mulvey, whose Pacific Palisades home became a retreat.

Wayne Martin made this snapshot of Harlow on Santa Catalina Island.

Catalina was a favored vacation spot and film location in the mid-1930s.

Francis had assumed that Loy and Powell, being married in *The Thin Man*, were married in real life; they booked the expensive Fleishhacker Suite for them. Harlow offered to solve the problem by bunking with Loy. "You would have thought Jean and I were in boarding school we had so much fun," recalled Loy. "We'd stay up half the night talking and sipping gin, sometimes laughing, sometimes discussing more serious things. She talked about Paul Bern. That was still very much on her mind after four years. She told me how terrible that had been, because she loved him."

Loy noticed that Harlow's usually creamy complexion was acquiring a gray cast. A doctor made a brief examination and thought that Harlow should undergo tests. Harlow agreed, but upon her return to Los Angeles, she decided against it. "I am the laziest female in the world when it comes to avoiding unpleasant issues," she said. And, besides, her mother believed that Harlow's condition was the result of nothing more than excessive drinking. It never occurred to her to ask why the cheerful, giving girl had to drink. It only occurred to her to stay out of her way when she did. Harlow had begun to drink at home. When she drank, the resentment of a lifetime found its deserving target. Harlow's maid Blanche Williams witnessed tirades that were "extremely frightening to her mother. The more Jean drank, the more she hated her mother. She became very verbally abusive."

When Harlow sobered up, she would grow contrite and then disappear. She would go to the home of Dr. Barnard and his wife and cook for them, often serving them breakfast in bed. One morning Barnard woke up to find Harlow lying against his back, talking to his wife, who was across from her in the other twin bed. Harlow had brought breakfast trays in while the couple was still asleep. Barnard shook his head and said, "I'm the only man that ever slept with Jean Harlow and didn't know it."

Jack Conway's *Libeled Lady* (1936) starred Powell, Harlow, Myrna Loy, and Spencer Tracy, right. The film was nominated for Best Picture by the Motion Picture Academy.

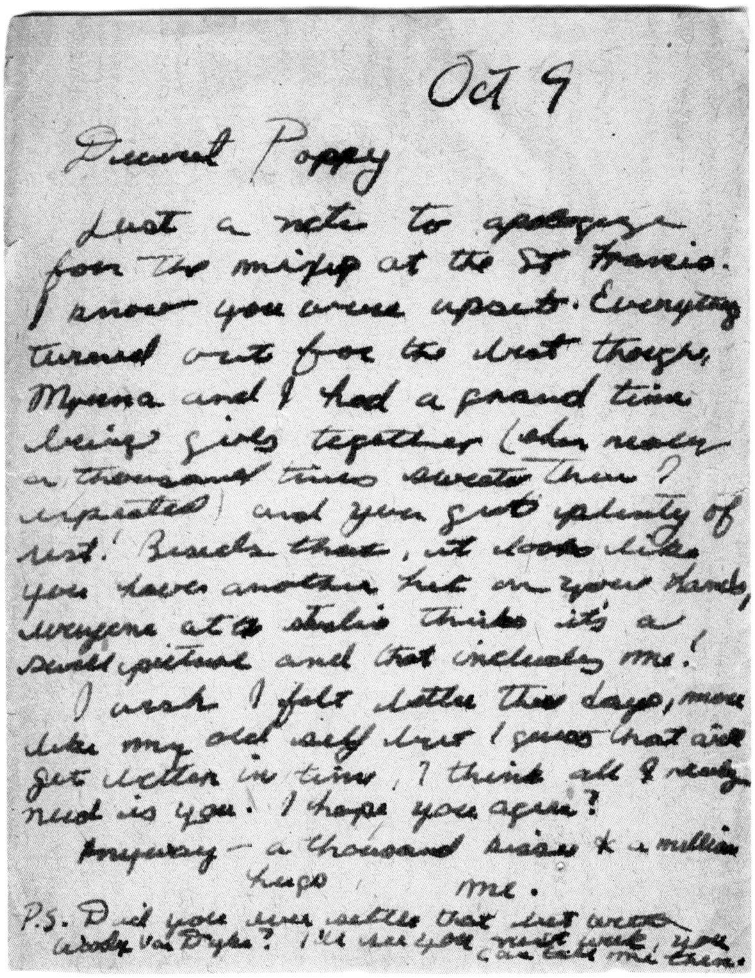

Oct 9

Dearest Poppy

Just a note to apologize for the mixup at the St Francis. I know you were upset. Everything turned out for the best though, Myrna and I had a grand time being girls together (oh, really a thousand times sweeter than I expected) and you got plenty of rest! Besides that, it looks like you have another hit on your hands, everyone at the studio thinks it's a swell picture and that includes me!

I wish I felt better these days, more like my old self but I guess that will get better in time. I think all I really need is you. I hope you agree?

Anyway – a thousand kisses & a million hugs

me.

P.S. Did you ever settle that bet with Woody Van Dyke? I'll see you next week, you can tell me then.

This draft of Harlow's 1936 letter to "Poppy," her nickname for William Powell, was found in the estate of Blanche Williams, Harlow's longtime maid. The letter reveals Harlow's tenderness, humor, and playful nature. Most poignant is her reference to not feeling well, a sign of advancing kidney disease.

In February 1936, Jean Harlow and William Powell visited Soboba Hot Springs and then dined at the Cocoanut Grove.

Directors W.S. Van Dyke and Wesley Ruggles posed with Harlow and Powell at the Café Vendome.

"We read books and go to see plays and laugh and cry over what happens to imaginary people," Harlow told an interviewer. "I'd rather laugh and cry over real ones." She did both in 1936.

On August 3, 1936, Harlow attended a Louella Parsons party for Marion Davies. Harlow is seen here with actresses Glenda Farrell, left, and Mary Carlisle.

At the Café Trocadero, even Harlow and Powell had to wait for a table.

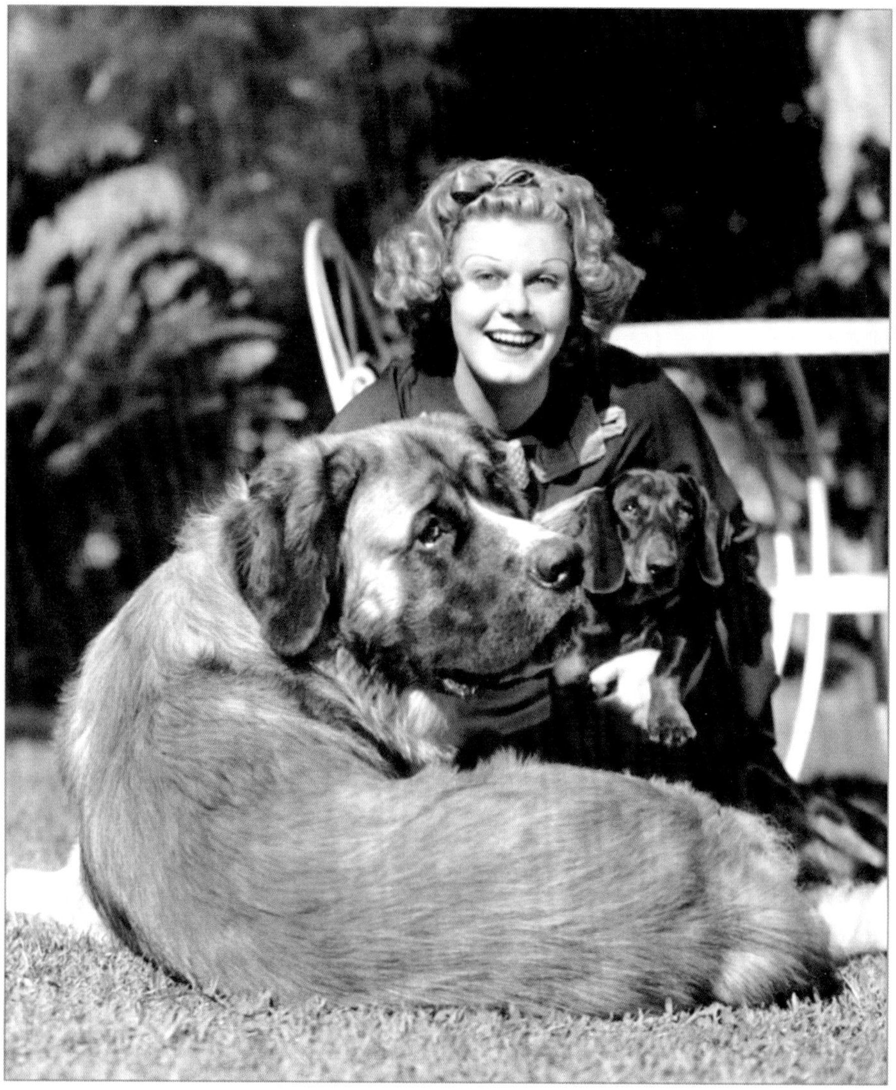

M-G-M photographer Bud Graybill shot Harlow in her garden with Nudger, seated at left, and The Flying Dutchman.

Harlow and Powell made the rounds of clubs and restaurants in 1936, dancing, drinking, and avoiding a basic issue.

[OPPOSITE] In 1936, Harlow's portraits were made exclusively by Ted Allan and her movie gowns by Dolly Tree.

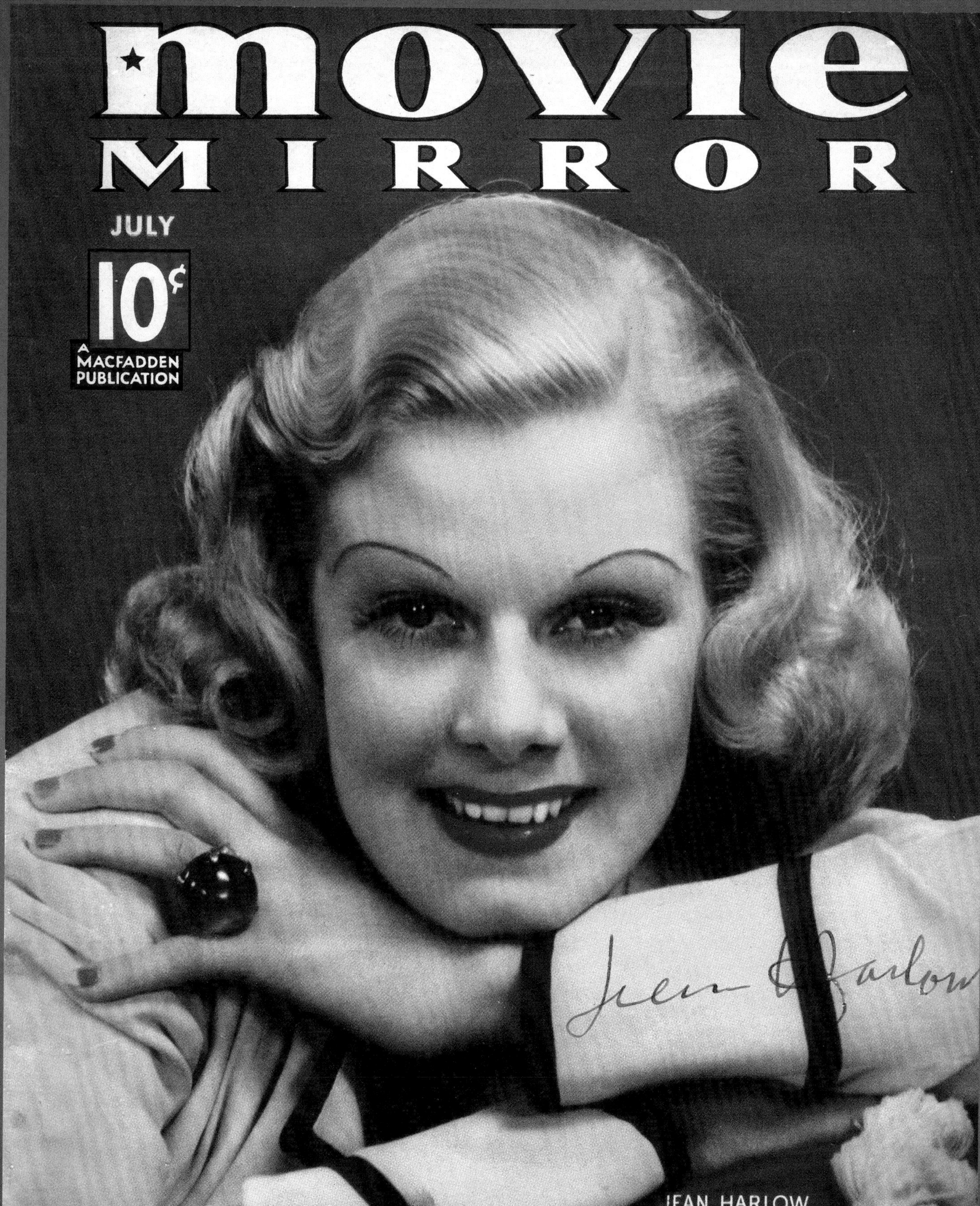
movie
MIRROR
JULY
10¢
A MACFADDEN PUBLICATION
Jean Harlow
JEAN HARLOW
Revealing The DUAL PERSONALITY of FRED ASTAIRE
The STARTLING Story Behind SPENCER TRACY'S ILLNESS

• The Woman in Possession •

JEAN HARLOW WAS TWENTY-FIVE YEARS OLD IN DECEMBER 1936, but few people called her Jean. To co-workers and intimates she was still "the Baby." She was childlike, still in thrall to her mother. Because of Harlow's innate gentleness, M-G-M had successfully modified her image. Gone was the porcelain glaze. In its place was the soft glow of a poised and respectable, amused and amusing young woman. The most impressive proof of Harlow's new image was an auspicious invitation. President Franklin D. Roosevelt was hosting a series of birthday balls to raise funds for the fight against polio. The main ball would be held at the Wardman Park Hotel in Washington, D.C., on January 30, 1937. Harlow was invited. It was a signal honor for the actress who had been vilified three years earlier in the Legion of Decency campaign. She was thrilled, but first she had work to do.

After the tremendous reception accorded *Libeled Lady* in late October of 1936, Harlow had found herself without an assignment. There were announcements of projects (*Love on the Run* and *The Foundry*) but nothing materialized. "I'm always the last one to find out what picture I'm playing in," said Harlow. "After all, I'm only the star." Without story conferences, fittings, or rehearsals, Harlow was left to her own devices. For once her mother was not there to decide them. Jean Bello was seeing a middle-aged man named H.V. ("Heinie") Brand, brother of Harry Brand, the powerhouse publicist of Twentieth Century-Fox. At forty-three, Heinie was four years younger than Jean Bello. He liked fishing on Catalina Island and frequently took her along.

Harlow spent her enforced leisure with friends, especially those who had children. She lavished attention on publicist Kay Mulvey's son, director Jack Conway's son, and gangster Bugsy Siegel's daughter. It was obvious that Harlow loved children. She enjoyed talking with them and making mud pies with them. She even enjoyed domestic chores. "Come on," she would say to Bobbe Brown. "Let's go do the dishes." Brown was perplexed at Harlow's interest in such mundane activities. "It's the only time I have peace," Harlow answered. Dr. Barnard saw Harlow's newfound domesticity as an escape. "She did it to get away from her mother," he said. Trips to Lake Arrowhead and evenings out were another way of avoiding conflict. "Some people like to suffer," said Harlow. "Mental sadists, I call them. And I don't want to be one of them. If I have a problem so baffling that it can't be solved, I tuck it away."

William Powell continued to be a baffling problem. He gave Harlow an eighty-five-carat star sapphire ring for Christmas. "I knew she'd like it," Powell said to a friend. "It's so vulgar." Harlow was thrilled by the gem, constantly lighting matches to highlight the star within the blue sapphire. She called it her "non-engagement" ring, a sad comment on her love life.

M-G-M had not found a suitable project for Harlow, so she made a radio appearance. She co-starred on *Lux Radio Theatre* with Robert Taylor in a digest version of Sardou and Moreau's historical comedy *Madame Sans-Gêne*. Harlow had never played in a period film. The broadcast showed why. Her Missouri accent was out of place in Napoleonic France. When her next film went into production, it was contemporary, and Taylor was her co-star. *Personal Property* was a remake of *The Man in Possession*, a minor 1931 comedy, but rewritten to favor the female lead. For the first time since *Dinner at Eight*, Harlow had William Daniels as her cameraman. He was known for the loving care with which he lit close-ups of Greta Garbo. On this film, he created equally effective images of Harlow, but not without work. Harlow was looking tired, almost dissipated. She was not well. "She constantly flubbed

[OPPOSITE] William Powell gave Harlow an eighty-five-carat star sapphire for Christmas in 1936, one of her precious possessions, but he belittled her enjoyment of it. Harlow autographed the cover of this *Movie Mirror* issue.

her lines and was noticeably distracted at times," recalled sound engineer Bill Edmondson. "Something was preying on her mind. She was not easygoing like she'd been during her *Red Dust* days."

There was additional stress when Louis B. Mayer declared that Harlow and Taylor could attend the Washington festivities, but only if they first completed *Personal Property*. Director W.S. Van Dyke was notorious for his fast pace, but even he was hard pressed to finish an A picture in three weeks. He shot everything in master shots and two-shots, assuming that, as usual, Richard Boleslawski and George Folsey would shoot the missing close-ups later. As the film neared completion, Harlow nervously readied herself for the trip. A small publication called *Screen and Radio Weekly* was granted a short interview with her. "I hate to bring anybody into this dressing room," Harlow apologized. "It's a mess. I'm sorry, but you've got to listen to my troubles. Here I am, going to the President's ball—and I haven't a thing to wear. The newest evening gown I own is two years old. I tried to buy something yesterday, but I couldn't find a thing that looked right on me. And then when I finally got permission to wear a copy of a gown I used in this picture, my dressmaker was sick with flu. I don't know what I'm going to do."

Influenza notwithstanding, the dressmaker completed the

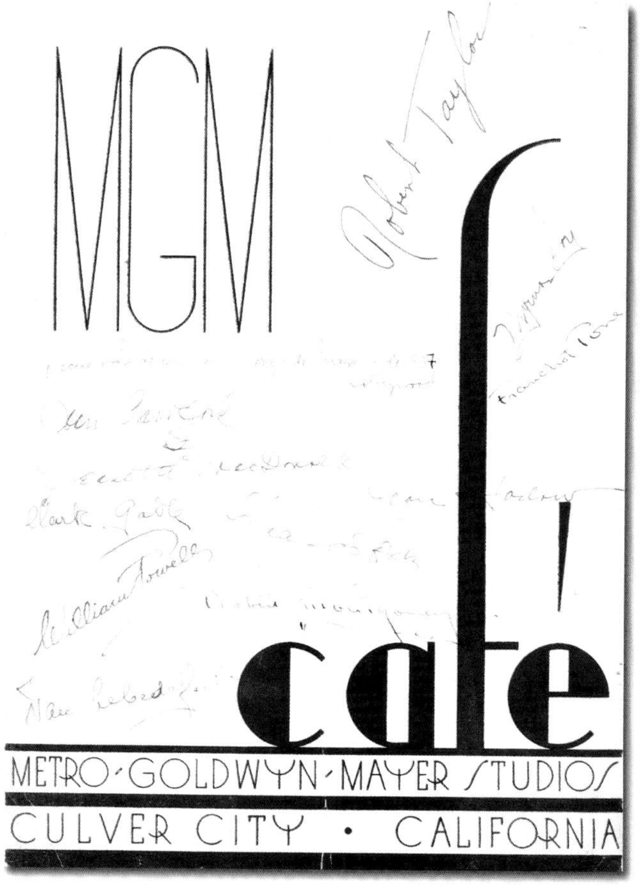

By 1937, the M-G-M commissary was as famed for its hearty fare as for its glamorous diners. Robert Montgomery, Joan Crawford, and Harlow, among others, signed this menu for a visiting South American journalist.

Harlow, Robert Taylor, the bespectacled Claude Rains, and C. Henry Gordon, right, gather at the December 10, 1936, rehearsal of *Madame Sans-Gêne,* for *Lux Radio Theatre.*

Argentine radio commentator Chaz de Cruz interviewed Harlow on the set of W.S. Van Dyke's *Personal Property* (1937). The PCA's Advertising Council made designer Dolly Tree add a second strap to Harlow's "revealing gown".

[OPPOSITE] In this Ted Allan photo, Blanche Williams holds Harlow's mirrored make-up case, and Edith Hubner smoothes her hair as she poses with Robert Taylor.

Harlow and Taylor rushed through *Personal Property* in order to make an important trip.

gown. Harlow and Taylor departed Los Angeles on January 23. The flu would be the recurring theme of their trip. First Taylor was confined to his compartment with it. Then it spread. "I'm the only one on this hospital train who does not have the flu," Harlow wired Van Dyke. The party detrained in Washington at 8:30 A.M. on January 29. By this time, Harlow, too, was ill. She could not give into it. In the next forty-eight hours she had twenty-two personal appearances, including one with First Lady Eleanor Roosevelt. The highlight of the trip was, of course, a visit to the Oval Office, where President Roosevelt greeted the entire Hollywood contingent. Harlow was moved by the experience. "My trip to Washington," she wrote, "was one of the greatest pleasures I have ever had." Ethel Ley was handling Harlow's correspondence since Bobbe Brown had left her employ to attend business school. This note was written to the *Platinum Page*, the official publication of the Jean Harlow Fan Club.

Fans in New Mexico waited for Harlow to greet them from the train on February 2, but she did not appear. Both she and her mother were so ill that they required the care of nurses. Upon returning to Los Angeles, Harlow rested and then reported to M-G-M for retakes on *Personal Property.* She did not feel fully recovered so she adjourned to William Powell's Palm Springs home for a rest. The visit was little more than that. There was no romance. Powell was resolved not to marry an actress. "Twice I've been married, and twice the marriages have failed," he told a writer. "It may be me. It may be the institution of marriage. Or it may be the institution of marriage in this business. I don't know. I only know that I am not married now." Harlow did not argue with him, but friends saw that she was deeply hurt. "He won't believe me when I say I only want him and a home," said Harlow. "He kisses me and laughs and says we'd never make a go of it."

When Harlow returned to Beverly Hills, she began complaining of pain in her gums. She was diagnosed with four impacted wisdom teeth. There was back-and-forth about whether to pull two or four. As usual she deferred to her mother, and oral surgery was scheduled for March 24. Harlow was at a beauty parlor with her hairdresser Peggy MacDonald when Louella Parsons came up to her and told her she looked tired. "I've been worn out since that personal appearance trip," Harlow answered. "It seems that everything tires me. I guess I'm just run down." Harlow's friends saw something more than fatigue. "After Bill's rejection," recalled Anita Loos, "Jean seemed to lose interest in everything.

This candid photo of Harlow and Taylor was taken at the Pasadena train station on January 23, 1937.

Both Harlow and Taylor were ill during their stay in Washington, D.C.

Wearing a copy of the redesigned gown, Harlow joins government dignitaries in celebrating the birthday of President Franklin D. Roosevelt.

Harlow was photographed with First Lady Eleanor Roosevelt while raising money for polio research and treatment.

[OPPOSITE] Three years after being maligned by churchmen and clubwomen, Harlow was the belle of the ball in Washington. A closer angle of this pose with North Carolina Senator Robert Rice Reynolds appeared in *Time* magazine on February 15, 1937.

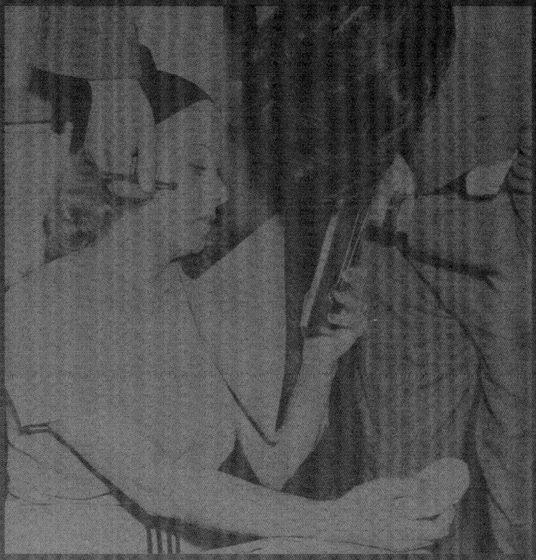

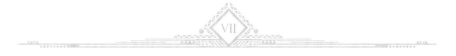

VII

THE FALLING COMET

- *Saratoga*
- "Film Star Dies in Hollywood"

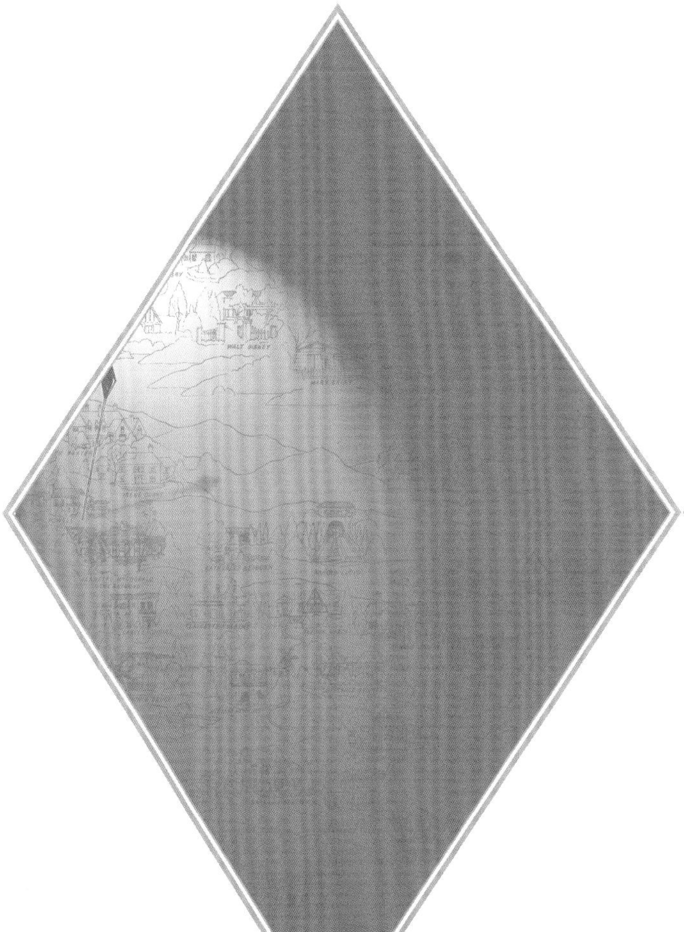

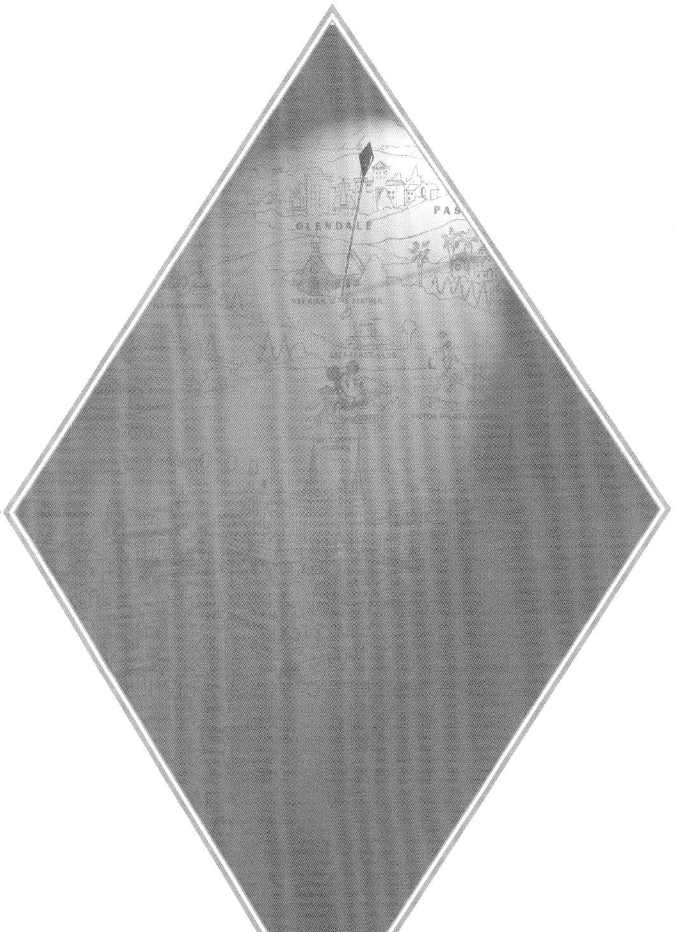

• *Saratoga* •

Jean Harlow's popularity continued to soar. Bringing M-G-M hit after hit, she was box-office insurance. The company was paying her five thousand dollars a week, which amounted to the deal of the century. The publicity, the interest, and the good will she brought M-G-M were inestimable. At this point, nothing would do for her but another film with Clark Gable. He was already slated for a racetrack film called *Saratoga Springs* with Joan Crawford. Producer Bernie Hyman replaced Crawford with Harlow, and assigned Anita Loos and Jack Conway, the team that had made *Red-Headed Woman*, to develop the project as *Saratoga*. Meanwhile, Harlow was in Room 826 of Good Samaritan Hospital. This was the same room in which she had undergone the appendectomy in 1933 and the abortion in 1936.

Harlow's dentist, Dr. Leroy Buckmiller, advised Jean Bello that her daughter was not strong enough to have four teeth extracted at once. Jean Bello had him replaced with a more compliant doctor. On March 24, Harlow was put under general anesthesia, and three physicians began the extraction. After the third tooth had been removed, loss of blood caused Harlow to go into shock. Her heart stopped beating. She was successfully revived, but the procedure was terminated. She spent the next two weeks regaining her strength. She returned to her home on April 10 for more rest, hoping that her swollen face would return to normal in time for her next film. During her recuperation, she visited Dr. Harold Barnard and his wife, mostly to evade her mother. On April 20, Jean Bello hosted a dinner for Skip and Ella Harlow. They had come for an extended stay, and Skip's first visit since 1929. The dinner was to celebrate their fifty-first wedding anniversary. In attendance were Jetta Belle Chadsey, Don Roberson, and other family members. Skip had reconciled himself to little Harlean's fame. When reminded that he had once threatened to disinherit her, he admitted taking back "them harsh words."

On April 22, *Saratoga* went into production. One day Harlow came to the set all smiles. William Powell had sent her a cake to remind her of the three-year anniversary of their first date. His card read: "To my three-year-old, from her Daddy." He was working on an adjoining soundstage with Myrna Loy on another comedy, *Double Wedding* (1937). He was also dating a young actress named Bernadene Hayes.

As *Saratoga* moved into its third week of filming, Harlow began to look sick. Publicist Teet Carle had worked with her at Paramount. He arranged an interview with W. Ward Marsh, the *Cleveland Plain Dealer* film critic. After the interview Marsh asked him: "Has she been ill?" Carle also sensed something wrong. Harlow appeared to be in discomfort. In fact, her gums had not healed. They were still infected and throbbing.

Harlow was not known to complain. She was unfailingly solicitous about the welfare of her co-workers, asking about their wives and children. On this film, her behavior was different. She rode in a limousine from the dressing room building to the soundstage, something she had never done. She was subdued. She kept to herself. It was known that her grandmother was not well. Ella had contracted pneumonia and been admitted to a hospital. It was also whispered that Harlow had broken up with William Powell. She had recently been seen on the town with publisher Donald Friede. Both Harlow and Friede maintained that their connection was solely professional. She still hoped to get her novel published. However, on Friede's thirty-sixth birthday, she gave him a note that

[OPPOSITE] In April of 1937, Jean Harlow attended a belated portrait session for *Personal Property*. She had not been able to pose after completing the film, as was customary, because she had been consistently—and dangerously—ill. When she finally came to George Hurrell's studio, *Personal Property* was already in release and she was starting *Saratoga* (1937), so she posed in costumes from both. Dolly Tree designed this ensemble for *Saratoga*.

said: "Love and no kidding. Me." This emboldened him to tell the press that Harlow was through with Powell. She denied it.

On May 12, Skip Harlow came to the *Saratoga* set to watch his granddaughter act. "I never knew they worked so hard in Hollywood," he said. A week later, his wife was well enough to board the train for home. But the trip weakened Ella, and she suffered a relapse. She was taken off the train in Albuquerque and hospitalized again. Harlow arranged for a nurse to accompany Ella and Skip back to Kansas City. On Sunday, May 23, Harlow attended a boxing match with Friede at Olympic Stadium in downtown Los Angeles. Afterwards, they dined at the Café Vendome. Although the weather was warm, Harlow wore a red fox coat and was more than subdued. She was listless.

As *Saratoga* moved into its fifth week of shooting, Harlow's appearance began to change. "Her face kept puffing up," recalled actress Maureen O'Sullivan, "and she was worried about how she would look on camera." Louella Parsons came to the set on Monday, May 24, and expressed concern at Harlow's wan expression. "I don't know why I get so dead tired," Harlow answered. "I really feel well." For the next few days, she complained of recurring headaches and was unable to arrive at the studio on time. "Jeanie, why didn't you tell us you were going to be late?" Conway teased her. "Then we could have all slept longer."

"You're lucky I'm here at all," Harlow said without a trace of humor. Conway was alarmed by her tone of voice.

On Tuesday, Bobbe Brown came to sit with Harlow in her dressing room while she picked at a cottage cheese salad. Harlow had tried to project enthusiasm for the camera. She was unable to do so for her friend. "Do you mind if we don't talk?" Harlow asked Brown. "I don't feel very well." Brown was taken aback. This was not the girl she had known for twelve years. Even more disturbing was the sight of Harlow draining infection from her mouth. She finished the day and managed to eat at a restaurant that night, even signing an autograph, but she was visibly unwell.

On Thursday, May 27, Harlow filmed a scene with Gable in the morning, retiring to her dressing room between shots to lie down. In the afternoon she went with Gable to the M-G-M portrait gallery, which was located at the top of the editing building, accessible only by a steep flight of stairs. After climbing them, she was unable to muster much energy for the sitting with Clarence Bull. She leaned against Gable through most of it. When she was leaving the gallery, she mouthed an odd farewell to Bull. "I'll never be here again," she said. Harlow chanced to encounter one of her schoolmates, Joel McCrea, who was now a star at Paramount. "She looked ill," recalled McCrea. He asked her how she was. "She said she was always tired. She said M-G-M worked her when she was ill—and she was afraid." Yet, when given a choice, she insisted on working.

On the morning of Saturday, May 29, O'Sullivan rode with Harlow in Jean Bello's chauffeured limousine, making the trip from Beverly Hills to Culver City. "She complained about not feeling well," recalled O'Sullivan. "But she didn't elaborate. She looked pale and fragile and that ring from Bill Powell looked too heavy for her hand." When she arrived at the studio, her co-workers saw a marked difference in her appearance. Assistant director Tom Andre was distressed to see how bloated she had become since the previous day. "It was obviously fluid retention," he said later. Makeup artist Violet Denoyer thought Harlow looked weak and sick. "Violet, you know," said Harlow quietly, "I have a hunch I'm going away from here and never coming back." Denoyer did not ask what Harlow meant. Wardrobe assistant Ted Tetrick saw Harlow sweating and appealed to Jack Conway. A nurse was called. She advised Harlow to go home. She said she could work.

Harlow gave a lackluster performance in her scenes that morning on Stage 9. Her scene with Walter Pidgeon was a light comedy exchange set in a library. Pidgeon was to hold her close to him. Harlow was barely able to rehearse. During a break, she asked script clerk Carl Roup to speak to Pidgeon for her. Could he hold her lightly when they did the take? "My stomach is killing me," she said. She did not make the shot.

"We were to do the shot just before lunch," recalled Pidgeon. "We were standing together for a final light check. She doubled up in pain."

"Baby's got a pain," Pidgeon said to Conway. Conway called lunch. Harlow was escorted to her dressing room.

Fifteen minutes later, Andre got a call from Harlow. He hurried to her dressing room. He found her on her day bed. "I don't know what's the matter with me," said Harlow. "I feel so ill. I haven't the strength to hold up my head or take off my makeup." Andre immediately called Conway, who in turn called studio manager Eddie Mannix. The studio doctor arrived and examined Harlow. "That was the end," said Pidgeon. "Instead of doing the scene after lunch, she went home. We never saw her again."

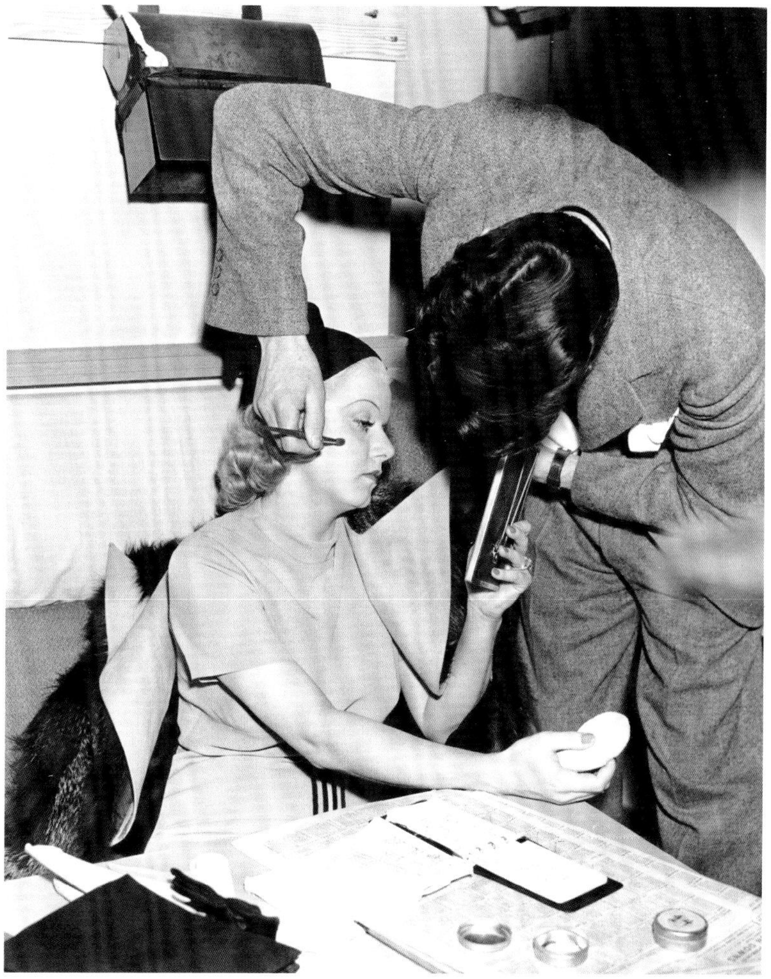

On April 22, Harlow began shooting *Saratoga*. Before long, she was causing her makeup artists extra work; she was constantly sweating.

On May 10, Harlow posed with makeup artist Peggy MacDonald on the steps of the dressing room building.

While making *Saratoga*, Harlow needed to seclude herself in her dressing room.

On Saturday, May 15, Harlow was shooting a *Saratoga* racetrack scene with, left to right: assistant director Tom Andre, cameraman Ray June, director Jack Conway, script clerk Carl ("Major") Roup, and Clark Gable.

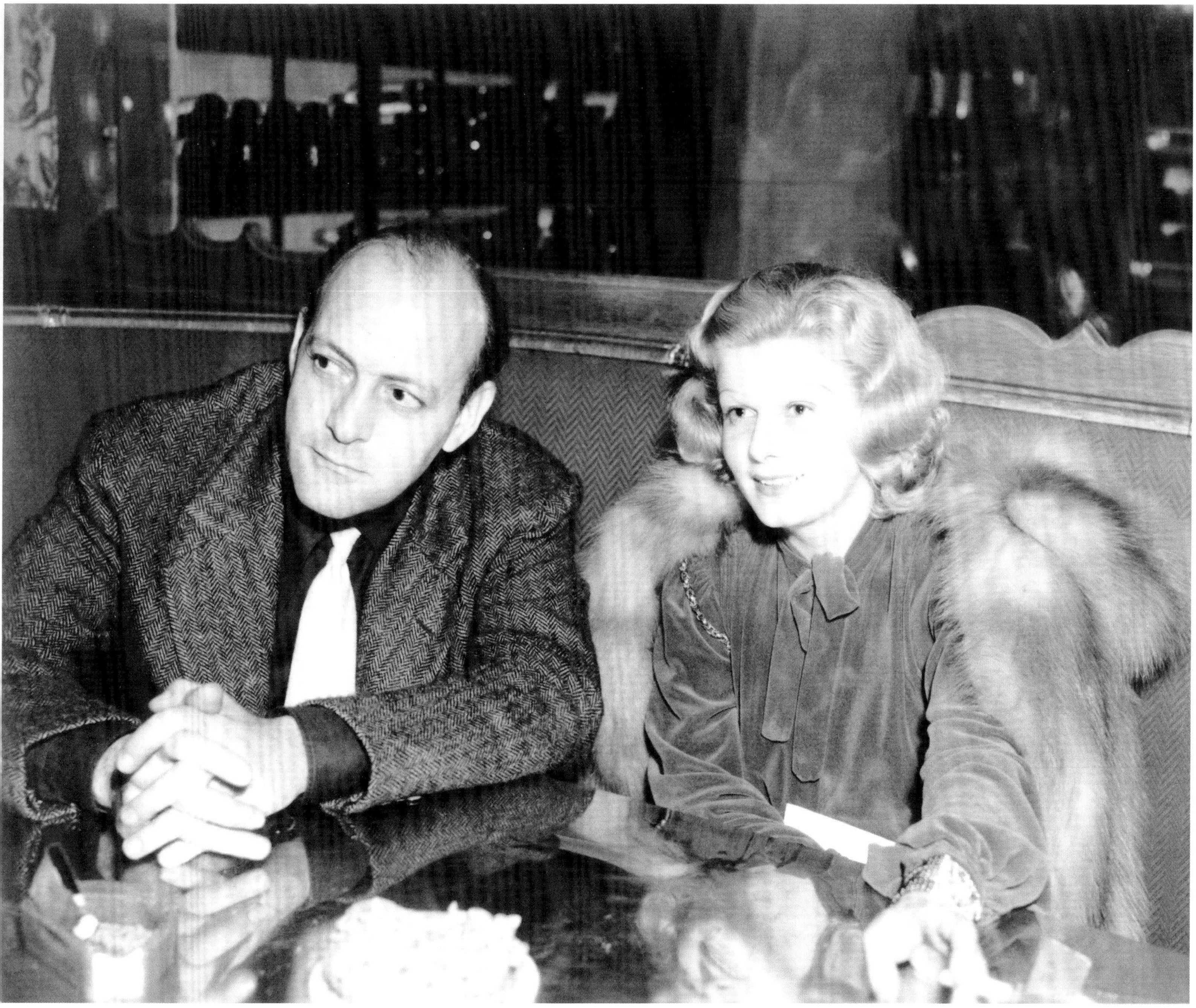

On May 23, Harlow watched a boxing match at Olympic Stadium with publisher Donald Friede and then dined with him at Café Vendome.

On May 27, Harlow posed with Gable for Clarence Bull, both of whom noticed that she was listless.

By May 28, Harlow was no longer walking from her dressing room to Stage 9; she needed a ride.

On May 28, Harlow was photographed entering Stage 9, the mansion set.

This unretouched proof of a May 28 photo shows a sadly debilitated Harlow struggling to work with Lionel Barrymore, left, and Walter Pidgeon.

This rare photograph was made on the morning of May 29, 1937. Harlow adjusts her shoe strap, her feet swollen due to the advanced stage of kidney disease.

• "Film Star Dies in Hollywood" •

In the 1930s, the Hollywood movie star epitomized glamour, a quality not easily defined but quickly recognized. Glamour could be wholesome, like Janet Gaynor, or exotic, like Marlene Dietrich, but it was always vital. Health was its basic component. Stars were shown exercising, playing polo, and swimming. Jean Harlow, a paragon of glamour, loved golf and tennis. It was odd, then, that no one noticed the signs of encroaching illness. George Hurrell was one of the few Hollywood photographers to shoot stars without a makeup base; he used retouching to create the alabaster sheen unique to his portraits. Seeing Harlow without pancake in 1932, he noticed that her eyes were deep set and that there were dark circles around her eye sockets. By the time he made her *Personal Property* portraits in April of 1937, there was a dark line of demarcation around each eye. Harlow was bloated. Her skin looked gray. Colleen Moore noticed that when Harlow drank alcohol, her ankles swelled. Occurring singly, these symptoms might mean anything. Occurring simultaneously, they were ominous. The star was not as healthy as her image. She had endured a year of illnesses and medical procedures. What was wrong with her?

When Harlow left the *Saratoga* set on May 29, she did not go directly home. She stopped by the set of *Double Wedding*. "Daddy," she said to Powell, "I don't feel good. I'm going home." There was no one home at Palm Drive, however. After Skip and Ella Harlow had returned to Kansas City, Jean Bello had accepted Heinie Brand's invitation to spend a week on Catalina Island. Bereft of her mother, Harlow chose to go to Powell's home. To all appearances, she had the flu. By Sunday night, she was looking worse than a flu victim. Powell called Catalina Island and had Jean Bello paged. Monday was Decoration Day, a national holiday, but Jean Bello was able to get home and bring her daughter to Palm Drive. Although Jean Bello subscribed to Christian Science, she was not a fanatic. "She had a reader in to look at Jean," recalled Kay Mulvey. "But she did not deny Jean medical attention." Jean Bello tried to get Dr. Leland Chapman. His wife was obdurate, so he sent his senior partner, Dr. Ernest Fishbaugh, who had treated Ella Harlow a month earlier. Dr. Fishbaugh made a series of tests and brought in a staff of nurses. His initial diagnosis was "severe cold and sore throat" and an unidentified stomach ailment.

On the morning of Tuesday, June 1, Harlow woke up and remembered that she was supposed to be working on *Saratoga*.

Harlow was taken to Good Samaritan Hospital on Sunday, June 6.

[opposite] A press photographer keeping vigil in front of Jean Harlow's home captured this image of her house while she lay ill in her bedroom. Its window is visible at the upper right.

She called Jack Conway. "Jack, I'm so sick," she said. "I can't come to work." She was crying, more worried about a film being delayed than she was about her health. Conway told her they could shoot around her but Harlow was not reassured. Her condition worsened. By Wednesday morning, she was delirious, suffering intense abdominal pain, too weak to be moved. Dr. Fishbaugh ordered equipment brought in, transforming the home into a private hospital.

In the early hours of Thursday, June 3, Harlow's condition stabilized. Jean Bello decided to speak to the press. "I feel like the whole world has been lifted from my shoulders," said Jean Bello. "This baby of mine is quite improved. Her doctor says she is out of danger." Dr. Fishbaugh maintained that the crisis had passed. "Miss Harlow is better," he said. "At her present rate of progress, she will be able to return to work soon." Powell believed—or preferred to believe—that Harlow had been suffering from nothing worse than the flu. "I was working," he said, "and I could get over to see her only three times that week. But no one was concerned, and she was expected back at the studio on Monday."

The optimism was short-lived. Yes, Harlow was able to sit up in bed, and she went back to her copy of *Gone with the Wind*. But her condition did not jibe with Dr. Fishbaugh's diagnosis. While she lost strength, he treated what he thought was cholecystitis, an inflammation of the gall bladder. He used intravenous dextrose. Jean Bello could see that her daughter was sinking. Dr. Fishbaugh insisted she was improving.

At this point, Jean Bello lapsed into denial, trying to cope with Harlow's deterioration by exerting tighter control over her environment. She refused entrance to Bobbe Brown, Donald Friede, and Jetta Belle Chadsey. Carmelita Geraghty Wilson refused to be put off. She pushed her way in. What she encountered shocked her. Harlow's room had a foul odor. Her skin was dark, and she was severely bloated. Wilson called her husband Carey. He and John Lee Mahin went to Jack Conway. "Mrs. Bello," pleaded Conway over the phone, "you must get the Baby to a hospital."

Jean Bello refused, citing Christian Science, which was irrelevant; her home was full of medical staff. Meanwhile, Jetta Belle Chadsey called Dr. Chapman and begged him to go to Palm Drive. Then Jean Bello called him. Harlow was in agony. "The Baby is dying," she wept. "Dr. Fishbaugh is killing her." Finally, one of Dr. Fishbaugh's nurses got on the phone. In a grim, calm voice she advised Dr. Chapman to come. Surprisingly, he defied his wife and agreed. Conway and Clark Gable got there first. Nothing had prepared them for what they saw. Gable later described Harlow's appearance as that of a "rotting person." Louis B. Mayer and Howard Strickling showed up and tried to convince Jean Bello to accept the services of another physician. She refused. Mayer called her behavior "legalized murder."

Dr. Chapman arrived. When he saw Harlow, he broke down and wept. After he regained composure and examined her, he knew what was wrong, what had been wrong for some time, what every other physician had failed to diagnose. The toxic levels of urea in her system indicated nephritis, a decline in kidney function. How had it started? Most likely when Harlean Carpenter had contracted scarlet fever in the summer of 1926. That ailment was not in itself sufficient to cause nephritis. It had been followed by glomerulonephritis, which is a post-streptococcal infection of the kidneys. Its side effects include high blood pressure and nephritis. Her kidneys had been degenerating for years, so the disease would be fatal.

Worse yet, Dr. Fishbaugh was injecting Harlow with fluids when he should have been draining her with diuretics. As a result, her tissues were swollen to twice their size. "It was too late," Dr. Chapman said later. "There wasn't anything I could do to save her." Unlike Dr. Fishbaugh (whose misdiagnosis could not be made public), Dr. Chapman had known Harlow, and he had

Jean Harlow died on Monday, June 7, 1937. Her chauffeur Herbert Lewis was photographed removing her effects from the hospital.

come to care deeply for her. Yet he had to face her flaws. She had medicated herself with alcohol to cope with her powerlessness. She had ignored her health while selflessly attending to the needs of others. The result was this grisly scene. Dr. Chapman tried to reverse what had gone before, but after two days of trying to rally his patient, he gave up. "She didn't want to be saved," he said later. "She had no will to live whatsoever." There was nothing to do but send her to Good Samaritan Hospital for a death watch—and try to soothe her anguished relatives and friends.

For a time, Jetta Belle Chadsey hoped for the best, writing to another relative on Saturday, June 4, that "Dr. Chapman just called me and said she is better."

> Dr. Chapman first told Jean he could not take care of Harlean, so he sent Fishbaugh, but I called Dr. Chapman yesterday and asked him to go. I said, "She will be better to know you are there." So he went and is going today again. The poor little thing was taken sick on the set a week ago. Jean was at Catalina the first three days Harlean was sick. Harlean did not let her know, and that was why she was so bad off, had gotten such a start. Harlean's a very sick girl yet. This inflammation of the gall bladder has her swollen from chin to legs. No solid food. She only can take it in through her veins, because she's vomiting all the time. Well, you know how little rest I've had this week between Jean keeping me out and everything else that's happened. We will drive up this evening after Don [Roberson] comes.

Chadsey was again refused admittance by Jean Bello, but Dr. Chapman got her into the hospital.

Once more secluded in Room 826, Harlow was slipping in and out of consciousness, dying of renal failure. Sitting in the room were Jean Bello, Marino Bello, Blanche Williams, Jetta Belle Chadsey and William Powell. Across the hall, actor Warner Baxter comforted Powell, who paced when he wasn't in her room. In the next room, a patient named Merritt Ruddock heard "the sounds of muffled and intense activity in the corridors, the soft padding of nurses' rubber-soled shoes, and the jerky, constant tread of a man in the room next door." In the hall were the few reporters who had managed to get into the hospital.

On Monday morning, just before nine o'clock, Dr. Chapman opened the oxygen tent so that Chadsey could slip her hand through and grasp Harlow's. Her niece was able to hear her. "Harlean," said Chadsey, "please try to get better."

"I don't want to," said Harlow. Chadsey rushed out of the room, overcome. "Where's Aunt Jetty," asked Harlow. "I hope she didn't run out on me." At nine, Harlow slipped into a coma. For the next two and a half hours, while a fire department inhalator squad worked to revive her, Jean Bello tried to reach

Harlow's status as a film star ensured that every aspect of her death was recorded by the press.

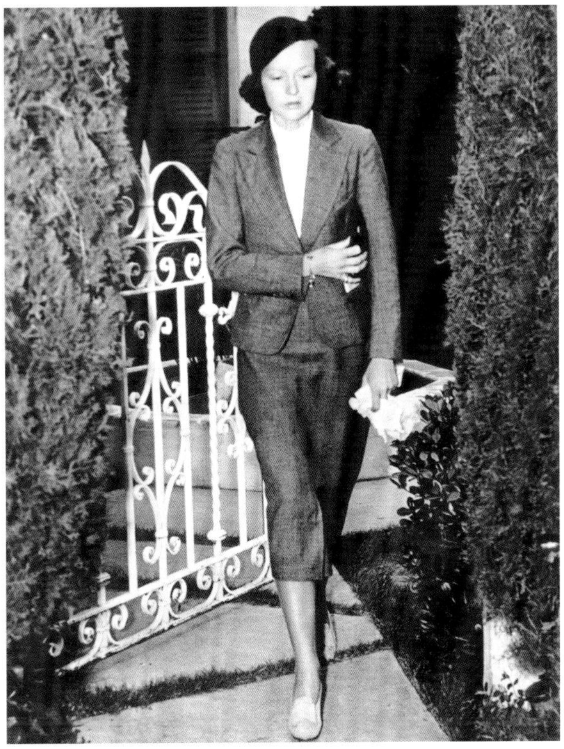

Harlow's friend Bobbe Brown was not spared by photographers as she left Harlow's home after visiting Jean Bello.

her. "Mother loves you, darling," she repeated over and over. "You know that, don't you? Mother needs you."

Jean Harlow died at 11:37 in the morning on June 7, 1937. Incredulous newspapers ran special editions. The headlines screamed: "Film Star Dies in Hollywood!"

Shocked fans passed an all-night vigil at the Pierce Brothers Mortuary, 720 West Washington Boulevard, Los Angeles.

"The day the Baby died there wasn't one sound in the M-G-M commissary for three hours," recalled writer Harry Ruskin. "Not one goddamn sound." M-G-M's switchboards were jammed with calls from around the world. In Kansas City, Harlow's grandparents were shaken. Skip Harlow had known his granddaughter was ill but had thought it was from the effects of dental surgery. Mont Clair Carpenter sat in his office, absentmindedly fingering the edge of his lab coat. "I can't believe it," he said blankly. "She always wrote me and visited me when she was here. She was such a dear girl."

Marino Bello worked with Howard Strickling and M-G-M to make funeral arrangements. Harlow's body was taken to Pierce Brothers Mortuary in Los Angeles. Even though the casket would be closed, Violet Denoyer, Peggy MacDonald, and Blanche Williams attended to hair and makeup of the remains, and dressed her in a pink organdy negligee from *Saratoga*, Jean Bello's last-minute change from the white gown she had first specified.

The following morning at exactly nine o'clock, the Hollywood studios observed one minute of silence. As limousines passed through the gates of Forest Lawn Memorial Park in Glendale, a crowd of autograph hunters peered into their windows.

On June 9, the funeral service at Forest Lawn Memorial Park in Glendale drew morbidly curious crowds.

Two hundred fifty mourners filled the Wee Kirk o' the Heather chapel. The service began with Jeanette MacDonald singing "Indian Love Call," one of Harlow's favorite songs. Mrs. Genevieve Smith, a Christian Science practitioner and family friend, read the Twenty-ninth Psalm. Nelson Eddy sang "Ah! Sweet Mystery of Life" with MacDonald until she faltered; he finished it. The service was concluded in twenty minutes. Three days later, Jean Harlow was entombed in a marble mortuary chamber in the Great Mausoleum in Forest Lawn in Glendale. She had lived twenty-six years.

Wee Kirk o' the Heather Chapel could accommodate only two hundred fifty. Floral displays had to sit outside.

Jean Bello arrived for her daughter's funeral with Carey Wilson and William Powell.

Mont Clair Carpenter and his wife Maude came from Kansas City. He had planned to visit his ailing daughter later that month; sadly, his first visit to Los Angeles was for her funeral.

On June 12, Jean Harlow's remains were interred in the Great Mausoleum at Forest Lawn.

JEAN HARLOW

The *Hollywood Reporter* ran this tribute to Jean Harlow the week she died.

♦ Epilogue ♦

Jean Harlow's fans clamored for *Saratoga*, so the studio hired a double and completed it without her. The film became a major moneymaker in 1937, an otherwise slow year. Its feverish attendance may have been due to morbid curiosity or simply the desire to see a beloved star one last time. It also may have been an attempt to comprehend the incomprehensible. A vital young woman was dead. For years afterward, fans would try to make sense of "uremic poisoning" with speculation of fatal sunburn, makeup poisoning, or toxic bleach. Even now, with the hindsight of seventy-four years, it is difficult to come to terms with this tragedy.

In the 1960s, when Harlow regained currency (partly because of a libelous biography), her contemporaries tried to explain her death. Some blamed Jean Bello. Others blamed the studio. It is true that both mother and studio sold this girl as a sex symbol, and that she sold well. But Harlow cooperated with the process, partly because her mother wanted her to and partly because she enjoyed it. She accepted what Hollywood had to offer: Beverly Glen swimming pools, Trocadero dinners, trysts with athletes, writers, and actors. She derived emotional sustenance from her fans, in an era when most observed basic etiquette. To her credit, she did try to keep the artificiality of Hollywood at bay, with trips to the beach and the mountains. If she had been a stronger person, she might have succeeded, yet even in rustic settings, she had to agree with Valentino. A star is a product, controlled by a company, subject to an image. The glow of Lake Arrowhead was a mirage; the flash of Hollywood was reality.

Harlow acknowledged her dilemma. "If I could put on the Harlow personality like a mask while I was working and then take it off when the day was done, that would be heaven." And if she had been strong enough to break free from her mother, she could have had a different life: writing, marriage, motherhood.

Harlow's mother, Jean Bello commissioned the painting *Farewell to Earth* by Tino Costa in 1937 to commemorate her daughter. After Mrs. Bello's passing, the painting all but disappeared and remained missing for more than fifty years. It had made its way to the Midwest, where it was purchased by Dr. James Idol Jr. for his private collection. In 2016, co-author Darrell Rooney and Dave and Dianne Reidy acquired the painting at auction to preserve the Costa work.

As long as she clung to Jean Bello, she functioned in a classic symbiosis, choosing emotionally unavailable men because her mother would not share her. If indeed she was an abused child, the crime was not only that it happened, but also that it continued in another form, preventing emotional maturity. Her mask served more than one purpose, and, for a time it worked, along with the glamour and the humor and the cocktails.

Eventually the person behind the mask, the one who loved books and writing and children, grew tired of the masquerade. Her greatest asset—that gentle, winning warmth—was subverted by resentment and fatigue. It's difficult to laugh when the joke's on you, when no one takes you seriously, when you're expected to be flashy and no more. The tension between Harlean and Harlow eventually took its toll. If Harlean had been stronger, if Harlow had been less strong, perhaps illness would not have ended in death.

Jean Harlow's death was, from any perspective, a tragedy, a loss of potential. Viewed in the context of film history, her death

Harlow at the entrance to her Club View Drive home in 1931, inset, and the same view in 2010.

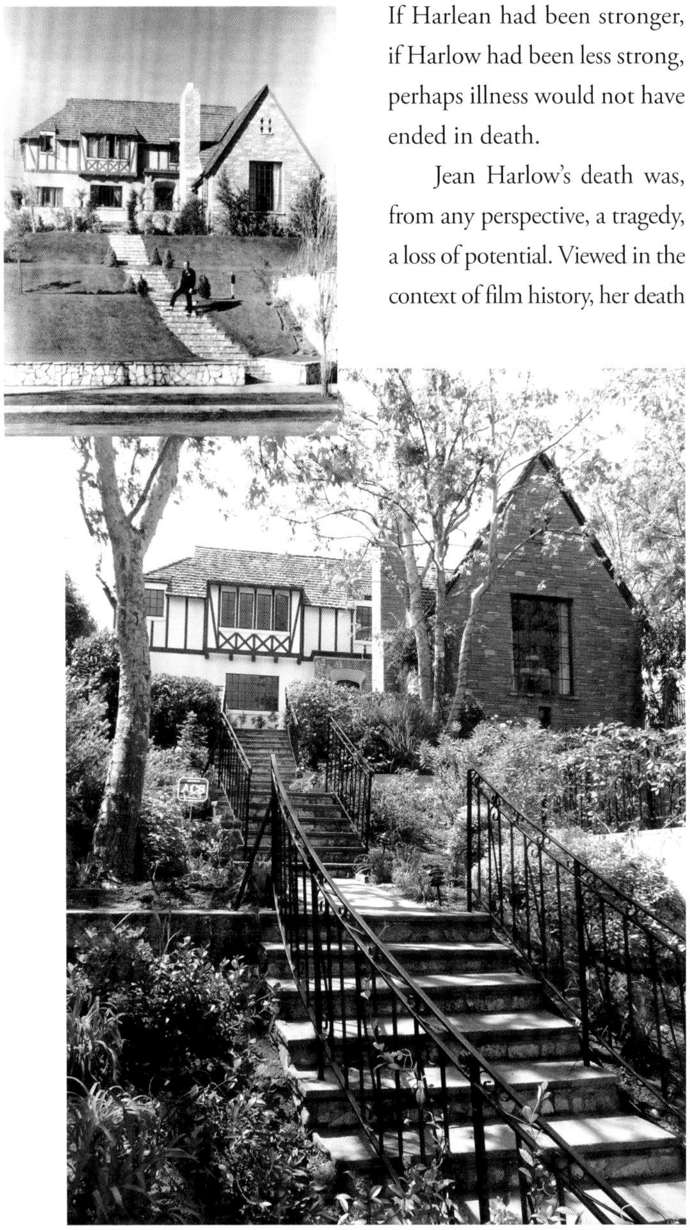

Harlow's home on Club View Drive in 1931, inset, and in 2010.

came at the end of an era. The period she typified—the glossy, naughty talkie years, later dubbed the Pre-Code Era—was evolving into the Golden Era, the zenith of the studio system, the apex of its productivity and brilliance. Harlow was not present when, in the last year of the decade, the studios produced a portfolio of great films. Her death precluded the plum role of Crystal in *The Women*, which Hunt Stromberg had bought with her in mind. 1939, the year that would go down in history for the number of greatly popular and truly great films, did so without Harlow.

It is intriguing to think what direction Harlow's career would have taken had she lived. Would she have continued in comedy? Would she have tackled more complex roles? Or would she have been put out to pasture by Louis B. Mayer? In 1942, to make room for Lana Turner, Judy Garland, and Hedy Lamarr, Mayer ended the tenures of his female stars. The Twilight of the Goddesses saw Jeanette MacDonald, Myrna Loy, Greta Garbo, Norma Shearer, and Joan Crawford leave Culver City. Perhaps Harlow would have done what Crawford did—gone to Warner Bros., found a new image, and won an Oscar. She might have taken the Rosalind

Russell route, starring as a series of career women. She might have joined Lucille Ball on television, creating a comic character. With her talent for writing, she might have followed Ida Lupino and become a combination of producer, writer, and director.

The loss of Harlow is most keenly felt when reading articles that pop up after her death. One is especially touching. In February 1942, the journalist Jimmy Starr, known mostly for his coverage of Hollywood in the *Los Angeles Herald-Express*, wrote a piece about Harlow for *Stardom* magazine. A journalist—under constant pressure to cover only the new—was looking back five years. As he explained in his article, he came across notes that he had taken during an interview with Harlow a month before her death. "I had known Jean a long time," wrote Starr, "since she had first tried to get into pictures at the Hal Roach and Al Christie comedy studios, even before Paramount gave her a chance." Sitting in Harlow's dressing room, Starr asked her to help him find an angle for a proposed newspaper article. Good scout that she was, she tried to get into the spirit of the thing.

"I like to cook," she winked, "but you'd better not print it, because no one would believe it. I like wire-haired terriers, and good phonograph records. I always wanted to be a newspaperwoman. You know I've written a novel. I haven't a good title for it. Oh, well. It probably won't be published anyway. And I—" She paused and looked across her dressing room. "I'm going to confess something." She went to her desk and took out paper and a fountain pen. She sat down. "I make up jokes. Twist phrases. Things like that. Is that bad?"

"You mean gags?" asked Starr.

"Sure," she answered. "That's it. Gags. They're wows. Well, some of 'em. Here, I'll show you. You think of the subjects. I'll think of the gags, or epigrams, or whatever you call them. How about 'Harlow-isms?'"

In the manuscript of her novel, Harlow had written a sentence that went: "An epigram is an amusing statement of an untruth designed to make the effect tasty if not digestible." She was no stranger to Oscar Wilde, but Starr had not expected this flight of whimsy. "Some are born great," Harlow

Harlow's 1932 Packard, now owned by Cliff and Joyce Gooding, returned to Club View Drive in 2009 and was parked in the same spot as in the classic 1933 photo.

The living room of Harlow's Club View Drive home looks much the same in 2010 as it did in 1932.

began. "Some have good press agents. Others have their love letters read in court." The interview turned into a game, one that lasted more than an hour. The results were uneven, but good enough for a spontaneous romp.

> The man with the wrinkled forehead isn't a character actor. He's a producer.
>
> Lesson to Hollywood about columnists: Don't feed the hand that bites you!
>
> In Hollywood they teach the wolf at the door to bark at the creditors.
>
> Usually a self-made man quits too soon.
>
> Familiarity breeds attempt.

Starr did not publish the article because of the shock of Harlow's subsequent death. "I put the interview notes away as a keepsake," he wrote, "as a remembrance to which I would one day return."

The most prominent keepsakes of Harlow's brief, bright tenure are her films. In the decades following her death, her films were reissued occasionally, but, not until the release of M-G-M's library to television in 1957, were they seen with any regularity. Since then, Harlow has been stamped in the popular consciousness as the Platinum Blonde, the first blonde sex symbol, the comedienne who was both desirable and lovable. Perhaps film history will begin to present the other Jean Harlow, the gentle, witty young woman who was so generous that she would spend a lunch break coining epigrams for a reporter.

The pool area of the home shared by Harlow and Paul Bern on Easton Drive in 1932 is little changed.

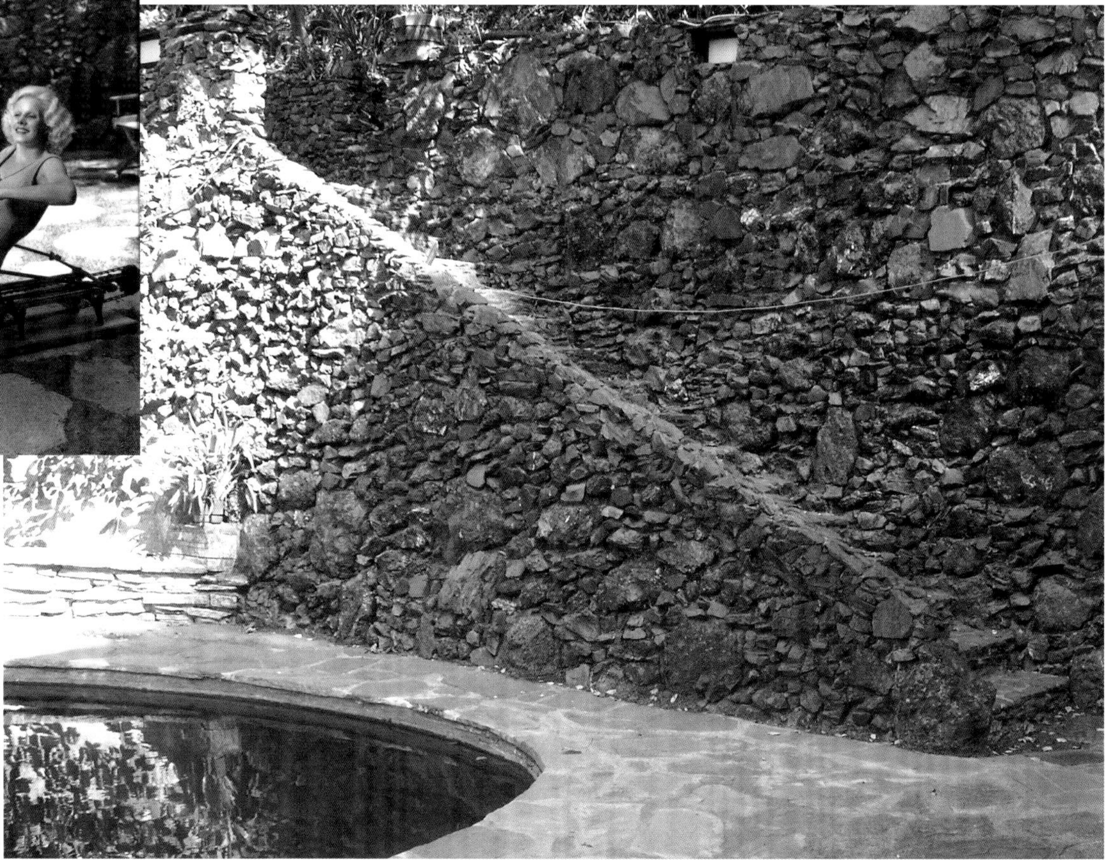

Adorned in a traditional Dutch bonnet, Harlow publicizes her film *Saratoga* in this 1937 natural-color photo by James Doolittle.

The theater where Harlow attended numerous premieres still bears her imprint.

She was a generous and thoughtful, amused and amusing young woman—who had the ability to mesmerize millions.

Acknowledgments

Telling the story of any historical figure is a daunting prospect. Bringing a much-maligned woman to life with honesty and integrity is impossible—unless you have a remarkable group of people behind you. Darrell and I did. I wish to thank the following institutions, archives, and individuals for helping Darrell and me write *Harlow in Hollywood*.

I thank Robert S. Birchard, Kenton Bymaster, Frank Coiro of Editions Iconix, Margot Gerber of the American Cinematheque, Richard Peterson of the Rafael Film Center, Christina Rice of the Los Angeles Public Library, and Marguerite Topping. I thank David Stenn for giving us the opportunity to build on the peerless research of his 1993 book. I thank my literary agent Alan Nevins.

I thank Marc Wanamaker of Bison Archives for supplying rare images of Los Angeles and Hollywood environs. I thank Thomas G. Coyle, Director of AICP in Kansas City; Gena Hall of City Planning and Development in Kansas City; and Bradley Wolf, Administrator, Historic Preservation Office of City Planning and Development Department in Kansas City, Missouri, for helping me understand the borders between Kansas and Missouri. I thank Richard and Disnalda Lewis, conservators of the Ignatieff mural, for the opportunity to record this unique artifact in a digital photograph. I thank Ron and Maggie Hale for making possible a stylized book jacket portrait.

I owe a personal thank-you each to Guy Vieira, Janine Faelz, Jann Hoffman, Harvey Stewart, P.R. Tooke, Michael Vera, Mae Friedman, Andrew Montealegre, Jonathan Quiej, Howard Mandelbaum, and Ben S. Carbonetto. Thank you for giving me support and encouragement while I burned the midnight oil.

I thank Darrell Rooney for including me in his heartfelt quest. I thank Tom Zimmerman for introducing me to Angel City Press. I thank Hilary Lentini of Lentini Design for realizing an ethereal concept in two marvelous dimensions. And, finally, I thank Paddy Calistro and Scott McAuley of Angel City Press for showing faith in this project and for shepherding it to a completion that is truly gratifying.

—Mark A. Vieira

Harlow in Hollywood would not exist without the contributions and extraordinary support of David Stenn, whose mentoring prepared me for this project; and of Dennis Lee Cleven, who shared the invaluable interviews he conducted with Harlean Carpenter intimates. I thank Pierre Casanova and Cliff's Edge Restaurant in Silver Lake, where this book was birthed.

I thank individuals who did not live to see it completed. For providing images: Ed Baker, Clare Cameron, and Erik Stogo. For recollections: M-G-M sound engineer Bill Edmondson and *Red Dust* actor Gene Raymond. For showing me around Kansas City: the late Michael Rudd and his widow Gloria. For sharing memories of their famous schoolmate, I thank three ladies whom I unfortunately never met: Helen Fieger Dawson, Virginia Bosch Eckstein, and Lamarr Schmit Ahearn.

I thank memorabilia dealers who found the images that made this book possible: Jack Condon at Backlot Books, Jim Cullen, Mack Dennard, Sabin Gray, Eduardo Orenstein, Danny Schwartz, Marci Siegel of Hollywood Legends, Mark Willoughby at Collectors Book Store, and Roy Windham at Baby Jane of Hollywood.

I thank the private collectors whose generosity with photographs, correspondence, and interviews has made us friends: Sandy Arcieri, Darin Barnes, Brian Bundy, E.J. Fleming, Bill Forbriger, Allen Gonzales, James Kaufmann, Bill and Richard Lewis, Wayne D. Murray, Marne Rafter, Caren Roberts-Frenzel, Jim Roup, Mark Santamaria, and Michael Yakaitis.

I thank those friends whose resourcefulness and support have made this book a reality: Jack Allen at Dream City Photo, Karie Bible, Ray Bradbury, Lisa Burks, Johnny Crawford, David Easter, Kathleen Violet Gray, Alex King, Bill Matthews, Skip O'Brien, Dave Stephan, John Silletti, Brent Vallens, Judith Vargas, Steve Vilarino, Sheree Puma Watson, and Reg Williams.

I would especially like to thank Dave and Dianne Reidy who worked with me to rescue the painting *Farewell to Earth* and helped make that dream come true.

I thank the owners of Harlow's former residences for opening their homes (and hearts) to me: Mark Walsh and Nancy Nadel, Dr. Charles Chandler and Rebecca Chandler, and Dr. Ron Hale and Maggie Hale. I thank Cliff and Joyce Gooding, owners of Harlow's 1932 Packard, for their time and support.

I thank Harlow's surviving relatives: Mrs. Sharon Barnes, Mallory Barnes Morton, and Briony Barnes.

I thank two Hollywood veterans who shared reminiscences with me: Mary Carlisle Blakely and Pauline Wagner McCourtney.

I thank my co-visionary on this project, Mark A. Vieira, for suggesting a book on Harlow. I thank designer Hilary Lentini for realizing our vision with taste and skill. I owe a special thank-you to Paddy Calistro and Scott McAuley of Angel City Press for saying yes and for their expertise and passion. They put the "angel" in Angel City Press.

Last but not least, I wish to express my heartfelt thanks to the family members and friends who gave me Harlow photos on my birthday and for Christmas; thank you to Kay Rooney, my mother; Cathy Cooke and Arvella Marshall, my sisters; Richard Rooney, my brother; Leslie Cooke Morris, my niece. I thank my friends Roger Allers, Leslee Hackenson, Leah and Aidan Allers, Pamela Stephan, and Richard Lee Stiles. They were always the very best presents.

—Darrell Rooney

Books

Behlmer, Rudy. *W.S. Van Dyke's Journal: And Other Van Dyke on Van Dyke.* Lanham, Maryland: The Scarecrow Press, 1996.

Conway, Michael, and Mark Ricci. *The Films of Jean Harlow.* New York: Cadillac Publishing, 1965.

Crowther, Bosley. *Hollywood Rajah.* New York: Holt, Rinehart, and Winston, 1960.

—. *The Lion's Share.* New York: E. P. Dutton and Company, 1957.

Davies, Marion, and Kenneth Marx. *The Times We Had.* New York: Ballantine Books, 1990.

Dressler, Marie, with Mildred Harrington. *Marie Dressler: My Own Story.* Boston: Little, Brown and Company, 1934.

Eyman, Scott. *Lion of Hollywood: The Life and Legend of Louis B. Mayer.* New York: Simon and Schuster, 2005.

Finler, Joel. *The Hollywood Story.* New York: Crown Publishers, Inc., 1988.

Granlund, Nils T. *The Three Most Beautiful: Blondes, Brunette and Bullets.* New York: David McKay, 1957.

Hamann, G.D. *Jean Harlow in the 30s.* Los Angeles: Filming Today Press, 2004.

Haver, Ronald. *David O. Selznick's Hollywood.* New York: Alfred A. Knopf, Inc., 1980.

Kobal, John. *The Art of the Great Hollywood Portrait Photographers.* New York: Alfred A. Knopf, 1980.

—. *People Will* Talk. New York: Alfred A. Knopf, 1985.

Kotsilibas-Davis, James, and Myrna Loy. *Being and Becoming.* New York: Alfred A. Knopf, 1987.

Lanchester, Elsa. *Elsa Lanchester, Herself.* New York, St. Martin's Press, 1983.

Lasky, Jesse Jr. *What Ever Happened to Hollywood?* New York: Funk & Wagnalls, 1973.

Levy, Emanuel. *George Cukor, Master of Elegance.* New York: William Morrow and Company, 1994.

Lewis, David, with James Curtis. *The Creative Producer: A Memoir of the Studio System.* Metuchen, New Jersey: The Scarecrow Press, 1993.

Lyon, Ben. *Life with the Lyons.* London: Oldham's Press, 1953.

Marx, Samuel. *Mayer and Thalberg, the Make-Believe Saints.* New York: Random House, 1975.

Nystedt, Robert. *The True Story of Jean Harlow.* Publisher's Development Corporation, 1964.

Parsons, Louella O. *Jean Harlow's Life Story.* New York: Dell Publishing, 1937.

Scott, Evelyn Flebbe. *Hollywood When Silents Were Golden.* New York: McGraw-Hill, 1972.

Stenn, David. *Bombshell: The Life and Death of Jean Harlow.* New York: Knopf, 1993.

Stine, Whitney. *The Hurrell Style.* New York: The John Day Company, 1976.

Thomas, Bob. *Joan Crawford: A Biography.* New York: Bantam Books, 1978.

—. *Thalberg: Life and Legend.* Garden City, New York: Doubleday & Company, Inc., 1969.

Articles and Documents

Beall, Harry Hammond. "She Tried to Dodge Stardom." *Movie Classic,* January 1937.

Bello, Jean. "Is Jean Harlow Dead? Her Mother Says No!" *Modern Romances,* March 1938.

Benham, Laura. "Hell's Smartest Angel." *Silver Screen,* January 1931.

Benson, Rachel. "How Long Will Hollywood Protect Harlow?" *Modern Screen,* August 1934.

Burke, Marcella. "The Inside Story of Jean Harlow's Whirlwind Romance." *Screen Book,* October 1932.

Burks, Lisa. "A Conversation with *Bombshell* Author David Stenn." *The Platinum Page,* March 1997.

Chrisman, J. Eugene. "Jean Harlow and Judge Ben Lindsey Discuss Sex." *Hollywood,* March 1934.

—. "Jean Harlow Answers Your Questions." *Motion Picture,* July 1933.

Douglas, W.A.S. "Harlow Meets Chicagoan to Whom She Penned Inmost Thoughts." *Chicago Herald and Examiner,* June 10, 1937.

Dowling, Mark. "'I Am Wise to Myself Now!' Says Jean Harlow." *Screen Book,* February 1936.

1931

Fidler, James M. "Jean Gets Married." *Screenland,* September 1932.

Flagg, James Montgomery. "Drawing a Million Dollars Worth of Beauty." *Photoplay,* November 1936.

Foster, Iris. "Unsophisticated Sex Appeal." *Film Weekly,* June 9, 1933.

Frink, Carol. "Jean Loved for Great Heart, Says Carol Frink." *Los Angeles Herald Examiner,* 1937.

—. "Parade? It's Just Jean Harlow and Admiring Throng." *Chicago Sun-Times,* June 14, 1933.

Gooding, Clifford, and Joyce Gooding. "The Three Lives of our Packard 903 Sport Phaeton." *The Classic Car Club of America,* Volume XLVI, June 1998.

Graham, Sheila. "Harlow—Fact or Fiction: Actor Labels Book on Star 'Vile.'" *Fort Worth Star Telegram,* January 10, 1965.

Hall, Gladys. "Jean and Clark Expose Each Other." *Movie Classic,* May 1936.

Keats, Patricia. "It's Easier in Fast Company." *Silver Screen,* September 1933.

Kingsley, Grace. "Time Out to Play." *The New Movie,* December 1934.

Lane, Virginia T. "Don't Scoff at Good Health." *Modern Screen,* October 1933.

Lee, Sonia. "I Love Bill Powell." *Screen Guide,* August 1936.

Loos, Anita. "Behind the Scenes with Jean and Clark." *Modern Screen,* August 1933.

—. "Harlow's Hollywood." *Cosmopolitan,* May 1974.

MacCulloch, Campbell. "Facts and Figure." *Motion Picture Classic,* September 1930.

Mack, Grace. "Jean Harlow Acquitted." *Hollywood,* April 1932.

Mank, Gregory. "Jean Harlow." *Films in Review,* December 1978.

Manners, Dorothy. "Looking Them Over." *Motion Picture Classic,* July 1930.

—. "Jean Harlow's Own Story of Her Future." *Movie Classic,* December 1932.

March, Joseph Moncure. "About *Hell's Angels.*" *Look,* March 1954.

1933

Marsters, Ann. "Struggles for Stardom Told in Last Interview." *Boston Sunday Advertiser,* June 1937.

Martin, Martha. "The Bern Mystery." *New York Sunday News,* June 20, 1937.

McGrew, Harlean. "Harlean Carpenter McGrew v. Charles F. McGrew 11." Los Angeles County Superior Court, September 28, 1929.

Moffitt, Mary. "Jean Harlow Loved Life, but Never Quite Found Happiness." *Kansas City Times,* June 9, 1937.

Mooring, W.H. "This Sex Nonsense." *Film Weekly,* December 14, 1934.

Mulvey, Kay. "Discrepancies in Shulman-Harlow Biography." Metro-Goldwyn-Mayer Inter-Office Communication, December 29, 1965.

Packer, Eleanor. "The Authentic Story of My Life by Jean Harlow." *The New Movie,* August 1934.

—. "Men I Have Loved on the Screen by Jean Harlow." *The New Movie,* January 1934.

—. "Now Hollywood Is Harlow Conscious." *Picturegoer Weekly,* December 9, 1933.

—. "The Story of My Romance and Marriage by Jean Harlow." *Picturegoer Weekly,* November 18, 1933.

—. "Jean Harlow Is Willing to Pay the Price." *Hollywood,* November 1933.

Parsons, Louella O. "Harlow's Real Life and Loves Related." *Los Angeles Examiner,* June 9, 1937.

—. "Jean Put Peace above Honors Won in Films." *Los Angeles Examiner,* June 9, 1937.

Ramsey, Walter. "The True Story of Jean Harlow." *Modern Screen,* November 1931.

Reid, James. "'I Have No Regrets' Says Jean Harlow." *Movie Mirror,* February 1937.

—. "My Advice to Myself by Jean Harlow." *Motion Picture,* March 1937.

Rhode, Edward. "What Now for the Blond Bombshell?" *Film Pictorial.* October 12, 1935.

Schallert, Elza. "Ben Lyon Ushers Jean Harlow into World of Platinum Fame."

—. "Jean Harlow Gives First Statement on Tragedy." *Los Angeles Times,* October 2, 1932.

—. "Jean Harlow, Modern Cleopatra, Thrills Men Whenever She Appears." *Kansas City Journal-Post,* September 23, 1932.

—. "Jean Harlow's Personality Is Startling Contrast to Her Artificial-looking Platinum Blond Locks." *Kansas City Journal-Post,* September 24, 1932.

Service, Faith. "Jean Harlow Is Watching Her Step." *Modern Screen,* September 1936.

Scott, Romney. "Tell It to Bern." *Picture Play Magazine,* April 1932.

Sharon, Mary. "Jean as I Know Her by Barbara Brown." *Screenland,* January 1935.

St. Johns, Adela Rogers. "Jean Harlow Tells the Inside Story." *Liberty,* November 26, 1932.

—. "Love, Laughter and Tears." *The American Weekly,* February 4, 1951.

—. "The Private Life and Loves of Jean Harlow." *Liberty,* December 16, 1933.

Stuart, Betty Thornley. "Movie Set-Up." *Collier's* Magazine, September 30, 1933.

Verrill, Virginia. "Confessions of a Film Canary." *Radio Guide,* June 15, 1935.

Wales, Clark. "What New Harlow?" *Screen and Radio Weekly,* March 14, 1937.

Waterbury, Ruth. "The Murder of Jean Harlow's Memory." *Motion Picture,* March 1965.

1936

Unsigned Articles

"All Mystery to Brother." *Los Angeles Examiner,* September 6, 1932.

"Bern Death Is Reopened." *The Tampa Daily Times,* February 28, 1933.

"Bill Powell Buys Crypt for Body of Jean Harlow." *Kansas City Times,* June 12, 1937.

"Bury Jean Harlow; Powell Collapses." *Chicago Herald and Examiner,* June 9, 1937.

"'China Seas' a New York Hit." *Los Angeles Times*, August 16, 1935, p. 8.

"Cinema: Dinner at Eight." *Time Magazine,* September 4, 1933.

"Four Million Dollars and Four Men's Lives." *Photoplay*, April 1930.

"Friendship the Finest Thing in Life, Says Jean Harlow." *The Seattle Sunday Times,* October 18, 1931.

"Gossip Blurb." *Movie Mirror,* December 1933.

"Grandmother's Illness to Keep Harlows from Funeral of Actress." *Kansas City Journal-Post,* June 8, 1937.

"Harlow Powell Lowdown." *Screen Guide and Life,* July 1937.

"If You Knew Suzy Like I Know Suzy." *Hollywood,* September 1936.

"Inheritance Lost by Films Regained." *Los Angeles Times*, August 20, 1929, p. A2.

"Jean Harlow Dead—Star Succumbs." *Los Angeles Evening Herald Express,* June 7, 1937.

"Jean Harlow Is Dead." *The Bellingham Herald,* June 7, 1937.

"Jean Harlow to Be Bride." *Los Angeles Times,* June 21, 1932.

"Jean Harlow, Who Changed Blond Standard from Gold to Platinum, in Chicago." *Chicago Sun Times,* December 12, 1931.

"Jean Steps Up." *Screen Book,* April 1933.

"The Little Father." *Los Angeles Times,* June 22, 1932.

"On and Off the Set." *Picture Play,* April 1937.

"The Platinum Blonde Bride and Her Wall of Screen Friends." *The Sketch,* August 17, 1932.

"Red-Headed Woman." *Variety*, July 5, 1932.

◆ About the Authors ◆

Mark A. Vieira is a filmmaker, photographer, and writer specializing in Hollywood history. His previous books include *Hurrell's Hollywood Portraits, Irving Thalberg: Boy Wonder to Producer Prince,* and, with Tony Curtis, *The Making of Some Like It Hot.* He maintains a portrait studio in the historic Granada Buildings in Los Angeles.

Darrell Rooney has one of the world's most significant collections of Jean Harlow photographs and memorabilia. A Hollywood insider, Rooney is an animator and director best known for his Annie Award-winning direction of *The Lion King 2: Simba's Pride. Harlow in Hollywood* is his first book. He resides in Los Angeles.

◆ Image Credits ◆

Ted Allan 182 top; 182 bottom; 183; 193; 197; 198 • **Virgil Apger** 94; 95; 158; 163 top left; 163 top right; 163 bottom right; 165; 166-167; 168 • **Max Munn Autrey** 17 • **Russell Ball** 6; 122 • **Clarence Sinclair Bull** 58; 67 top, middle, and bottom; 68; 70 center; 72 top left, top right, and bottom left; 73; 80 top left, top right, bottom left, and bottom right; 81 left; 82; 96 left; 126 top and bottom; 127; 128; 144; 145; 146; 147; 180 top left; 210; 214 • **James N. Doolittle** 6, 194 • **Preston Duncan** 33; 56 • **Empire Studios** 14 • **Hyman Fink** 99 • **Elmer Fryer** 50 top left • **Durward ("Bud") Graybill** 192; 207 left, top right, and bottom right; 208; 211 top left, top right, and bottom; 212; 213 • **William Grimes** 78 bottom; 79 top and middle; 81 right; 141 top right, left, and center • **Edwin Bower Hesser** 26; 28 left and right; 29 left and right; 30 top and bottom; 31 • **George Hurrell** 66 bottom right; 70 top left and bottom right; 100; 109; 111; 114; 124 bottom left and bottom right; 137; 153 bottom right; 154; 170; 171; 174; 204 • **Ray Jones** 47 top; 50 upper right; 51 • **Victor Mascaro** digital color enhancement, 212, 229 • **Martin Munkácsi** 161 • **Carl Roup Collection** 213 • **Frank Tanner** 102 top and bottom; 105; 155; 156; 157 • **Mark A. Vieira** 40, 82-83; 236 portrait of authors • **Harvey White** 92; 101; 103; 104 • **Dick Whittington** 153 bottom left • **Witzel Studio** 16

The authors have made a good faith effort to ascertain the photographer of each image. If an error is detected, please notify the publisher.

Harlow In Hollywood: The Blonde Bombshell in the Glamour Capital, 1928-1937
Darrell Rooney and Mark A. Vieira ◆ Copyright ©2022 by Darrell Rooney and Mark A. Vieira ◆ Design by Hilary Lentini

ISBN-13: 978-1-62640-220-1

ANGEL CITY PRESS

www.angelcitypress.com

Library of Congress Cataloging-in-Publication Data is on file.

PRINTED IN CANADA

Index

MORE MAP ON INSIDE FRONT COVER